Spenser's Allegory of Justice
in Book Five of
The Faerie Queene

Most sacred vertue she of all the rest,
Resembling God in his imperiall might;
Whose soveraine powre is herein most exprest,
That both to good and bad he dealeth right,
And all his workes with Justice hath bedight.
That powre he also doth to Princes lend,
And makes them like himselfe in glorious sight,
To sit in his owne seate, his cause to end,
And rule his people right, as he doth recommend.

Spenser's Allegory of Justice

in Book Five of

THE FÆRIE
QUEENE

BY T. K. DUNSEATH

PRINCETON UNIVERSITY PRESS

PRINCETON, NEW JERSEY

1968

Publication of this book has been aided by
the Whitney Darrow Publication Reserve Fund
of Princeton University Press

This book has been composed in Caslon type.

Printed in the United States of America
by Princeton University Press, Princeton, New Jersey

For Don Cameron Allen

Acknowledgments

THE Samuel S. Fels Foundation generously supported me in 1961-1962, when I completed the major portion of the research and writing of this book. The University of Wisconsin thoughtfully permitted me to continue my studies by means of a fellowship from the Alumni Research Foundation, which relieved me of a semester's teaching duties in the spring of 1963.

I wish to thank the staffs of The Johns Hopkins Library and The Folger Shakespeare Library for their helpful consideration and expert assistance.

My wife Diana Fenn Dunseath sustained me in this work and listened through its various versions. I am obliged to Howard Schultz for early advice and encouragement. John Huber, a former student of mine at the University of Wisconsin, stimulated me into clarifying my ideas on important issues concerning the theme of justice in the poem. I am grateful to Earl R. Wasserman, who read critically the first finished version of the book and made useful suggestions for improvement. My special debt is acknowledged in the dedication.

Contents

Spenser's Allegory of Justice
in Book Five of
The Faerie Queene

Introduction

Spenser was the instrument of a detestable policy
in Ireland, and in his fifth book the wickedness he
had shared begins to corrupt his imagination.
C. S. Lewis

The political fifth is the dullest of all.
Sir Herbert Grierson

Spenser's fiction seems to break down in Book Five.
A. C. Hamilton

A survey taken today to determine the least popular of
Spenser's major works would probably reveal that
Book Five of *The Faerie Queene* holds few poetic attractions for the reader. Book Five has not suffered from a
lack of critical attention, however. Because of an evident
abundance of apparent historical allusion, it has drawn the
interest of scholars primarily desirous of determining as
exactly as possible event and character. This long-standing
interest has been extensive enough to generate the necessary scholarly acrimony that the pursuit of exactitude requires. Upon a matter of politics and perhaps filial pride,
James VI, unknowingly as in so many things, became the
first officially recorded annotator of Spenser's many topical
allusions when he complained to Lord Burghley of the
portrayal of Duessa at Mercilla's Palace.[1] Since John Up-

---

[1] "The K[ing] hath conceaved great offence against Edward
Spencer publishing in prynte in the second book p[ar]t of the
Fairy Queene and ixth chapter some dishonorable effects (as the
k. demeth thereof) against himself and his mother decessed. He
alledged that this booke was passed with priviledge of her mats
Commission[er]s for the viewe and allowance of all wrytinges to
be receaved into Printe. But therin I have (I think) satisfyed that
it is not given out with such p[ri]viledge: yet he still desyreth that
Edward Spencer for his faulte, may be dewly tryed & punished."
This letter of Robert Bowes to Burghley is included in Frederick
Ives Carpenter's *Reference Guide to Edmund Spenser* (Chicago,

Introduction

ton in his great edition of *The Faerie Queene*[2] conjectured
that some characters of Book Five are thinly veiled historical personages, critics following him have been able to
find more and more historical references, often with dis-
quieting critical implications. Historical allusions clearly
abound in the whole of *The Faerie Queene* and should be
identified wherever possible, as Josephine Waters Bennett,
Edwin Greenlaw, Ray Heffner, and others have percep-
tively done. But in time the exclusive search for historical
possibilities has diminished.[3]

The search for historical allusions also has had the unintended effect of discouraging further inquiries into the
implications of the poetry. The solving of historical equations in general tends to limit the suggestibility of Spenser's
poem and in particular has led to the low critical fame of
Book Five. A brief example may be permitted here. When
the Amazon Radigund subdues Artegall, dresses him in
woman's clothing, and forces him to perform menial tasks,
the poet remarks that such is the cruelty of women when
they have revolted against the law of nature to "purchase
a licentious libertie."

> But vertuous women wisely understand,
> That they were borne to base humilitie,
> Unlesse the heavens them lift to lawfull soveraintie.
>
> (V.v.25.7-9)

1923) pp. 41-42. See *Variorum, Book Five,* 244. All citations in
this book refer to *The Works of Edmund Spenser: A Variorum Edition,* eds. Edwin Greenlaw et al. (Baltimore, 1932-1957).

[2] *Spenser's Faerie Queene,* II (London, 1758), 612-635.

[3] René Graziani has proposed a slightly different political interpretation of the episode at Isis Church, in which he reads Britomart's dream as Spenser's fictive rendering of the differences between Elizabeth and Parliament over the disposition of the case of
Mary Queen of Scots ("Elizabeth at Isis Church," *PMLA,* LXXIX
[Sept. 1964], 376-389). Graziani goes as far as anyone in making
a large part of Book Five read like a dossier of the Queen of Scots.

The last line is sometimes read as Spenser's bow to Queen Elizabeth to save himself censure or as the necessary result of contemporary political doctrine.[4] Knowing Elizabeth's humor, we may beguile ourselves with a poet's compromise and compliment him for his knowledge. Such readings are neither alternative nor contradictory. Emphasis upon the local implications of these lines, however, diverts the reader's attention from their place in the overall design of the poetry. In contrast to the unnatural Radigund, Spenser has created the character of Britomart, whose actions at important intervals in the narrative are specifically placed within a providential framework. From the outset, the arch-artificer Merlin assures her that her vision of Artegall in his magic mirror was not accidental but the "streight course of heavenly destiny/ Led with eternall providence" (III.iii.24.3-4). Later, when he depicts her trapped in Dolon's Castle and in imminent danger from his snares, Spenser reminds the reader that her rescue is owing as much to "Gods grace" as it is to "her good heedinesse" (V.vi.34.6). Finally, she has a divine vision in the Church of Isis, which when interpreted confirms her in her love for Artegall. The priest's last words to her, significantly enough, are "So blesse thee God, and give thee joyance of thy dreame" (V.vii.23.9). The lines in question fit into this pattern of imagery and clearly show that Spenser is directing his reader's attention to a divine meaning rather than making an obvious effort simply to soothe Elizabeth with philosophy. Even the trial of Duessa, the most topical reference in Book Five, bears a strict relationship to the whole of *The Faerie Queene*. This is not only the final arraignment of the Queen of Scots but also of Duessa, who, in the course of a notorious career, has succeeded in subverting at one time or another all levels of society in Faery Land. It is consistent with Spenser's purpose that each

---

[4] See *Variorum, Book Five*, 204.

charge brought against Duessa at the trial matches point for point her malefactions in the poem. Spenser is employing nice irony, literal poetic justice, when he has Arthur, who was the instrument of Duessa's first discomfiting, assent to her final condemnation.

Unless the study of historical allegory can further the larger understanding of Spenser's poem, its single pursuit becomes self-serving, a pointless exercise in scholarly ingenuity.[5] A. C. Hamilton has realized the limits of historical application to the poetry of Book Five. Yet in his final analysis, he relies upon historical allegory to make his point: "The last three cantos are distanced from fact by the increasing element of fairy tale—the final episode is pure fairy tale—and the obvious emphasis upon the ideal."[6] The apparent incompatibility between historical fact and the way it is presented in Book Five has led Hamilton to this untenable conclusion. Nothing could be further from Spenser's purpose than to give his readers the impression that these cantos are "fairy tales" and approximations of the ideal.

Renaissance critics thought history was the necessary

[5] The problem of "historical allegory" also has long occupied Dante scholars. In a brilliant article concerning two famous cruxes in the *Commedia*, R. E. Kaske succinctly places political allegory in its proper perspective when he writes that "such literature, if it is to become much more than a series of arbitrary and imaginatively jejune equations, must by its very nature draw strongly on other more fundamental and universally significant meanings, already somehow implicit in the figures it is made to inhabit" ("Dante's 'DXV' and 'Veltro,'" *Traditio*, xvii [1961], 202). I feel that Kaske's strictures especially apply to *The Faerie Queene* in general and Book Five in particular. In Book Five Spenser's use of history for the purpose of poetry is always directly related to his moral meaning. In depicting Prince Arthur's mission to rescue Belgae, Spenser, as we shall see, carefully continues his major theme of justice, illustrating it with the matter of history.

[6] *The Structure of Allegory in* THE FAERIE QUEENE (Oxford, 1961), p. 170.

background for an epic; and while Spenser uses at least two kinds of history (Faery and British), the actual shape of events in his poem need not agree with history precisely. By emphasizing history as such, we often lose sight of the poem and Spenser's artistic purpose. Book Five is the most heavily "historical" because its subject is justice, and justice has as its province governments and men. Artegall and Arthur ride through several "realms." All of the conflicting governments in the sixteenth century (Spain, England, France, and the Netherlands, to mention those alluded to in Book Five) were based upon law. The question posed poetically in Book Five is not whose is the better cause but whose is the just cause.[7] As a loyal Englishman, favorably committed to Elizabeth I's policies, Spenser could hardly be expected to honor the Catholic powers with the dispassionate objectivity we expect—and sometimes receive—from modern historians.

Long before the age of Augustus, rulers had subsidized, inspired, or otherwise influenced poets, artists, and historians to make common cause. In this regard Elizabeth I had no equal. The endless parade of her literate public admirers bore little resemblance to her parsimonies. Few writers balked at supporting her. For the most part, Shakespeare seems in the history plays to follow the Tudor party line, and has yet to provoke the animus Spenser receives when dancing to the same piper.[8] The art of writing good history

[7] According to sixteenth-century English legal theory, Ireland was not a properly constituted nation, neither *de jure* nor *de facto*. Ireland was considered an outlaw province of the realm and had no rights under natural law. England perpetuated this legal fiction well into the twentieth century. Repressive measures against Tyrone or against the Fenians differ only in degree and time, not in legal justification.

[8] Sigurd Burckhardt convincingly argues that in *King John* Shakespeare subjects the "Tudor Doctrine" to searching criticism ("*King John*: The Ordering of This Present Time," *ELH*, xxxiii [June 1966], 133-153).

is almost invariably aided by the passage of time—time after the conflict to gather facts, to weigh them objectively, to develop a more mature perspective. Spenser is not a gifted historian of his age, and Rudolf Gottfried has taught us to read the *View of the Present State of Ireland*, his formal attempt at the art, as a contemporary exercise written according to the Elizabethan formula.[9] Spenser is a great poet, however; and his expert handling of "history" —whatever his propaganda purposes—enlarges it to encompass the theme of justice in Book Five. This is his major poetic concern and should also be ours.

The almost universal critical disesteem for the poetry of Book Five is commensurable with our lack of understanding of its structure and meaning. This misunderstanding, arising as it does from undue emphasis upon historical allegory and exclusive concentration upon the episodes at the Church of Isis and Mercilla's Palace, has blurred the fact that many perplexing critical problems raised in previous books of *The Faerie Queene* find adequate explanation in Book Five.

The great theme of this book is justice, the queen of the four cardinal virtues, without which civilized society as we know it would perish and Faery Land itself would disappear. In Book Five Artegall and Britomart temper their basic differences and bring nearer the day when their marriage will make possible the continuation of the British nation—a nation of felicitous people whose common ancestors bequeathed them an uncommon tradition of justice and equity. The quest of Florimell for Marinell, amply shown by Kathleen Williams, A. C. Hamilton, and A. R. Cirillo to be a unifying motif of Books Three and Four, reaches both its natural and divine end with their virtuous marriage in Book Five. With this marriage and the in-

---

[9] "Spenser as an Historian in Prose," *Transactions of the Wisconsin Academy of Sciences, Arts, and Letters*, xxx (1937), 317-329: see *Variorum, Prose Works*, 502-503.

evitable union, albeit temporarily delayed, of Artegall and Britomart, Spenser continues his exploration of the nature of false and true love. Nowhere else in *The Faerie Queene* do we find Spenser's method of teaching by *ensample* so profusely illustrated as we do on this theme in Book Five. Artegall and Britomart, Marinell and Florimell, Bracidas and Lucy, Amidas and Philterra, the "squallid Squire" and his lady, Sanglier and his, Bellodant and Radigund, Bourbon and Flourdelis—not to mention Braggadocchio and False Florimell—all contribute to Spenser's continuing investigation of the dialectics of love.[10] Here Duessa feels the curb of justice. False Florimell melts away and Braggadocchio is unmasked. Guyon recovers his stolen horse, Brigadore, and Florimell recovers her girdle. All these strands are tightly woven into the fabric of Spenser's poem and are not dependent for meaning upon historical allegory. If so many major (and minor) themes in *The Faerie Queene* are resolved by the poetry of Book Five, it is not unreasonable to begin with the premise that Spenser worked with artistry and integrity to clarify his great argument. We should examine the poetry with at least as much diligence and care as has been justifiably lavished upon his other efforts.

Since critical opinion hopefully tends, for good or ill, to shape and direct readers' interests, a periodic revaluation of accepted critical responses is both salutary and necessary. The modest revival of interest in Spenser owes its being in large part to this impulse, beginning, if a landmark is needed, with Kathleen Williams' fine essay on "eterne in mutabilitie."[11] Certain unqualified characterizations of Arte-

[10] Alastair Fowler unduly limits Spenser's treatment of the subject when he writes, "in so far as V deals with love, it is concerned with its expression in marriage *considered as an institution*" (*Spenser and the Numbers of Time* [New York, 1964], p. 35).

[11] "Eterne in Mutabilitie: The Unified World of *The Faerie Queene*," *ELH*, XIX (1952), 115-130; reprinted in *That Soveraine Light: Essays in Honor of Spenser*, eds. D. C. Allen and W. R.

gall and Britomart still seem valid, however: Britomart is perfection herself; Artegall is "the warrior who must either subjugate or be subjugated, who is either all pride or 'humbleness meek.' "[12] But Miss Williams has misconstrued as a pejorative description of Artegall's character a philosophical and moral point about humility and meekness Spenser is trying to make about him in Britomart's dream.[13] Britomart's and Artegall's careers in *The Faerie Queene* are inextricably intertwined, however seemingly oblique their separate journeys; for we know from the beginning that they share a common destiny guided by eternal Providence. It is difficult to imagine that this great union—destined for such far-reaching consequences not only for Faery Land but for the British nation and history itself—is to be achieved by an arbitrary joining.

Unqualified praise for Britomart does an injustice to her character and a disservice to Spenser's poetry.[14] Britomart is not incarnate perfection since the poet reserves that honor for Queen Elizabeth in the Proem to Book Three and

Mueller (Baltimore, 1952). The recent studies of Berger, Fowler, Frye, Hamilton, Nelson, and Roche have sustained this interest.

[12] Kathleen Williams, "Venus and Diana: Some Uses of Myth in *The Faerie Queene*," *ELH*, xxviii (June 1961), 117.

[13] For the importance of Artegall's humility and meekness and their relationship to the pursuit of justice, see my analysis of Mercilla's judgment in Chapter IV.

[14] Thomas P. Roche's reading of Britomart's character is a helpful corrective to the prevailing view (*The Kindly Flame* [Princeton, 1964], pp. 51-95). My general assessment of Britomart's character is similar to Roche's; but our interpretations of the action differ—sometimes slightly, sometimes greatly. Roche tacitly claims to explain the whole love affair of Britomart and Artegall; any explanation, however, of the romance of Britomart and Artegall which does not include Book Five, where that romance itself has its most crucial trials, is partially incomplete. My analysis (Chapter III) of Britomart's career in Book Five supplements Roche's analysis. Since our readings are based upon different poetic criteria, I have not thought it necessary to mention all the times we agree or disagree.

Mercilla in Book Five. Britomart is the exemplar of "mag-nificke chastity," which, as Professor Lewis teaches us, always leads to virtuous marriage. We should consider Britomart's actions throughout the poem with this larger end in view. Just how firm is her initial commitment to Artegall? Her second? For we know Faery Land is a world where one step in the dark wood is error, where a slackening of pace brings temptation, where doubt breeds spiritual malaise and despair. She has many successes, which are not to be treated lightly; but she also undergoes spiritual vicissitudes. Britomart starts her pilgrimage in *The Faerie Queene* as a love-sick young girl, guided by the dubious offices of an aged nurse. She has much to learn and needs to become spiritually mature before she can look upon Artegall with compassion born only of a love which is unwavering and true.

In emphasizing Britomart's defections, both large and small, I in no way wish to detract from her great achievements. Nevertheless, since Britomart is to be the exemplar of chastity, any declination from the ideal, no matter how slight, must be regarded as potentially wrong. On the whole, to identify Britomart's peccadilloes as part of the romance tradition or to relate her behavioral lapses to a vague standard by which we read romances in general is to overlook Spenser's serious purpose in even considering such a character for his epic. Whatever his faults in execution, and I think some critics have found more ghosts than bodies, Spenser's ultimate design for *The Faerie Queene* is everywhere appropriate and consistent. The creation of Britomart is the magnificent poetic result of a century of sustained interest in the problem of love in society. Beginning with Ficino and continuing through Leone Ebreo and his successful imitators, love reached its zenith as a subject for serious philosophical speculation. *The Faerie Queene* is filled with lovers—good, bad, indifferent. In a way, love (or its perversions) affects all the titular heroes and heroines in the poem and many of the minor characters as well. Britomart's willful but erratic journey in Faery Land until her visit to the Church of Isis is everywhere consistent with Spenser's investigation of the problem of love. Britomart's character must be taken as a whole, as we must all Spenser's characters. Her conversion is a prime exemplum of her good offices and character. The story of Britomart's conversion is the final poetic embodiment of the shadowing of Divine Providence which manifests itself in the many thousands of lines devoted to her career in *The Faerie Queene*.

If Britomart suffers from an excess of critical praise, Artegall starves for want of any. Critics have preached against his pride, warned of his wrath, and smiled at his concupiscence. The consensus is that Artegall is thoroughly disagreeable and not at all like the other glorious champions of *The Faerie Queene*. His faults are usually ascribed to the harshness of being a justiciar or the pressures of historical allegory and his peccadilloes to Spenser's surprising lapses in taste. These outcries against Artegall have the curious, unintended, effect of swelling the chorus of *Envie, Detraction*, and the *Blatant Beast*, a phenomenon unique in Spenserian scholarship. The place to assess the final development of Artegall's character is at the end of Book Five after he has completed his quest, and Artegall here seems to need no apologist. He is serene and unmoved by the attacks of *Envie* and *Detraction*, the two sure signs that he has achieved success in public undertaking, the two things Pindar never tired of cautioning his jubilant victors to expect when they went to receive the laurel. The poetry of Book Five wants careful review and the character of Artegall surely deserves at least as much attention and enthusiasm as the late H. S. V. Jones once gave to it when he saw it as the defense of Lord Grey.

Artegall is, after all, the patron of justice, an officer of the law. He can and does attract the animosities natural to those of his calling, especially when, and this is one of Spenser's points, he reveals weaknesses common to all. It is quite understandable to allow Red Cross, Guyon, Britomart, and Calidore imperfections in character, both major and minor. They are exemplars of private virtues, and while their departures from the ideal have public implications, their sins remain essentially private. Red Cross, whatever his ultimate goal, is an individual man beset with personal problems. His escapade in Errour's Den, his sexual fantasies and jealousies, his visit to the House of Pride, his bestial wallowing with Duessa are all extremely personal, and while ultimately cosmic in scope are nevertheless private. With Artegall it is quite a different matter; his virtue is a specific matter of public concern. Aristotle first made the special distinction that justice was practiced toward others as well as oneself while the practice of the other virtues largely pertained to private affairs.[15] As the advance publicity given him by Guyon shows (II.ix.6.5-9), Artegall is in every way a public figure. His actions affecting society are everywhere open for inspection. Since his earlier trials are compromising and unsatisfactory, we view his every rash action and suspect his wisdom in the same way we would any judge whose unusual sexual proclivities or drinking habits came to light. Everything a justiciar does is subject to immediate public appraisal, and actions short of the ideal must be censured simply because society at large bases its immediate and future well-being upon the impartial execution of justice. Spenser's gentle reader should react strongly and emotionally to Artegall (as people in Faery Land do) because by implication he has a stake in his successes and is sure to share immediately in his failures.

[15] *Nichomachean Ethics*, v.i.15. Moralists, such as Cicero and Aquinas, noted that this quality of the virtue gave it its preeminent position. See Thomas Aquinas (*Summa Theologica*, i.ii.Q.66.4; ii.ii.Q.58.1-2; *Commentary on the* NICHOMACHEAN ETHICS, v.L.ii).

Spenser optimistically holds, however, that present shortcomings need not spell ultimate failure. Indeed, the whole of *The Faerie Queene* is expressly designed with hopes of educating a virtuous gentleman. Since education is both practical and theoretical, we expect to pay more visits to Errour's Den than to the contemplative mountain. As the school of the world is the forge of experience, Spenser does not present his heroes and heroines with clear-cut choices of right and wrong. To the reader viewing the whole sweep of the narrative, the choice of ways is clear. But the character engaged in making the decision usually has a difficult time in separating the good from the expedient—always in the heat of a moment, often trapped by illusion or reality. Spenser, however crudely in modern eyes, attempts an analysis of human character and exposes it to view. Of course, some of his observations are formulaic, commonplace, and scientifically indefensible, as are some of Shakespeare's. Self-control, inner concord, and self-knowledge are the three related goals of Spenser's educational program. Spenser presents his characters with conflicts between duty and inclination, between freedom and license. As the most visible of characters in this regard, Artegall needs to be studied in depth to reveal Spenser's creation of a justiciar perfected.

Since the search for precise analogues between Spenser's fiction and the facts of history has led only to fragmentary and partial views of Book Five, little or no notice has been taken of the organic wholeness and thematic integrity of the narrative. The purpose of this book is to investigate precisely these aspects of the poem and to demonstrate the relevance and coherence of the ethical and structural materials of Spenser's poetic world. Richard Hooker once told his readers "if any complaine of obscuritie, they must consider, that in these matters it commeth no otherwise to passe then in sundry the workes both of art and also of nature, where that which hath greatest force in the very things we see, is notwithstanding itself oftentimes not seene." Since Hooker has set himself the task of investigating causes and obscure origins of ecclesiastical polity in order to explain and defend current practices, he cautions against hasty judgments by explaining his method.

> For as much helpe whereof as may be in this case, I have endevoured throughout the bodie of this whole discourse, that every former part might give strength unto all that followe, and every later bring some light unto all before. So that if the judgments of men doe but hold themselves in suspense as touching these first more generall meditations, till in order they have perused the rest that ensue: what may seeme darke at first will afterwardes be founde more plaine, even as the later particular decisions will appeare, I doubt not more strong, when the other have beene read before.[16]

Hooker refuses to play the critical/apologetical game of deducing facts from assumptions. With the necessary critical qualification, Hooker's statement could very well serve not only as a general description of Spenser's poetic technique in *The Faerie Queene* but also as a warning for readers to suspend judgment until all poetic evidence for each quest is presented.

The meaning of Book Five encompasses and transcends

[16] *Of the Lawes of Ecclesiastical Politie* (1593), p. 48. For his translation of Ovid, Arthur Golding argues similarly in his preface to the general reader (*The XV Bookes of . . . Metamorphosis* [London, 1567], sig. A.iii.verso):

And even as in a cheyne eche linke within another wynds,
And both with that that went before and that that followes binds;
So every tale within this booke dooth seeme too take his ground
Of that that was reherst before, and enters in the bound
Of that that followes after it: and every one gives light
To other: so that whoo so meenes to understand them ryght,
Must have a care as well too know the thing that went before,
And that the which he presently desyres too see so sore.

the historical allegory in a poetic context where every situation is totally relevant to Spenser's avowed purpose of fashioning a virtuous gentleman. In Book Five, as in any other Book in *The Faerie Queene*, the hero, like every man, begins his quest under very definite personal handicaps. He undergoes a series of adventures which reveal his weaknesses and ultimately perfect him in his virtue. It is only when the meaning of these adventures, apart from their real or supposititious historical framework, is understood that the reader sees Spenser's fiction does not "break down" in Book Five. Here, the precise ordering of Spenser's poetic vision imparts to his fiction an artistic integrity which makes it worthy of his other efforts in *The Faerie Queene*.

CHAPTER I

Character and Theme

NONE OF Spenser's titular heroes in *The Faerie Queene* appears in the action of the poem before the book in which he specifically begins his quest except Artegall, the patron of justice in Book Five, and the Red Cross Knight. Red Cross is a justifiable exception since he begins the action of the whole poem and sets the pattern for what is to follow. Even before he begins his specific quest to free Irena from Grantorto, Artegall's whole character, with its attendant virtues and blemishes, is investigated and revealed. In Book Two Guyon holds Artegall up to Arthur as a sterling example of a Knight of Maidenhead. In Book Three Artegall appears in the magic mirror to Britomart, and she falls in love with his manliness and beauty. Britomart's vision is interpreted by Merlin to mean that she and Artegall will unite to continue the lineage of the Trojans in the British nation. In Book Four Artegall fights in "salvage" armor and is defeated by the magic lance of Britomart. He woos Britomart, and they plan to wed.

Spenser's elaborate investigation of the character of Artegall even before he begins his quest is most important. On the one hand, Spenser has provided the rationale that forms a background to the romance of Artegall and Britomart, giving it a kind of believable inevitability. On the other, Spenser has portrayed in Artegall a noble knight whose character shows great potential but is marred by the flaws of pride, wrath, and concupiscence. In this general sense Artegall is no different from Red Cross, Guyon, Britomart, Cambell, Triamond, and Calidore. Spenser's careful delineation of Artegall's character in these earlier books foreshadows his fall by his own hand to Radigund and also promises his resurrection. In these books preliminary to his Book of Justice, Spenser has deliberately portrayed Artegall in an ambivalent light. In the artist's world of nature, Artegall is an ideal knight expressed as "potential." In the fallen world of nature, he is an intemperate synthesis of the passions expressed as "fact." This apparent division in character between the potential and the actual corresponds to the differing treatments of him in Book Three and Book Four. The manner in which Spenser has subtly compounded the character out of these higher and lower elements prepares his readers to grasp the full import of Artegall's first judgment in Book Five, a judgment which presents in fine all the difficulties to be encountered on his journey to free Irena from Grantorto.

i

The first mention of Artegall in Book Three comes as a result of Britomart's crude, but psychologically sound, attempt to find out about him and his reputation from the Red Cross Knight. In this case the narrative sequence does not correspond to the actual order of events; for after Britomart hears of the prowess and good deeds of Artegall, Spenser reveals that she knew all along about her lover (III.ii.17) and then proceeds to show how she first became aware of Artegall's existence and how he became fastened upon her consciousness. In contrast to the narrative, the true order of events follows a logical sequence: 1) Britomart has a vision of Artegall in the magic glass; 2) Merlin explains her lover's role in helping continue the British nation; and then 3) Britomart seeks firsthand accounts of her lover's prowess. In following this logical pattern, Spenser prepares the reader (and Britomart) for the actual appearance of Artegall in Book Four.

The magic mirror devised by the "great Magitian *Merlin*" which serves as the vehicle for Britomart's vision, her first knowledge of Artegall, was long considered by the critics to be just another device rescued by Spenser from the ruins of romance. It remained for Kathleen Williams to see that this mirror is the world, the mirror of truth that signifies her love.[1]

> The great Magitian *Merlin* had deviz'd
> By his deepe science and hell-dreaded might,
> A looking glasse, right wondrously aguiz'd,
> Whose vertues through the wyde world soone were
>   solemniz'd.

> It vertue had to shew in perfect sight,
> What ever thing was in the world contaynd,
> Betwixt the lowest earth and heavens hight,
> So that it to the looker appertaynd;
> What ever foe had wrought, or frend had faynd,
> Therein discovered was, ne ought mote pas,
> Ne ought in secret from the same remaynd;
> For thy it round and hollow shaped was,
> Like to the world it selfe, and seem'd a world of glas.
>   (III.ii.18-19)

This is a truly wonderful glass, but it has its limitations. In the first place it is confined to the world, the fallen world of friend and foe, the world of illusion and error. Being "man made" and sharing the imperfections of its maker, it cannot penetrate the mysteries of "lowest earth" or "heavens hight." Yet the maker of this little world is a great man, the magician Merlin; and within limits Merlin has transmuted the nature of the world into a kind of ideal nature. For Merlin is the magician, the archetype of the artist, who refashions the world into an ideal image.[2] As

---

[1] "Venus and Diana: Some Uses of Myth in *The Faerie Queene*," *ELH*, xxviii (June, 1961), 116.

[2] I am conscious here of adopting Hamilton's use of Sidney's phrase. For a generalized account of Sidney's theory of poetry see Hamilton's *Structure of Allegory in* THE FAERIE QUEENE, pp. 1-29. See also the article "Sidney's 'Golden World,'" by John P. McIntyre, S.J., in *Comparative Literature*, xiv (Fall 1962), 356-365.

artist, Merlin has created a mirror of the world, a mirror in which truth may be seen.

When Britomart, daughter and sole heir of King Ryance, wanders into her father's closet, she sees the magic mirror and is filled with curiosity. At first she is naturally desirous to find out about herself, but "when she had espyde that mirrhour fayre,/ Her self a wile therein she vewd in vaine" (III.ii.22.5-6). Since Britomart first looks into the magic glass to gain self-knowledge, the fact that she seeks this "in vaine" in the mirror points up another limitation of Merlin's work. However gifted the artist or inspired his efforts, it is not within his power directly to show the secrets of the soul since this is the work of the divine artist, God. Whatever the artist may do to help a man in the highest sense to know himself is done obliquely through innuendo and suggestion. A direct revelation which produces self-knowledge, as we shall see in Britomart's vision in the Church of Isis, is the province of God, not of the artist. Yet despite being confined to the world and denied the powers of direct revelation, the artist may recreate the world into an "ideal image,"[3] Merlin's magic mirror, on which the specters of truth perform the dance of destiny.

Being a practical young woman, Britomart soon gives up her quest for herself in the mirror.

> Tho her avizing of the vertues rare, [of the mirror]
> Which thereof spoken were, she gan againe
> Her to bethinke of, that mote to her selfe pertaine.
>
> But as it falleth, in the gentlest harts
> Imperious Love hath highest set his throne,
> And tyrannizeth in the bitter smarts

McIntyre's study firmly establishes the philosophical basis of Sidney's poetic theory.

[3] Spenser's practice here perhaps anticipates the modern artist's preoccupation with his own art. By having Merlin demonstrate the limits of his art, Spenser explores the limits of his own.

Of them, that to him buxome are and prone:
So thought this Mayd (as maydens use to done)
Whom fortune for her husband would allot,
Not that she lusted after any one;
For she was pure from blame of sinfull blot,
Yet wist her life at last must lincke in that same knot.

(III.ii.22-23)

Denied self-knowledge by the limitations of the mirror, Britomart naturally thinks of love and marriage. This holy crown of desire was the commended means of fulfilling God's providential plan—the order to increase and multiply. Spenser knew desire in some form impels all men, and Pierre La Primaudaye gave it first consideration in *The French Academie*: "The Philosophers teach us by their writings, and experience doth better show it unto us, that to covet and desire is proper to the soule, and that from thence all the affections and desires of men proceed, which draw them hither and thither diversly, that they may attaine to that thing, which they think is able to leade them to the enjoying of some good, whereby they may live a contented and happy life."[4] In *The Faerie Queene* those women engaged solely in the pursuit of lascivious desires—evil women like Acrasia, Hellenore, Malecasta, Radigund— are destined to remain barren. Britomart's desire is pure, free from lust or "sinfull blot," and leads to marriage, a marriage we later learn, to be blessed with royal offspring. She is a potential embodiment of Spenser's "Vertue of chast love,/ And wivehood true."

As she is chaste and true to her nature, Britomart sees her lover as the ideal knight.

Eftsoones there was presented to her eye
A comely knight, all arm'd in complet wize,
Through whose bright ventayle lifted up on hye

---

[4] "The Author to the Reader," *The French Academie*, trans. Thomas Bowes? (London, 1618).

His manly face, that did his foes agrize,
And friends to termes of gentle truce entize,
Lookt foorth, as *Phoebus* face out of the east
Betwixt two shadie mountaines doth arize;
Portly his person was, and much increast
Through his Heroicke grace, and honorable gest.

His crest was covered with a couchant Hound,
And all his armour seem'd of antique mould,
But wondrous massie and assured sound,
And round about yfretted all with gold,
In which there written was with cyphers old,
Achilles armes, which Arthegal did win.
And on his shield envcloped sevenfold
He bore a crowned litle Ermilin,
That deckt the azure field with her faire pouldred skin.
(III.ii.24-25)

This is not the knight we are to meet in Book Four. True,
Artegall's natural beauty remains constant. Britomart can
see that the "fayre visage written in her hart" which she
saw in the mirror is the same as the one she sees when she
vanquishes the Salvage Knight in Book Four; for "She
gan eftsoones it to her mind to call,/ To be the same which
in her fathers hall/ Long since in that enchaunted glasse
she saw" (IV.vi.26.4-6). But everything else about Artegall in nature seems opposed to his appearance in art. In the
world of nature Artegall is crude, vengeful, proud, wrathful, petty, and concupiscent. Through the artist's looking
glass, however, Britomart sees the true Artegall in all his
potential, not the Artegall in fallen nature who tries to
excuse his first defeat at the hands of Britomart by telling
Scudamour that he was tired (IV.vi.6.8).

After Britomart has the first fleeting look at Artegall in
the artist's glass, she feels the wound of love, opened by
the "false Archer, which that arrow shot" (III.ii.26.7).
What follows, of course, is a most virulent case of love

melancholy which runs its full course. Britomart's pride
humbled, she becomes "Sad, solemne, sowre, and full of
fancies fraile." Whenever she does fall asleep, she is immediately beset with fantastic dreams. Awakening with a
start, she immediately begins to "thinke of that fayre visage, written in her hart." Britomart's disease is even au-
thenticated by the required confidant, Glauce, who performs
as ineffectually as her literary predecessors.

When Glauce divines Britomart's sickness, her efforts
to comfort her only augment her pain. What makes this
attack particularly unbearable is that Britomart is in love
with an idea and she knows it. In response to one of Glauce's
exasperating platitudes, Britomart reveals the true cause
of her "despeire."

> For no no usual fire, no usual rage
> It is, O Nurse, which on my life doth feed,
> And suckes the bloud, which from my hart doth bleed.
> But since thy faithfull zeale lets me not hyde
> My crime, (if crime it be) I will it reed.
> Nor Prince, nor pere it is, whose love hath gryde
> My feeble brest of late, and launched this wound wyde.
>
> Nor man it is, nor other living wight;
> For then some hope I might unto me draw,
> But th'only shade and semblant of a knight,
> Whose shape or person yet I never saw,
> Hath me subjected to loves cruell law:
> The same one day, as me misfortune led,
> I in my fathers wondrous mirrhour saw,
> And pleased with that seeming goodly-hed,
> Unwares the hidden hooke with baite I swallowed.
>
> (III.ii.37-38)

Britomart realizes what she has seen in the magic glass is
an unkind fiction, her emphasis upon negatives underscor-
ing her despair: *nor Prince, nor pere, nor man, nor other*

living wight. Britomart thinks her love is "only shade and semblant of a knight," who "pleased with that seeming goodly-hed." Since she is unable to equate the vision Merlin's artful glass has presented to her eye with fact in nature, she gradually pines away. Despite Glauce's homely remedies, Britomart "still did waste, and still did wayle,/ That through long languour, and hart-burning brame/ She shortly like a pyned ghost became,/ Which long hath waited by the Stygian strond" (III.ii.52.3-6). Britomart has become a shade just like her lover in the magic glass.

Since no natural means will staunch her wound, both Britomart and Glauce disguise themselves and go in search of the great artificer, Merlin, who lives in the earth (III.-iii.7) and is able to penetrate the secrets of the world (III.iii.15.4-5). In other words, like any artist, he works in nature. But he is able to transmute nature and make it obey his will.

> For he by words could call out of the sky
> Both Sunne and Moone, and make them him obay:
> The land to sea, and sea to maineland dry,
> And darkesome night he eke could turn to day.
> (III.iii.12.1-4)

With such powers, Merlin easily penetrates their flimsy disguises. He then tells them of Artegall's strange childhood and that the heavens have ordained that he should wed Britomart. He describes Artegall and tells the beadroll of the British nation which Britomart and Artegall are to continue. As he projects this history into Elizabeth's reign (III.iii.49), he breaks off the narrative, "As overcomen of the spirites powre," with "suddein fit and half extatic stoure" (III.iii.50.1-5). This, of course, is the artistic frenzy of the creative genius who has the gift of prophecy.

Through his powers as an artist, Merlin also acts as an agent of Providence, a point he implicitly makes when he first comforts Britomart.

It was not, *Britomart*, thy wandring eye,
Glauncing unwares in charmed looking glas,
But the streight course of heavenly destiny,
Led with eternall providence, that has
Guided thy glaunce, to bring his will to pas:
Ne is thy fate, ne is thy fortune ill,
To love the prowest knight, that ever was.
Therefore submit thy wayes unto his will,
And do by all dew meanes thy destiny fulfill.
(III.iii.24)

Since God usually works through second causes, Merlin, the artist, has created the mirror in which Britomart caught that fleeting glimpse of her destiny. His admonition to Britomart that she must submit herself to God's will is particularly apt and serves as a piece of epic foreshadowing. For only when Britomart submits herself to divine will in the Church of Isis is she confirmed in her love for Artegall.

After Britomart hears Merlin's prophecy and dresses herself in Angela's armor,[5] she sets out for Faery Land where she meets the Red Cross Knight. In order to find out more about Artegall she feigns he has done her dishonor for which she seeks revenge (III.ii.8). Britomart's deviousness is one of the prerogatives of a young girl in love, especially since at this stage in her quest she is still unsure of her lover and is buffeted by an internal storm, whose force and intensity she later laments on Marinell's Rich Strond (III.iv.6-10). Her bit of girlish hypocrisy produces the desired result, however; for in admonishing Britomart, Red Cross answers her unvoiced question.

Certes ye misavised beene, t'upbrayd
A gentle knight with so unknightly blame:
For weet ye well of all, that ever playd

---

[5] Spenser intends us to notice that Britomart's armor is surprisingly like Artegall's in the magic mirror. Since it is so similar Dolon later mistakes her for her lover.

> At tilt or tourney, or like warlike game,
> The noble *Arthegall* hath ever borne the name.

(III.ii.9.5-9)

Although inwardly pleased by Red Cross's reply, Britomart persists in her vagrant charges intent upon ferreting out Artegall's whereabouts. Red Cross further dilates Artegall's honor.

> Ne soothlich is it easie for to read,
> Where now on earth, or how he may be found;
> For he ne wonneth in one certaine stead,
> But restlesse walketh all the world around,
> Ay doing things, that to his fame redound,
> Defending Ladies cause, and Orphans right,
> Where so he heares, that any doth confound
> Them comfortlesse, through tyranny or might;
> So is his soveraine honour raisde to heavens hight.

(III.ii.14)

While these verses seem to be the deciding arguments in Artegall's favor, they also anticipate the delays and turnings before Britomart and Artegall actually meet to share a common destiny, and the lines also suggest their ultimate thorn of conflict, the dilemma of love and duty.

In her emotional response to Red Cross's portrayal of her lover and in Spenser's analysis of the source of her feelings, we can see in retrospect how he has carefully created the idea of Artegall in Britomart's mind and how he has brought her to accept Artegall as a lover even before she has seen him in the World of Faery.

> His feeling words her feeble sence much pleased,
> And softly sunck into her molten hart:
> Hart that is inly hurt, is greatly eased
> With hope of thing, that may allegge his smart;
> For pleasing words are like to Magick art,
> That doth the charmed Snake in slomber lay.

(III.ii.15.1-6)

Britomart's whole idea of Artegall as a lover is planted in her mind and is nurtured by the artist. Her first vision of Artegall is in the magic glass of Merlin, the great artificer, who works as an agent of Providence. When common nature, Glauce, cannot heal her wound, Britomart goes to the artist himself. In a fit of prophetic frenzy, Merlin reveals the workings of Divine Providence, as expressed in the course of history. Even the Red Cross Knight's "pleasing words are like to Magick art."

From first to last in Book Three, Britomart's (and the reader's) awareness of the character and estate of Artegall is developed and controlled by art. As Britomart's knowledge of Artegall progresses from the one-dimensional shadow flitting in the magic mirror to the full image of a stalwart knight, defending ladies and orphans and overthrowing tyranny, so also does the reader's knowledge of him increase. The reader rides with Britomart; and as the image of Artegall progressively emerges from shade to substance, both reader and Britomart share in the artistic revelation. At the same time Spenser is developing the character of Artegall (using that evolution as a metaphor of art) and exploring his potential as a goodly knight, he is also nudging Artegall closer and closer to the progress of the poem, closer and closer to the nature of Faery Land.

This movement corresponds to the three revelations that Britomart has of Artegall. The first is just an evanescent shadow trailing across the mind. Then Merlin in his prophecy places this shadow in history by giving Artegall the dress of time. Finally the Red Cross Knight puts Artegall in Faery Land and describes his estate, thereby hastening Britomart in her quest for him in Faery Land. Metaphorically Artegall has already become a part of the nature of Faery Land, and Britomart frames him in her mind as its finest citizen.

> A thousand thoughts she fashioned in her mind,
> And in her feigning fancie did pourtray

Him such, as fittest she for love could find,
Wise, warlike, personable, curteous, and kind.

(III.iv.5.6-9)

This is the final touch in the portrayal of Artegall's character before he actually appears on the scene in Faery Land, and significantly this last touch is also the product of thought—Britomart's "feigning fancie." But Britomart's fancy ties Artegall securely to the Land of Faery and prepares the way for his entrance in Book Four. Artegall is fully accoutred for life in the world of "faerie," since he now has the complement of the courtly virtues.

ii

The apparent dichotomy between the idealized portrayal of Artegall and his actual appearance in Faery Land poses an essential crux in the reading of *The Faerie Queene*. The absence of a generally accepted interpretation of these differences in character has led to the hypothesis that Spenser must have changed his mind between the writing of Book Three and Book Four and, more recently, to various archetypal readings. The one is impossible of proof, slights Spenser's poetic integrity, and questions his grand design. The others have the unintended effect of flattening the character just when the poet is giving it point. As a matter of dramatic interest, we perhaps should ask ourselves how poetically satisfying would a perfect Artegall be? Artegall is, if nothing else, interesting and controversial, and no reader views him with the indifferent admiration perfection seems to inspire. Since Faery Land is no less than Spenser's fictional rendering of the world, the idealized Artegall of Book Three should not be expected to spring to flawless life in the mud of the Tournament of Beauty in Book Four. Even so, Spenser softly prepares his readers for the sudden apparent change of character by having Artegall arrive at the battle in disguise, a disguise which fools most of the participants (IV.iv.42). His unexpected arrival and his "new" character are intimately related to the context of Satyrane's Tournament of the Girdle. When this is established, the reasons for Artegall's appearance will become more clear.

The manner in which Satyrane gains possession of Florimell's girdle and his failure to understand its significance lead directly to the establishment of a tournament supposedly in her honor. Solely devoted to seeking her true lover, Florimell dashes into the forest to resume her quest and to escape the foul embraces of the witch's son, at whose hut she has had a reluctant but necessary rest. In sympathy for her son's loss, the witch calls up a spotted beast from a hidden cave and charges "him" to bring Florimell back or to devour her (III.vii.22-23). In this case the only thing that would restore Florimell to her son's embraces is the unbridled passions, the devouring power of lust. Florimell escapes by boarding a fisherman's small boat, an act which symbolically links her to the sea and anticipates her achieving final safety from the beast by marriage to the man of the sea, Marinell. She loses her girdle in her haste, and the witch's beast attacks and devours her weary horse. At this moment Satyrane arrives, and recognizing Florimell's horse, begins to fight the beast.

Satyrane's battle with the beast confirms that it is an emblem of the unrestrained passions. They are the chief enemy of the natural man (Satyrane) and Spenser's elaborate description of his struggle emphasizes this fact. This beast is not to be subdued by ordinary sword play (III.vii.32) nor is it ever to be completely vanquished. As to be expected from the beast's nature, Satyrane is fighting an unfamiliar battle.

> He wist not, how him to despoile of life,
> Ne how to win the wished victory,
> Sith him he saw still stronger grow through strife,
> And him selfe weaker through infirmity;

Greatly he grew enrag'd, and furiously
Hurling his sword away, he lightly lept
Upon the beast, that with great cruelty
Rored, and raged to be under-kept:
Yet he perforce him held, and strokes upon him hept.
                                        (III.vii.33)

After a laboriously protracted struggle in which he succeeds in checking the beast and abating its fierceness,
Satyrane tries to prolong its pain in order "to avenge the
implacable wrong,/ Which he supposed donne to *Florimell*" (III.vii.35.5-6); these lines, by the way, cast serious
doubt upon Hamilton's view that Florimell has lost her
maidenhead.[6] To make sure his readers do not miss his
point, Spenser has Satyrane tie Florimell's girdle about the
beast. Since the girdle represents unwonted restraint to
intractable lust, the witch's beast roars in despite; yet fearing Satyrane's furious rage, it trembles "like a lambe, fled
from the pray" and meekly follows his new master (III.-
vii.36). The girdle we are later to learn is the girdle of
virtue, a diaphanous reminder symbolic of the strength of
Florimell's chastity in particular and the good offices of
chastity to Faery Land in general. When Satyrane becomes
distracted and falls to the nymphomaniac Argante, the
beast is no longer liable to control.

Thence backe returning to the former land,
Where late he [Satyrane] left the Beast, he overcame,
He found him not; for he had broke his band,
And was return'd againe unto his Dame,
To tell what tydings of faire *Florimell* became.
                                        (III.vii.61.5-9)

---

[6] *Structure*, p. 150. It is difficult to see how Hamilton has come
to this conclusion, inasmuch as the poetry makes clear Florimell's
escape. Then, too, if Hamilton is correct, how can Florimell lose
her maidenhead (i.e., the girdle) here and then recover it intact
after the wedding tournament in Book Five?

Satyrane's fall frees the beast, whose return to his mistress hastens the creation of a false Florimell.

The girdle has come to Satyrane by default, and although he wears it for Florimell's "sake," his subsequent actions show he has no idea of its office or value.[7] It is now of no use to him and only brings him envy's sting.

> But when as she her selfe was lost and gone,
> Full many knights, that loved her like deare,
> Thereat did greatly grudge, that he alone
> That lost faire Ladies ornament should weare,
> And gan therefore close spight to him to beare:
> Which he to shun, and stop vile envies sting,
> Hath lately caus'd to be proclaim'd each where
> A solemne feast, with publicke turneying,
> To which all knights with them their Ladies are to bring.
>
> (IV.ii.26)

Satyrane is only as virtuous as his nature and training allow; and while his achievements in Faery Land are not inconsiderable, he nevertheless has a primitive understanding of chivalry. The tournament he calls demonstrates this primitivism. The prize for the fighting ostensibly provides the tournament's rationale and sets the tone for the action; for according to Satyrane's rules, the fairest lady will win the girdle; the strongest knight, the fairest lady (IV.ii.27). Since the only test for the winning of the girdle is beauty, ironically the snowy Florimell can claim the prize.

From the very beginning, we know that this will be a mock tournament, inasmuch as Satyrane is offering that which he has already proved is not his to offer—Florimell's girdle. The avowed reason for parting with the virtuous girdle is his wish to be free of envy, a vain wish since the reader will learn with Artegall at the end of Book Five that the battle against envy is a lifetime struggle that only death

---

[7] An irony Spenser exploits by having the False Florimell claim the girdle.

vanquishes. Satyrane has carefully hedged his bets in setting up his own tournament. He gives up the girdle hoping to escape envy and then contests for the fairest lady—who wins it. Satyrane is true to his nature when he establishes strength and beauty as the rules for his tournament. But strength and beauty, while admirable attributes in themselves, are worthless in Faery Land if not linked with virtue.

The tournament itself is a travesty and Satyrane himself is to blame. His entrance sets the tone of the proceedings.

> Then first of all forth came Sir *Satyrane,*
> Bearing that precious relicke in an arke
> Of gold, that bad eyes might it not prophane:
> Which drawing softly forth out of the darke,
> He open shewd, that all men it mote marke.
> A gorgeous girdle, curiously embost
> With pearle and precious stone, worth many a marke;
> Yet did the workmanship farre passe the cost:
> It was the same, which lately *Florimell* had lost.
>
> (IV.iv.15)

Although Satyrane's behavior here may be reminiscent of the supposed offices of Courtly Love, in this context it is a parody of religious ceremony, not a facsimile. As Spenser has already revealed in Satyrane's partial success with the witch's beast, the natural man can achieve virtue by controlling his passions. Since his defeat at the hands of Argante, however, he has given up such pretensions. Beauty for its own sake has become his god, and chaos at the tournament is the result.

It is customary to pass hurriedly over the minor battles in *The Faerie Queene* in order to gain time to wander slowly through the gallery of paintings that supposedly emphasize Spenser's strongest point—his powers of sensuous description. Nevertheless, the neglected battles are every bit as important to the argument of the poem, and an understanding of them is essential. In these seemingly insignificant and endless Iliads, what seems occasional metaphor becomes, upon closer examination, an elaborate poetic order in which every image contributes to the progress of the argument. For Spenser has so carefully organized and drawn the individual encounters that image and meaning become one.

Satyrane's tournament is a perfect example of his mastery of this technique. The course of the individual battles at this contest is indicative of the emphasis upon beauty and strength rather than upon virtue—the beast in man rather than the mind in him which aspires to virtue. Because Satyrane is three-quarters man, and one-quarter beast, he has very definite personal handicaps imposed upon him by nature. That his energies are solely devoted to seeking "adventures wild" (III.vii.30) rather than directed toward a specific end indicates he lacks the moral awareness necessary for the unwavering pursuit of virtue. When he fights for beauty, ultimately the false Florimell, the ambiguity of his character is emphasized and only the bestial side of his nature is apparent. Accordingly, his first opponent is a brown horse, Sir Bruncheval, who battles with equal animalistic savagery.

> So furiously they both together met,
> That neither could the others force sustaine;
> As two fierce Buls, that strive the rule to get
> Of all the heard, meete with so hideous maine,
> That both rebutted, tumble on the plaine.
> (IV.iv.18.1-5)

This simile is apt and not just another commonplace of battle rhetoric; it accords well with the brutalizing rules of the tourney since both Satyrane and Bruncheval are out to win the beauteous heifer, the snowy Florimell. Although animal imagery was ready to hand for descriptions of the battle and tournament, Spenser nowhere else in *The Faerie*

Queene relies exclusively upon this device to point his meaning.

Another bestial combatant, Ferramont (φηρομονής) rides to Satyrane's rescue. When Satyrane recovers, he forces Triamond, who had gained apparent mastery, to retire wounded from the field. Satyrane then is judged victor of the first day's fighting.

The next day, Cambell seeks him out to avenge the wound given Triamond.

> There *Satyrane* Lord of the field he found,
> Triumphing in great joy and jolity;
> Gainst whom non able was to stand on ground.
> (IV.iv.28.1-3)

Although "Lord of the field" is an accurate phrase for his success, it is subtly ironic; for Satyrane has domination over the beasts of the field and nothing else, certainly not over himself. Cambell, in envying Satyrane's glory as the ruler of beasts, becomes animal-like in turn. When they charge one another, they fight "As two wild Boares together grapling go,/ Chaufing and foming choler each against his fo" (IV.iv.29.8-9). Together Cambell and Triamond win the second day's fighting, however. Their style of battle is appropriate and not out of keeping with the standards established by Satyrane.

> As when two greedy Wolves doe breake by force
> Into an heard, farre from the husband farme,
> They spoile and ravine without all remorse,
> So did these two through all the field their foes enforce.
> (IV.iv.35.6-9)

In the tournament it is difficult to keep track of the action. Since Spenser is to make patent that the glories of the Tournament of Beauty are illusory, he has subtly implicated all the contestants. For the participating knights all act like animals, metamorphoses especially demeaning for the Knights of Maidenhead.

On the final day Satyrane reestablishes his "superiority" over the rest of the field, a tournament now reduced to chaos in which mockingly Spenser notes that "the knights of Maidenhead the better wonne" (IV.iv.38.9).

> Till that there entred on the other side,
> A straunger knight, from whence no man could reed,
> In quyent disguise, full hard to be descride.
> For all his armour was like salvage weed,
> With woody mosse bedight, and all his steed
> With oaken leaves attrapt, that seemed fit
> For salvage wight, and thereto well agreed
> His word, which on his ragged shield was writ,
> *Salvagesse sans finesse*, shewing secret wit.
>
> (IV.iv.39)

The appearance of this "salvage" knight makes explicit the degrading effects of the pursuit of beauty for its own sake. As the one most closely identified with raw nature, the knight has no trouble in his encounters with the other beasts. He quickly overthrows Sir Sangliere, the wild boar (IV.iv.40.3) and then defeats the entire field—false knights, Knights of Maidenhead, and paynims. Since this is truly a beastly battle, he fights as the king of beasts, faring wrathfully "like a lyon in his bloodie game" (IV. iv.41.5). The tournament becomes a rout when all flee the lion's wrath.

Spenser's deliberate delay in establishing the identity of the Salvage Knight as Artegall until after he has humiliated all rivals is a stroke of poetic brilliance. Although many threads of the narrative are to converge here, Spenser's immediate concern is the brutalizing Tournament of Beauty. The Salvage Knight may well be reminiscent of the "wild man" of the Middle Ages and the Renaissance. But

Artegall's "quyent disguise" is appropriate for such a low pursuit. We should remember also that to staunch beauty's wound Britomart goes to Merlin disguised in "straunge" and "base attyre" (III.iii.7.1-2). Since premature identification of Artegall would divert his readers' attention, Spenser first brings him into the action and exposes his weaknesses. He identifies Artegall at the appropriate dramatic moment; for suddenly Britomart appears and smites him "in middest of his pryde" with her magic spear (IV. iv.44.2), a rather inauspicious beginning for a romance, however providentially inspired. Because the other knights thanklessly envy her success and attempt to overthrow her, Britomart overcomes them one by one.

> Like as in sommers day when raging heat
> Doth burne the earth, and boyled rivers drie,
> That all brute beasts forst to refraine fro meat,
> Doe hunt for shade, where shrowded they may lie,
> And missing it, faine from themselves to flie.
>
> (IV.iv.47.1-5)

In quelling the "beasts," Britomart restores the *prize* to "knights of Maydenhead" (IV.iv.48.2).

The pattern of imagery used in the battle scenes suggests that the participants at the tournament lose their separate identities, especially those supposedly committed to the pursuit of virtue. The defeat of Artegall, Cambell, Triamond, and the other "brute beasts" by Britomart completes the pattern. It is significant to Spenser's imagistic scheme that Satyrane's mock tournament ends when the "trompets loudly gan to bray" (IV.iv.48.5).

Britomart's victory over the baser contestants is a triumph of virtue—chastity which apparently brings order out of chaos. But Spenser knows that force is at best only a temporary restraint upon the body and is of no use in reforming the mind. The followers of beauty have yet to reveal their true selves.

So fitly now here commeth next in place,
After the proofe of prowesse ended well,
The controverse of beauties soveraine grace;
In which to her that doth the most excell,
Shall fall the girdle of faire *Florimell*:
That many wish to win for glorie vaine,
And not for vertuous use, which some do tell
That glorious belt did in it selfe containe,
Which Ladies ought to love, and seeke for to obtaine.

(IV.v.2)

Spenser's irony puts the tournament in its proper perspective. We already know how those that fought for the girdle for the wrong motives debased themselves. It remains for the poet to examine the women who wish to obtain it for vain reasons. This, of course, gives him an opportunity to trace the history of the girdle, how Vulcan fabricated it to "bind lascivious desire" and how his wife Venus betrayed him, leaving it behind when she visited Mars. When the false Florimell wins the beauty contest, she claims the girdle as her right despite the fact that only Amoret, Britomart's ward, can wear it. The girdle truly is now the Snowy Lady's, however. Whether she is able to wear it is of little consequence here, simply because she meets the one measurement fixed by Satyrane—beauty. Her later possession of the girdle, confusing to some critics, is directly related to this "victory." The knowledge that she is not virtuous inspires the crude jest of the Squire of Dames which strikes a responsive chord of laughter in the warriors but does not deter them from wanting to be her consort.[8]

[8] Spenser has contrived to remove Gloriana's knights from any further involvement with the snowy Florimell, even though they have more or less priority by virtue of their exploits at the tournament: 1) Britomart (thought to be a man) will not forgo Amoret; 2) Artegall has already withdrawn from consideration, having "gone / In great displeasure" (IV.v.21.6-7); 3) Triamond has his beloved Canacee (IV.v.21.8-9). The prize then devolves upon 4) Satyrane, the imperfect knight, under whose auspices the tournament began.

The rival claims for her favor threaten to begin the battle anew, since Britomart has denied an interest and the Salvage Knight has left the field.

Satyrane proposes that their beautiful lady be permitted to choose freely among them.

> They all agreed, and then that snowy Mayd
> Was in the middest plast among them all;
> All on her gazing wisht, and vowd, and prayd,
> And to the Queene of beautie close did call,
> That she unto their portion might befall.
>
> (IV.v.26.1-5)

Satyrane's trick of physically substituting the false Florimell for virtue is emblematic of the whole degenerate progress of the tournament, for the spectacle of the suitors whining and slavering for her questionable favors shows what abject beasts they have become. It follows that when she chooses the "capon," Braggadocchio, to be her consort, "they chaft and rag'd,/ And woxe nigh mad for very harts despight" (IV.v.27.1-2). This is the unending discord created by the indiscriminate pursuit of beauty for its own sake. Britomart wisely decides to leave the senseless turmoil.

In Artegall's brief appearance at the Tournament of Beauty, Spenser has laid bare the principal flaws in his character—concupiscence, wrath, and pride. As he slinks away to lick his wounds, he meets Scudamour, who also bears a grudge against Britomart, falsely thinking she stole away his fair Amoret. They exchange confidences and find they have a common grief against Britomart. Just as Britomart once slandered Artegall for her own designs (III.ii. 8.7-9), Artegall uses almost exactly the same words to malign her and to justify revenge.

> This other day (sayd he) a stranger knight
> Shame and dishonour hath unto me donne;

On whom I waite to wreak that foule despight,
When ever he this way shall passe by day or night.
(IV.vi.5.6-9)

Artegall's shameful detour from his true quest is another manifestation of the workings of Providence in the texture of the poem, for he is now on a collision course with his destiny. And his physical defeat on the field of beauty prepares the reader for his subjugation, first by Britomart and then by Radigund.

When they finally see Britomart approaching, Scudamour has the honor of the first attack.

>   he his threatfull speare
> Gan fewter, and against her fiercely ran.
> Who soone as she him saw approaching neare
> With so fell rage, her selfe she lightly gan
> To dight, to welcome him, well as she can:
> But entertaind him in so rude a wise,
> That to the ground she smote both horse and man;
> Whence neither greatly hasted to arise,
> But on their common harmes together did devise.
> (IV.vi.10)

The contrast in their styles of fighting is important. Since he thinks Britomart has stolen Amoret, Scudamour attacks in a "fell rage" full of despite. On the other hand, Britomart is almost nonchalant: "she lightly gan/ To dight." Like a good hostess, she welcomes him. But the entertainment she provides at their meeting is not to Scudamour's liking. By playing on the words *lightly, welcome,* and *entertaind,* Spenser humorously makes the point that kindness turns away wrath. Britomart can afford to relax in her encounters, however. So long as she stays on her horse and keeps her magic spear, all her battles are like mild calisthenics. Britomart was long associated in antiquity with Diana; and her ebony spear is just another link in the chain of associations that evoke an implicit relationship. Spenser surely knew Pliny's account of Diana's temple at Ephesus,[9] and knew of the statue that it contained, the famous *Diana simulacrum mammosum*,[10] made of ebony.[11] Since Britomart subsumes both the chastity and the fecundity of the two fair Dianas in her own character, she can "beat downe licentious lust" *and* bear a race of kings. In her encounter with Scudamour she overcomes his wrath kindled by his impure desire for Amoret and thus prepares the way for true marriage. Her encounter with Artegall, however, marks a significant variation in her fighting technique, partly occasioned by necessity but primarily brought about by her personal involvement with her antagonist. She is enjoying a long string of victories when Artegall encounters her in a rematch.

In the first clash with Britomart at Satyrane's tournament, Artegall falls in the "middest of his pryde." In the second, he falls in the midst of his wrath, seeking vengeance for having been disappointed in the winning of the fairest lady (IV.vi.11). The course of this fight, however, follows a different pattern, since Artegall recovers quickly and battles Britomart from the ground with his sword.

> So as they coursed here and there, it chaunst
> That in her wheeling round, behind her crest
> So sorely he her strooke, that thence it glaunst
> Adowne her backe, the which it fairely blest
> From foule mischance; ne did it ever rest,
> Till on her horses hinder parts it fell;
> Where byting deepe, so deadly it imprest,
> That quite it chynd his backe behind the sell,
> And to alight on foote her algates did compell.
>   (IV.vi.13)

[9] Spenser specifically mentions the temple in IV.x.30.1-4.

[10] Natali Conti includes an excellent representation of the Ephesean Diana in his handbook *Mythologiae* (Padua, 1637), p. 141.

[11] *Historia naturalis*, xvi, 79.

Mr. Hamilton suggests that this is the blow of concupiscence and has subtly explained the significance of the sexual
imagery.[12] But the overall pattern of the battle reveals
just how similar Britomart is to Artegall. As soon as her
feet touch the ground, Britomart literally and metaphorically descends into nature. Where before she fought on
her own terms upon her lofty horse with her magic spear
of chastity, now she fights on equal footing with Artegall
on his terms. Her calm demeanor gone, "furiously she
strooke in her first heat" (IV.vi.15.1). She wounds Artegall
severely and forces him to retreat. Long accustomed to
easy victory, she is not prepared for the long battle of the
sexes in nature. When Artegall sees "her hastie heat/Abate,"
he rises in his strength and attacks her fiercely. Spenser's
description of his attack shows how completely Britomart
has been absorbed into nature. Artegall's huge strokes fall
"as thicke as showre of hayle" (IV.vi.16.5), beating Britomart, the tender plant, into the ground. Spenser confirms
this identification with an obvious poetic footnote:

> What yron courage ever could endure,
> To worke such outrage on so faire a creature?
> And in his madnesse thinke with hands impure
> To spoyle so goodly workmanship of nature,
> The maker selfe resembling in her feature?
>
> (IV.vi.17.1-5)

This is the culmination of a progress that began in Book
Three. From the instant of his appearance in the mirror,
Artegall has gradually added substance until he becomes a
full-fledged knight in the nature of Faery Land. Parallel-
ing his gradual emergence in nature is Britomart's descent
into it. This is as it should be. When Britomart had only
the idea of Artegall to content her fancy, she pined away
to a shadow. The more she knows about her lover and the
closer she rides to him the closer she will come to the time

---

[12] *Structure*, p. 182.

when she is to fulfill Merlin's prophecy and help perpetuate the British nation.

In this fight between man and woman the outcome is
uncertain at first; "But toward th'end Sir *Arthegall* re-
newed/ His strength still more, but she the more de-
crewed" (IV.vi.18.4-5). As masculine strength waxes, feminine power to resist wanes. With a sudden blow Artegall
shears away Britomart's vizor and discovers her beauty.

> And as his hand he up againe did reare,
> Thinking to worke on her his utmost wracke,
> His powrelesse arme benumbed with secret feare
> From his revengefull purpose shronke abacke,
> And cruell sword out of his fingers slacke
> Fell downe to ground, as if the steele had sence,
> And felt some ruth, or sence his hand did lacke,
> Or both of them did thinke, obedience
> To doe to so divine a beauties excellence.
>
> And he himselfe long gazing thereupon,
> At last fell humbly downe upon his knee,
> And of his wonder made religion,
> Weening some heavenly goddesse he did see,
> Or else unweeting, what it else might bee;
> And pardon her besought his error frayle,
> That had done outrage in so high degree:
> Whilst trembling horrour did his sense assayle,
> And made ech member quake, and manly hart to quayle.
>
> (IV.vi.21-22)

This marks Artegall's third fall. Having previously succumbed to pride and wrath, he now bows to concupiscence.
This pattern is repeated in Artegall's battle with Radigund,
with one important difference. The imagery of this passage
(IV.vi.21) shows that Artegall's abandoning his sword, the
symbol of his manhood, is not a willful act. It is all involuntary. His arm is powerless, numbed with secret fear,

as Spenser makes the point that there is some question whether the hand or the sword or both hand and sword felt pity for such a divine beauty.

Although he is not to be blamed when the sword falls from his hand—that is providential—Artegall is guilty of prostrating himself at beauty's shrine. Scudamour, who has burned his share of candles at beauty's altar, knows exactly who Britomart is. As he draws near, "he plaine descride/ That peerelesse paterne of Dame natures pride,/ And heavenly image of perfection" (IV.vi.24.4-6). When both Artegall and Scudamour then worship at beauty's shrine, Glauce, a spectator at the battle, is now "full glad of so good end" (IV.vi.25.3). Of course, it is she who gets Britomart to agree to a truce and the knights to raise their vizors. The manner in which she does this is with "seemely belaccoyle." The word *belaccoyle*, calling to mind associations from the *Roman de la Rose*, is particularly appropriate. In the *Roman*, it is *Belacoil*, as an aspect of the lady, who first extends a welcome to the lover. Belacoil is the first step in the dance of love.

As soon as Britomart sees Artegall, her wrath changes to meekness. She begins to withdraw her sword.

> Yet she it forst to have againe upheld,
> As fayning choler, which was turn'd to cold:
> But ever when his visage she beheld,
> Her hand fell downe, and would no longer hold
> The wrathfull weapon gainst his countnance bold:
> But when in vaine to fight she oft assayd,
> She arm'd her tongue, and thought at him to scold;
> Nathlesse her tongue not to her will obayd,
> But brought forth speeches myld, when she would
>   have missayd.
>
> (IV.vi.27)

Britomart's reaction is exactly like Artegall's capitulation to beauty. Her wrath changing to desire, she becomes meek and powerless to harm him. Spenser is having a little merriment at the expense of womankind when Britomart's secondary weapon of attack, her tongue, will not obey her will. This final detail points up just how helpless Britomart has become in the sight of Artegall's beauty, the one thing that Merlin's art did not improve upon.

By observing the change in Britomart's nature, Glauce "gan wisely all upknit" to the spectators in her own platitudinous style (IV.vi.30). When she sees that Artegall and Britomart are receptive to one another, Glauce assumes the role of matchmaker, a role that is true to the "course of kind."

> And you Sir *Artegall*, the salvage knight,
> Henceforth may not disdaine, that womans hand
> Hath conquered you anew in second fight:
> For whylome they have conquered sea and land,
> And heaven it selfe, that nought may them withstand,
> Ne henceforth be rebellious unto love,
> That is the crowne of knighthood, and the band
> Of noble minds derived frome above,
> Which being knit with vertue, never will remove.
>
> And you faire Ladie knight, my dearest Dame,
> Relent the rigour of your wrathfull will,
> Whose fire were better turn'd to other flame;
> And wiping out remembrance of all ill,
> Graunt him your grace, but so that he fulfill
> The penance, which ye shall to him empart:
> For lovers heaven must passe by sorrowes hell.
>
> (IV.vi.31-32.1-7)

While here, clearly, Glauce is promoting marriage, what she is describing however is love in the world. Circumscribed by nature, Glauce does not know that the crown of knighthood is love of virtue, that the marriage of true minds breeds no sorrow. Apparently having forgotten

Merlin's remark on Providence, Britomart becomes a normal woman who puts her lover through his paces. The love game, as played in nature, is a circular contest; and Britomart finally consents to be Artegall's love "Till they with mariage meet might finish that accord" (IV.vi.41.9). After they have plighted their troths, Artegall, "who all this while was bound/ Upon an hard adventure yet in quest,/ [found it was] Fit time for him thence to depart," after he has given her a "thousand vowes from bottom of his hart" and promises to return to her in three months.

Spenser's portrayal of Artegall in Books Three and Four serves as a background against which the specific episodes in Book Five are set. In Book Three Spenser delineates the ideal aspects of Artegall's character through the endeavors of art. Merlin, the arch-artificer, has created the magic mirror in which Britomart sees Artegall in his true potential. Merlin's prophecy, Red Cross's "Magick words," and Britomart's "feigning fancie" contribute to the illusion that Artegall is a perfect knight. In every degree, their "visions" are true; for Artegall does become the perfect knight at the end of his quest in Book Five. When he finishes his quest, the perfected Artegall approximates the ideal Artegall represented in art. We should not overemphasize the disparities existing between the Artegall of Book Three and the Salvage Knight in Book Four. This is one of Spenser's basic artistic techniques in writing *The Faerie Queene*. A knight, the patron of a particular virtue, undertakes a difficult quest. This knight is the patron of his virtue only in potential, but not in fact, since he is temporarily deterred from the achievement of his quest because of certain flaws in his character. When he receives grace or gains wisdom, he triumphs over his weaknesses and succeeds in his quest.

Artegall is no exception. In Book Four Spenser presents in fine all the defects of Artegall's character—pride, wrath, and concupiscence, to which he has succumbed in turn. At

Satyrane's Tournament of the Girdle, Britomart defeats him "in the middest of his pryde." In his second encounter with Britomart, she smites him down in his wrath. He himself is the instrument of his fall to concupiscence, when he slavishly prostrates himself before Britomart's beauty. All of the defects of Artegall's character presented in Book Four anticipate his specific problems in Book Five and foreshadow his fall. The idealized portrayal of him in Book Three likewise anticipates his triumphs over his passions and his ultimate perfection in justice. With Artegall's character (both ideal and actual) in mind, we are now able to consider his childhood and training and the significance of the first episode in his quest to free Irena from Grantorto.

iii

In addition to the elaborate analysis of Artegall in the preceding books, Spenser further enlarges upon his character at the beginning of Book Five because he is making doubly sure that his readers have a complete understanding of the personal barriers standing between him and the successful completion of his quest. The very nature of Faery Land itself is a barrier. Except for infrequent oases, Spenser's Faery Land shares dominion with the fallen world, and his beautiful Proem for Book Five serves to reinforce this unhappy fact in our minds. Civilized society now especially depends upon and is maintained by virtuous endeavor. Occasionally a great man arises who fights for right and establishes justice.

> Such first was *Bacchus*, that with furious might
> All th'East before untam'd did overronne,
> And wrong repressed, and establisht right,
> Which lawlesse men had formerly fordonne.
> There Justice first her princely rule begonne.
> Next *Hercules* his like ensample shewed,
> Who all the West with equall conquest wonne,

And monstrous tyrants with his club subdewed;
The club of Justice dread, with kingly powre endewed.

And such was he, of whom I have to tell,
The Champion of true Justice *Artegall*.

(V.i.2-3.1-2)

Through the work of Alice Sawtelle, Upton, and Lotspeich, readers of Spenser have long known of some of the treatments of the myths of Bacchus and Hercules in this context.[13] When we consider that Spenser's problem was similar to those of the historians in antiquity, we will begin to see how Spenser is using myth in Book Five. Unlike the modern historian who can draw upon the sciences of anthropology and linguistics to arrive at an appraisal of events, the early Greek and Latin compilers of "history" had to deal with the origins of cultural traditions, many of which were flourishing when they were writing, a problem some perceptive historiographers recognized as important. In this regard, Diodorus Siculus attempts to rationalize "deification" by considering it a reward for work well done.

Now it is an excellent thing, methinks, as all men of understanding must agree, to receive in exchange for mortal labours an immortal fame. In the case of Hercules, for instance, it is generally agreed that during the whole time which he spent among men he submitted to great and continuous labors and perils willingly, in order that he might confer benefits upon the race of men and thereby gain immortality; and likewise in the case of other great and good men, some have attained to heroic honours and others of great praise, since history immortalizes their achievements. For whereas all other memorials abide but a brief time, being continually destroyed by many vicissitudes, yet the power of history which extends over the whole

[13] *Variorum, Book Five*, 162.

inhabited world, possesses in time, which brings ruin upon all things else, a custodian which ensures its perpetual transmission to posterity.[14]

As did Diodorus, Dionysius of Halicarnassus had to choose from the welter of conflicting stories about Hercules conquering the West.

> But the story which comes nearer the truth and which has been adopted by many who have narrated his deeds in the form of history is as follows: Hercules, who was the greatest commander of his age, marched at the head of a large force through all the country that lies on this side of the ocean, destroying any despotisms that were grievous and oppressive to their subjects, or commonwealths that outraged and injured the neighboring states, or organized bands of men who lived in the manner of savages and lawlessly put strangers to death, and in their room establishing lawful monarchies, well-ordered governments and humane and sociable modes of life.[15]

In a similar way, when Spenser draws upon material from history or mythology, it is always appropriate to the action of the poem. By mentioning the legends of Bacchus and Hercules at the beginning of Book Five, Spenser has given his subject universal implications, as they divided the world between them—one taking the East, the other, the West.

Of the two commanders, Hercules is the more important for Spenser's purposes. From the tosspot and indefatigable lecher of the *vetus comedia* to the exemplar of the virtuous life for the stoics, Hercules held a certain fascination for readers in the Renaissance. Born a little lower than the

---

[14] *Library of History*, Loeb Library trans. C. H. Oldfather (London, 1932), 1.ii.3-5.

[15] *The Roman Antiquities*, Loeb Library trans. Earnest Cary (London, 1927), 1.xii.

gods, as man himself was born a little lower than the angels, Hercules fought valiantly for the benefit of mankind, finally triumphed over his own discordant nature, and was translated to the stars. Spenser was alive to the artistic possibilities inherent in the ambiguous character of Hercules and was especially diligent in using details of his mythical life to give point to his argument. Inasmuch as Christ is the true Hercules,[16] Red Cross's sufferings in fighting the dragon are greater than Hercules' final agony (I.xi.27). Arthur's battle with Maleger is deliberately reminiscent of Hercules' fight with Antaeus (II.xi.38-49). In the books of love and friendship Spenser twice invokes the love and friendship of Hercules and Hylas (III.xii.7; IV.x.27). Calidore binds the Blatant Beast as Hercules once chained Cerberus (VI.xii.35). The mythical Hercules once fought in the West, and Faery Land, the fallen world, is in the West. Artegall himself fights in the West, assuming some of the labors of Hercules and sharing all of his faults. Spenser has so carefully integrated the character of Hercules with that of Artegall and has implicitly or explicitly presented some of the labors of Hercules that the myth emerges as a major image of Book Five, the myth determining the structure and controlling the imagery. In this case, the myth of Hercules is a vehicle for the action in which image and meaning coalesce.

In some respects Artegall's childhood and early training are similar to Satyrane's. Although they both spend part of their childhood in controlling wild beasts, the ends for which they are trained differ greatly. Satyrane was born of the unlawful union of a "satyre" and Thyamis (his mother being already "married" to Therion, a *wild beast* who loved to "chase the salvage beast with busie payne" [I.vi.21.8]). Since Therion neglects her for the chase, "The forlorne mayd did with loves longing burne,/ And could not lacke

[16] A Renaissance commonplace, for which see the popular *De asse et partibus eius* of Budé (Lyons, 1551), pp. 706, 779.

her lovers company" (I.vi.22.1-2). One day following her husband into the woods, she finds exactly what she was looking for and commits adultery with a satyr who makes "her person thrall unto his beastly kind" (I.vi.22.9). The issue of this random woodland meeting is Satyrane, whom his father keeps as "ransome" and tries to educate.

He noursled up [Satyrane] in life and manners wilde,
Emongst wild beasts and woods, from lawes of men exilde.

For all he taught the tender ymp, was but
To banish cowardize and bastard feare;
His trembling hand he would him force to put
Upon the Lyon and the rugged Beare,
And from the she Beares teats her whelps to teare;
And eke wyld roring Buls he would him make
To tame, and ryde their backes not made to beare;
And the Robuckes in flight to overtake,
That every beast for feare of him did fly and quake.
                                        (I.vi.23-24)

As is to be expected from such a teacher, the emphasis in Satyrane's early education is upon the animalistic side of man's nature, and Spenser makes the obvious point that such training is "from lawes of men exilde." Satyre teaches his son the law of the jungle, and the whole purpose of his curriculum of studies is designed to get him to "banish cowardize and bastard feare."

In direct contrast, Artegall's parentage is mysterious and is unknown to him (III.iii.26). He has however been taught by a virtuous lady, Astraea, who symbolizes justice in the Golden Age. She singles him out for instruction when he is a child playing with his peers because she finds him "fit, and with no crime defilde" (V.i.6.4). She recognizes his potential as a patron of justice; and here Spenser reinforces the artist's vision of Artegall's promise in Book

Three. Like Satyre, Astraea has isolated her pupil from the world of men.

> So thence him farre she brought
> Into a cave from companie exilde,
> In which she noursled him, till years he raught,
> And all the discipline of justice there him taught.
>
> There she him taught to weigh both right and wrong
> In equall ballance with due recompence,
> And equitie to measure out along,
> According to the line of conscience,
> When so it needs with rigour to dispence.
> Of all the which, for want there of mankind,
> She caused him to make experience
> Upon wyld beasts, which she in woods did find,
> With wrongfull powre oppressing others of their kind.
>
> (V.i.6-7)

Even though Artegall is far from the company of men, Astraea teaches him the most civilized art, the art of administering justice. Her whole plan for his early training prepares him to protect and sustain civilization.

If we examine closely the particular details of Artegall's character from his youth to his maturity, we will see how Spenser has carefully prepared us for accepting Artegall as a type of Hercules. Each particular detail in itself is not wholly convincing; but in sum they make up irrefragable evidence that Spenser intended his readers to see his patron of justice as Hercules, compounded of the same faults, promising the same virtues. In this context, even Artegall's infancy anticipates the identification.

> For *Artegall* in justice was upbrought
> Even from the cradle of his infancie,
> And all the depth of rightful doome was taught

By faire Astraea, with great industrie,
Whilest here on earth she lived mortallie.

(V.i.5.1-5)

Hercules too started his indoctrination in the cradle. It is well known that Juno, incensed by Jupiter's infidelity with Alcmena, sent two serpents to destroy the offspring of their union. Hercules proved equal to the challenge by strangling the snakes. As the story is told in Apollodorus (2.4), both Hercules and his half brother Iphicles were sleeping when Juno sent the serpents. When they were awakened by the intruders, Iphicles screamed for help but Hercules manfully faced the danger. Lilio Giraldi in his *Vita Herculis* glosses the infant's behavior as representing the choice of ways, indicating that he has chosen virtue over vice, courage over cowardice.[17] T. A. d'Aubigné makes this an example of God's grace working in nature: "Commençant dès le berceau, comme dès lors sanctifié à Dieu par une générosité naturelle, à esteindre les malices, les cholères, despite et mauvaistiez de la première jeunesse, figurées par ces deaux serpens qui se couloyent dans le maillot d'Hercules, et dès lors rendent quelque preuve que les infans de Dieu sont sanctifiés dès le ventre de la mère."[18] The cave to which Astraea brings Artegall may also be reminiscent of Chiron's Cave. Since his father was Chronos,[19] Chiron like Astraea was identified with the Golden Age. It was upon this Centaur that the early rearing and educating of Hercules, Jason, Aesculapius, and Achilles devolved.[20]

[17] *Vita Herculis* in *Opera*, 1 (1696), 574a. The classic treatment of this aspect of Hercules' career is Erwin Panofsky's *Hercules am Scheidewege* (Berlin, 1930).

[18] *L'Hercule Chrestien*, in *Oeuvres complètes*, 11, eds. Reaume and de Caussade (Paris, 1877), 227.

[19] Appollonius Rhodius' *Argonautica*, 1, 547-558; see scholia included in Henri Estienne's edition *Argonauticon* (1574), pp. 26-27.

[20] This was handbook information in the Renaissance. See Charles Estienne's *Dictionarium Historicum, geographicum, poeticum* (Oxford, 1671), p. 276b.

Since Astraea has taken Artegall to a cave of learning far removed from the haunts of men, her pupil must get his practical experience among animals, to whom he restores peace[21] and measures out equity, weighing both "right and wrong" (V.i.7). After long practice he reaches the stage where "wilde beasts did feare his awfull sight,/ And men admyr'd his overruling might" (V.i.8.4-5). That Hercules conquered wild beasts is one of the commonplaces of antiquity. Diodorus' account of him is typical: "And with regard to Heracles they [the Egyptians] say that he was born among them and they assign to him, in common with the Greeks, both the club and the lion's skin. Moreover, as their account tells us, he was far superior to all other men in strength of body and in courage and cleared both land and sea of their wild beasts."[22] In discussing the virtuous life of Crates in his *Florida*, Apuleius draws a comparison between Hercules' conquering human or brutish monsters and the philosopher's overcoming the monsters and vices of the human soul: "As poets tell, Hercules once subdued by his courage those frightful human and bestial monsters and cleansed the world. Similarly that philosopher was a Hercules against wrath, envy, avarice, lust, and other monsters and shameful acts of the human mind; he drove out all these diseases from the minds of men, rid families of them, and overcame malice."[23] With the passage of time and the preservation of the writings of antiquity by rededicating them to *moralitas*, Apuleius' valiant Hercules and virtuous philosopher merged together in the steady flow of what has been called the allegorical tradition. Consonant with this tradition, Claude Mignault,[24] Alciati's annotator, and

[21] This contrasts with Satyrane's treatment of beasts "That his beheast they feared, as a tyrans law" (I.vi.26.9).

[22] *Library of History*, II.xxxix.2.

[23] *Opera*, ed. Alban Thorer (Basel, 1533), p. 367 [xiv].

[24] *Emblemata* (Lyons, 1614), pp. 491-496.

Natale Conti[25] in the sixteenth century proceed to equate each experience of Hercules with a moral achievement, and the learned Piero Valeriano holds that Hercules' conquest of animals and monsters represents virtues overcoming the vices.[26] Knowing fully of their enriching resonances, Spenser draws metaphors for poetry from similar funds of traditional material in his portrayal of Artegall's career and moral development.

The sword Chrysaor which Astraea gives to Artegall serves as another link between him and Hercules.

> Which steely brand, to make him dreaded more,
> She gave unto him, gotten by her slight
> And earnest search, where it was kept in store
> In *Joves* eternal house, unwist of wight,
> Since he himself it us'd in that great fight
> Against the *Titans*, that whylome rebelled
> Gainst highest heaven; *Chrysaor* it was hight;
> *Chrysaor* that all other swords excelled,
> Well prov'd in that same day, when *Jove* those Gyants
>   quelled.
>
> For of most perfect metall it was made,
> Tempered with Adamant amongst the same,
> And garnisht all with gold upon the blade
> In goodly wise, whereof it tooke his name,
> And was of no lesse vertue, then of fame.
> For there no substance was so firme and hard,
> But it would pierce or cleave, where so it came;
> Ne any armour could his dint out ward,
> But wheresoever it did light, it thoroughly shard.
>   (V.i.9-10)

Fowler suggestively shows that Chrysaor is a surname of

[25] *Mythologicae Libri* (Padua, 1637), pp. 355-375.
[26] *Hieroglyphica, sive de sacris Aegyptiorum* (Basel, 1575), p. 23 verso.

Jupiter—which fits in nicely with Spenser's text.[27] And in addition, this is the sword with which Jupiter fought the giants, who could be defeated only with the help of Hercules.[28]

If the details of Artegall's training in nature by Astraea suggest parallel details in the life of Hercules, we should expect Britomart's view of him in Merlin's mirror of art to provide us with similar information. In her vision she first notices Artegall's physical beauty and then his battle dress.

His crest was covered with a couchant Hound,
And all his armour seem'd of antique mould,
But wondrous massie and assured sound,
And round about yfretted all with gold,
In which there written was, with cyphers old,
Achilles armes, which Arthegall did win.
And on his shield enveloped sevenfold
He bore a crowned little Ermilin,
That deckt the azure field with her faire pouldred skin.

(III.ii.25)

For Spenser the most important piece of armor is the shield, inasmuch as a knight advertises his worth and purpose by it. Artegall later gives a lecture to Burbon when he abandons his shield, advising him that it represents his "honours stile" (V.xi.55.6). The construction of Artegall's shield is unique, sevenfold—a shield like those of the heroes of antiquity and is in keeping with the "antique

[27] *Spenser and the Numbers of Time*, p. 201.

[28] "Now the Gods had an oracle that none of the giants could perish at the hands of gods, but that with the help of a mortal they would be made an end of. Learning of this, Earth sought for a simple to prevent the giants from being destroyed even by a mortal. But Zeus forbade the Dawn and the Moon and the Sun to shine, and then, before anybody else could get it, he culled the simple himself, and by means of Athena summoned Hercules to his help" (Apollodorus, *The Library*, I.vi 1-2).

mould" of Achilles' armor. Merlin's interpretation confirms this point.

> Behold the man, and tell me *Britomart*,
> If ay more goodly creature thou didst see;
> How like a Gyaunt in each manly part
> Beares he himselfe with portly majestee,
> That one of th'old *Heroes* seemes to bee.
>
> (III.iii.32.1-5)

Artegall's "stile" is made clear by the ermine on his shield which refers to his nobility (with Britomart he is to help perpetuate the British nation) and also symbolizes his office as patron of justice.

In addition to these general resonances suggestive of Artegall's office and royal destiny, his shield specifically inspires the character of Hercules. It is consistent with Spenser's poetic design that his hero display such an emblem on his shield, as the ermine (any weasel which turns white in winter) is the animal held sacred to him. We know a retelling of the myth's origin in the writings of a well-known Roman poet and in the work of an early chronicler of the strange habits of animals and the stranger beliefs they inspired. Through the efforts of the compilers of mythological dictionaries, the glossators of Ovid, and the natural and unnatural historians, the association of Hercules with *mustela* became a Renaissance commonplace.

When Ovid, who industriously wove the uneven tapestry of the lives and loves of the gods in his *Metamorphoses*, tells of the birth of Hercules, he comments at length on the method Juno chooses to exact revenge upon Alcmena, who is bearing Jove's child. As the time nears for her to be delivered of Hercules, Juno forces Lucina, goddess of childbearing, to stay the birth. Alcmena suffers for seven long days and finally gives birth only after Galanthis, her maidservant, tricks Lucina into believing her efforts were in vain.

Fate is not kind to Galanthis, as she feels the fury of Lucina's wrath.

> They say Galanthis laught at this deceit:
> Whom straight the flouted Goddesse, in a fret,
> Drags her by the haire; nor suffers her to rise:
> Forth-with her armes convert to leggs and thighes:
> Agility and colour still abide:
> Her shape transform's. In that her mouth supply'd
> Help to that childbirth, at her mouth she beares.
> Nor now our still frequented houses feares.[29]

The writer of the *Ovide Moralizé* knew of Galanthis' transformation—"c'est la moustele, à mon avis."[30] And Raphael Regius provided the standard gloss for the sixteenth and seventeenth centuries when he wrote "The other goddess, indignant over the trick by Galanthis, quickly changed her into a weasel that she may give birth through her mouth which had lied."[31]

Confirming Galanthis' new destiny while making his contribution to social anthropology, the eclectic Aelian smiles disapprovingly upon the myth's being the basis of religious exercise.[32] In his *Hieroglyphica* Valeriano slips in a reference to this account,[33] while the enterprising natural

---

[29] *Ovids Metamorphosis Englished by Geo. Sandys* (London, 1638), ix. 317-324.

[30] "Neuvième livre," 1307; eds. C. de Boer et al., iii (Amsterdam, 1931), 252.

[31] *Metamorphoses* (Venice, 1509), folio xciii. All the early annotated editions of Ovid that I have been able to check adopt his gloss, with or without acknowledgment.

[32] "But the Thebans, in fact a nation of Greeks, humorous to behold, worship the weasel, and they say it was the nurse of Hercules, or was not even the nurse, but when Alcmena was in labor and was not able to deliver Hercules, it broke the chains of childbearing running by . . ." (*Opera quae extant omnia* [Zurich, 1556], p. 250a).

[33] Page 99 verso.

historian, Ulisse Aldrovandi, expands upon it, adding Clement of Alexandria as an authority.[34] From among the many meanings of *mustela* in general—both good and bad—Aldrovandi's moralization of this ambiguous animal as symbolizing the true dispenser of justice and mercy nicely agrees with Spenser's text.[35] Since the association of *mustela* with Hercules is unmistakable in the Renaissance, the inclusion of the ermine as a symbol of Artegall's "stile" shows just how carefully Spenser has worked to make his hero a type of Hercules.

Symbolically related to the nature of Artegall's quest is the color of his shield, as we learn from Legh's popular book of heraldry that azure is particularly appropriate to the virtue of justice. "[The shield] is a paire of ballance of Silver, in a field blewe, which signifieth Justice, who as well upholdeth the dignitie of everie estate, as also the common wealth, and yieldeth to everie one his due, and telleth what to doe, and what to leave undonne. Justice giveth reward after merite, as to the benefactour made, and to the transgressor punishment."[36] It is perhaps well to remember also that in the famous Hesiodic poem, *The Shield of Heracles*, the plates of this wonderful guard are of blue enamel: κυάνου δὲ διὰ πτύχες ἠλήλαντο (line 143). By substituting an ermine for the trite pair of balances customary to justice, Spenser again adds a detail that enhances further speculation rather than discourages it. Probably the equating of the weasel/ermine with justice is the responsibility of the many patient observers in antiquity of animal life. As

[34] "Clement of Alexandria noted this was true because they believed the mother of Hercules was helped in childbearing by a weasel." (*De quadrupedibus digitatis viviparis* . . . [Bonn, 1645], p. 322).

[35] *Ibid.*, pp. 321-322.

[36] *The Accendence of Armorie* (London, 1591), sig. A.vi.verso. This was revised and reprinted five times during the sixteenth century.

their observations (real or imagined) were grist for the mills of the emblem makers, Hadrianus Junius can speak confidently of *mustela* having the qualities of a justice: *Audito multa, loquitur pauca.* That the shield of Artegall is of universal significance while simultaneously particularizing him as a type of Hercules is a glory of Spenser's poetic technique.

Miss Williams has suggested that in wearing Achilles' armor Artegall shares some of his personality traits[37]— which is true but is a distinction without a difference, inasmuch as both were known to have similar faults of pride, wrath, and concupiscence. Achilles' armor here is Spenser's sly reference to the fact that Hercules fought at Troy, and Artegall as the new Hercules is to unite with Britomart, thereby continuing the Trojan line in Britain. That Artegall wears the armor of Achilles and carries the shield of Hercules should not be confusing. In antiquity they were closely associated with one another and attended the same school and had the same headmaster—Chiron. Since in mythology they receive their early training from a centaur, although a gifted one, they have rather aggravated personality problems which emphasize the ambiguity of their mentor.

Keeping in mind the rich associations with which Spenser has freighted his hero, we should be able to understand the significance of Artegall's progress in Book Five, the most roundly condemned and least understood book of *The Faerie Queene.* One of the most perceptive critics of Spenser writing today, A. C. Hamilton, has especial demurrers about the quality of the poetry in the Book of Justice. In his critical treatment of Book Five, Hamilton is torn between an analysis of the imagery and a desire to subsume the "historical allegory" into the context of that imagery. A consideration of historical allegory is incidental to an un-

[37] "Venus and Diana," 103.

derstanding of *The Faerie Queene*—even if we grant Spenser tickled the risibilities of his contemporary audience when he wrote of Burbon's excuses for wanting Flourdelis and probably made them pause to think how Divine Providence stood watch over England when he wrote of Arthur's miraculous victory over the Soldan. These passages, however, have a significance central to the narrative and consistent with its moral meaning. They are not dependent for meaning upon history.

Another serious obstacle blocking an understanding of Book Five is to consider it a sport of Spenser's poetic imagination, never, thankfully, to be repeated. Hamilton thinks the pattern here is different from the other books of *The Faerie Queene.*

> Spenser's fiction seems to break down in Book V. Probably for this reason the book is the least popular. C. S. Lewis finds part of its unpopularity in our changed concept of justice. . . . Surely it is that we are here more aware of the virtue itself than in the other books. When Spenser introduces an episode with the remark that "so much as to my lot here lights,/ That with this present treatise doth agree,/ True virtue to advance, shall here recounted be" (V.iii.3), his didacticism takes over the fiction. Professor Lewis considers Artegall to be one of the most disagreeable characters in the whole poem, and most readers would agree with him. I know it does not make him any less disagreeable to remind ourselves of Spenser's special problem with him; but for the first time among his titular heroes, the virtue must be separate from the man. . . . Justice must be impersonal. While the Red Cross Knight learns to frame his life in holiness, Guyon displays temperance, Britomart's chastity is herself, and Calidore's courtesy is as natural as breathing, Artegall must stand apart from the justice he administers.

Though he wields the sword of justice, he may use it
only once in the book; and that is in his final battle
against Grantorto.[38]

As Mr. Hamilton's serious objections will be handled in
the course of the following chapters, it is appropriate to
raise here a few general questions central to criticism of
The Faerie Queene. It seems unlikely that Spenser would
expend so much creative energy in developing Artegall's
character both in nature and art and then not take advantage of the opportunities it offers for his poetry. Although
readers may have found Artegall disagreeable, orphans and
ladies he has rescued in Faery Land love him. Astraea
thought enough of his potential to spend her last energies
on earth in training him in "justice lore," and Irena is
eternally grateful to him.

Why should the reader think the poet has a "special
problem" with his hero, when the text of the poem has
made it abundantly clear that Artegall, not Spenser, is the
one having difficulties? If what Hamilton says about Artegall is true, he has no business as an exemplar of justice
because any Renaissance reader of Plato or Aristotle or
Cicero (to name but a few) knew that a just man is one
who first resolves the discords within himself before undertaking to administer to others. Since one of the greatest
attributes a justiciar can have is to deal "Justice with indifferent grace" (V.ix.36.4), how is Artegall to "stand apart"
from his virtue? Self-control is a necessary prerequisite for
good judgment, and with fine artistry, Spenser has shown
Artegall's problems to be largely internal not external.
Hamilton is absolutely right in saying justice must be im-

---

[38] *Structure*, p. 170. If Hamilton is correct about Artegall's using
the sword of justice but once, and that in the final battle with
Grantorto, the reader may be mystified as to what sharp instrument
Artegall uses when he crops off Guizor's head and performs similar
service for Pollente, inasmuch as in the latter case he specifies
Chrysaor (v.ii.18.2).

personal (who would want it otherwise?), but Artegall's problem is that he is not impersonal; until he is imprisoned by Radigund he becomes emotionally involved in every episode.

The chief error (besides those occasioned by the historical mania) in most criticism of Book Five of *The Faerie Queene* is to consider justice as an end in itself. Hamilton thinks the book can be divided into two parts—one in which Artegall establishes justice by the use of force, the other in which Britomart tempers his rough justice with mercy. The more complex discrimination of justice, equity, and mercy would be more appropriate here, since we later learn Osiris is justice and Isis represents "That part of Justice which is Equity" (V.vii.3.4). In fact one of the structural patterns in Book Five determines this strict progress from justice absolute, to equity, and finally to mercy. Even this division tends to blur the significance of Artegall's quest. If however we consider Spenser's handling of the specific quests of the patrons of virtue in the first three Books of *The Faerie Queene*, we will see a definite pattern for their accomplishments. The Red Cross Knight becomes perfected in holiness in order to redeem Una's parents and to enter the heavenly Jerusalem. Guyon becomes temperate in order to defeat the enchantress Acrasia and to destroy her Bower of Bliss. Britomart becomes the exemplar of chastity in order to celebrate true married love and to help perpetuate the British nation. Should the analogy hold for Book Five, we should expect Artegall to achieve perfection in justice and then to succeed in his quest to free Irena and reestablish her rightful place. Although justice and equity and mercy are important, an emphasis upon them distorts Spenser's overall pattern.

The course of Artegall's quest plainly follows lines sanctioned by biblical, philosophical, legal, and popular traditions. If we defer a consideration of the historical allegory and think of Irena's name in its etymological sense, we will

be better able to understand the implications of Artegall's
arduous journey. Irena or εἰρήνη means peace, and Artegall's mission is to restore her to her rightful place. When
the goddess Astraea, Artegall's teacher, lived among man
in the Golden Age, "Peace universall rayn'd mongst men
and beasts" (V.Proem.ix.6). From Isaiah we learn of a
similar function of justice: "And the work of justice shall
be peace, even the worke of justice and quietnesse, and assurance for ever" (xxxii.17; Geneva version). Calvin[39] and
the Fathers[40] read this passage as prophetic of the great
justiciar Christ, who will establish a peace, both internal
and external, which surpasses all understanding. Erasmus,
the great *defensor pacis* of the Renaissance, uses these lines
to support his thesis that "Peace of all thinges that nature
gave unto man is best,"[41] an argument which he later extends to embrace the preservation of society.[42]

William Lambarde's legal handbook draws similar distinctions. His aptly titled *Eirenarcha*, a practical treatise on
the duties and privileges of the justices of the peace, was
extremely popular, and went through seven editions in
Spenser's lifetime.[43] In his book Lambarde carefully defines the ends of justice before he sketches the means to
achieve it. For him, peace also is of two kinds, one relating
to man's inner concord inspired ultimately by *pax apud*

[39] *Commentary upon Isaiah* (London, 1609).

[40] Jerome, "Commentariorum in Isaiam Prophetam libri duo-
deviginiti," *Patrologia Latina*, xxiv, 375. See also Hugh of St. Cher's
explanation, "In libros prophetarum," *Opera*, iv (Venice, 1703),
70 and Thomas Aquinas' qualifications, *Summa Theologica* (trans.
Fathers of the Dominican Province), ii.ii.Q.29.a.3. This translation
will be used throughout this book. For a useful compilation of glosses
on this passage, consult Lapide's *Commentaria in Quattor Prophetas
Maiores* (Antwerp, 1689), pp. 283-284.

[41] *The Complaint of Peace*, trans. Thomas Paynell (London,
1559), sig. B. vi recto.

[42] *Ibid.*, sig. C.iiii verso.

[43] First edition (London, 1581).

Deum, the other to man's dealings with society at large.[44] Lambarde does not spend much time in detailing the private aspects of peace, since he is primarily interested in providing a useful guide for the justice of the peace in dealing with the public.[45] With the same regard, Gentili reminds his readers in his influential *De jure belli* that man should war only to gain peace.[46]

Filtering through the vernacular, these precise ideas became part of a popular conception of justice. The anonymous poem, *A pretye complaynt of peace*, describes the peregrinations of Dame Peace, who wanders for years from country to country in continental Europe, searching for a suitable climate for her talents.[47] When she finds all these nations inhospitable to her, she sails for England, where after many more trials she finally encounters Justyce, befriends Wealthe, and lives happily ever after. The title page of this poem is bordered by a series of woodcut figures, representing *Fides, Spes, Patientia, Obedientia, Prudencia, Charitas*; but dominating the top center of the page is an armed knight with a sword in his right hand and a pair of scales in his left, labeled, of course, *Justicia*. (See Plate I, following page 68.) Early in the next century Robert Aylett dipped his pen in moral earnestness and scratched out a long poem called *Peace with her Foure Garders*.[48] Although it is subtitled *Five Morall Meditations of Concord, Chastitie, Constancie, Courtesie, Gravitie*, it is not a series of meditations but is a sort of verse sermon in loose epistolary style. It is marginal poetry at best, but provides for the common reader a digest of traditional notions concerning peace. To Aylett—the Erasmus of the

[44] *Eirenarcha*, p. 4.
[45] *Ibid.*, p. 5.
[46] (Hanau, 1612), iii.i: "Sic et victoria finis artis imperatoriae Aristoteli: quum ea honestatem habet, et Justitiam, quae pax est."
[47] London, 1538.
[48] London, 1622.

working class—the relationship between peace and justice
was quite clear.

> *Eternal, inward,* and *externall* peace,
> *Eternal Peace* is that with God alone,
> From which our *inward* Life hath and increase,
> The third's the *peace* we have with ev'ry one;
>   No farther yet than it concernes our owne:
> For when we wrong'd or injuride behold
> Those that with us in godly League are growne,
> We breake our League, if *peace* with them we hold.
> Inseparable friends are *Righteousnesse*
> And *Peace*, they one another meet and kisse:
> Except thou *Justice* love, thou do'st professe
> In vaine thy love to *peace:* Him that doth misse
>   True love to *Justice, peace* will never blisse:
> What more than Peace do all mankind admire?
> But Righteousnesse to them a stranger is:
> Sweet Fruits of Peace all earnestly require,
> But to the workes of *Justice* no man hath desire.

                       (pp. 3-4)

In Book Five the overall pattern of Artegall's quest closely
approximates the traditional ends of justice since he functions primarily as a peacemaker. His attempts to establish
concord, by restoring order, satisfying claims, and defending the weak, are substantiated in every episode. His quest
for Irena is metaphorically and actually a quest for peace.

    Since the effective working of the justiciar depends first
of all upon his state of mind, Artegall will succeed in his
outward quest only after he has established concord and harmony within himself. In the Fourth Book of *The Republic*
Socrates delineates the relationship between the just man
and the just act.

> But in reality justice was such as we were describing,
> being concerned however, not with the outward man,
> but with the inward, which is the true self and concern-

ment of man: for the just man does not permit the several elements within him to interfere with one another, or any of them to do the work of others,—he sets down in order his own inner life, and is his own master and his own law, and at peace with himself; and when he has bound together the three principles within him, which may be compared to the higher, lower, and the middle notes of the scale, and the intermediate intervals—when he has bound these all together, and is no longer many, but has become one entirely temperate and perfectly adjusted nature, then he proceeds to act, if he has to act, whether in a matter of property, or in the treatment of the body, or in some affair of politics or private business; always thinking and calling that which preserves and co-operates with this harmonious condition, just and good action, and the knowledge which presides over it, wisdom, and that which at any time impairs this condition, he will call unjust action, and the opinion which presides over it ignorance.[49]

It is here that Artegall fails; for his chief obstacle to success is his own nature—Spenser has already shown him as a proud and petty, a wrathful and concupiscent knight. In the opening cantos of Book Five Spenser will reveal how his inward discord affects his public judgments.

When Artegall finally begins his quest to rescue Irena from Grantorto, he is accompanied by the iron man Talus, the club of justice given to him by Astraea. Ever since Upton, critics of Spenser have known of the Hephaestian man of brass who made the rounds of Crete upholding the laws of Minos.[50] Given the Elizabethan penchant for

[49] *The Republic of Plato*, trans. Jowett, 3rd edn. (London, 1888), [443] pp. 136-137.
[50] *Variorum, Book Five*, 165-166.

etymologizing (which Spenser's poetic technique so amply illustrates), it seems likely also that the poet's iron man shadows the principle of *talion*, since in many respects he functions as a retributive force. In addition to these rather obvious meanings, Spenser has added a simple detail to the equipment of Talus which subtly suggests the mythological basis of Artegall's character: "Who in his hand an yron flale did hould,/ With which he thresht out falshood, and did truth unfould" (V.i.12.8-9). Since everyone knew of Hercules' club, Spenser simply endows the flail of Talus with virtues known to be inherent in it. While the club is naturally a symbol of power and strength, Cartari tells of its related virtues of prudence and wisdom.[51] To Valeriano the knots on the club expose the crowd of errors attacking from all directions; and with the club's guidance we should be able to perceive true virtue (*veram virtutem agnoscere possimus*).[52]

Just as the club of Hercules is an instrument of his power and an emblem of his virtues, so Talus is an actual and metaphoric extension of the forces of justice, since Astraea instructs her iron groom to "doe what ever thing he [Artegall] did intend" (V.i.12.5). By adding Talus to the armory of justice, Spenser has fully accoutred Artegall, the new Hercules, in his quest for peace.

Artegall and Talus ride but a short way before they see a "Squire in squallid weed" crying and lamenting.

> To whom as they approched, they espide
> A sorie sight, as ever seene with eye;
> An headlesse Ladie lying him beside,
> In her owne blood all wallow'd wofully
> That her gay clothes did in discolour die.

[51] *Imagines deorum* (Lyons, 1581), p. 234.
[52] *Hieroglyphica*, p. 396.

Much was he moved at that ruefull sight;
And flam'd with zeale of vengeance inwardly,
He askt, who had that Dame so fouly dight;
Or whether his owne hand, or whether other wight?

(V.i.14)

Crying forth anew in his despair, the Squire says that it would be little loss if he were to confess to the crime that another has done, since he has lost his own love. At the further questioning of Artegall, the Squire resumes his tale of misadventure, and in so doing, reveals his own weakness of character. His grief, though understandable, is excessive. When he marks his activities, he says that "This day as I in solace sate hereby/ With a fayre love, whose losse I now do rew" (V.i.16.6-7), thereby pointing up his own inadequacies. The Squire shows his unworthiness even as he is telling the cause of his sorrow when he describes a rival knight.

He, whether mine seem'd fayrer in his eye,
Or that he wexed weary of his owne,
Would change with me; but I did it denye;
So did the Ladies both, as may be knowne,
But he, whose spirit was with pride upblowne,
Would not so rest contented with his right,
But having from his courser her downe throwne,
Fro me reft mine away by lawlesse might,
And on his steed her set, to bear her out of sight.

Which when his Ladie saw, she follow'd fast,
And on him catching hold, gan loud to crie
Not so to leave her, nor away to cast,
But rather of his hand besought to die.
With that his sword he drew all wrathfully,
And at one stroke cropt off her head with scorne,
In that same place, whereas it now doth lie.

Plate I: Anon., *A pretye complaynte of peace*, London, 1538?
The Folger Shakespeare Library

EMBLEMATA

POST MORTEM CESSAT INVIDIA.

Lib. 2.
Epift. 1.

—— diram qui contudit Hydram,
Notáque fatali portenta labore fubegit,
Comperit Inuidiam fupremo fine domari.
Vrit enim fulgore fuo, qui prægrauat artes
Infra fe pofitas: exftinctus amabitur idem.

Plato.

Iter facientes per folem, neceffariò comitatur vmbra : inceden‑
tibus verò per gloriam, comes eft Inuidia.

Ouid.

Pafcitur in viuis liuor, poft fata quiefcit;
Tunc fuus ex merito quemque tuetur honos.

Philo.

Honefta, etiamfi per Inuidiam ad tempus obfcurentur : atta‑
men fuo tempore foluta, iterum fplendent.

Den Hercules vermaert, die monfters
heeft vervvonnen,
En alles 'tonderbraght, dat vvederftant
hem boodt,
Seyd'dat de Nijdicheyt hy noyt hadt tem‑
men konnen.
Door niemandt wert de nijt ghetemt dan
door de doodt.

l'Inuincible Hercules ayant fçeu furmon‑
ter
Tous monftres & brigans, comblez de fe‑
lonnie,
Dit que la feule Enuie iamais n'a fçeu dom‑
pter.
Par autruy que la mort ne fuccombe l'En‑
uie.

N E-

Plate III: Veen, *Emblemata Horatiana*, Antwerp, 1607, pp. 172, 173.

Plate II: Giraldi, *Vita Herculis*, in *Opera*, I, Leyden, 1696, p. 570.
The Folger Shakespeare Library

Plate III: Veen, *Emblemata Horatiana*, Antwerp, 1607, pp. 172, 173.

So he my love away with him hath borne,
And left me here, both his and mine owne love to morne.

(V.i.17-18)

Spenser has given here an emblem of two people who are
willing to die for love, which shows that excessive love is
self-destroying. Having lost his lady, the Squire wishes for
death, an almost unnecessary wish, since he has already for-
feited his manhood and has reduced himself to "squallid
weed." When the other knight steals his lady from him,
he cannot defend her and later weeps like a woman. The
knight's lady, denied the pleasure of his company, actually
begs for death, which she speedily suffers. The irony is
reinforced by the "non" man weeping for the "non"
woman, because the Squire complains that the outlaw
knight has left him "both his and mine owne love to
morne." While we learned at Satyrane's tournament that
love of beauty for its own sake is brutalizing, we now see
here that excessive love brings death, the woman suffering
physical death, the Squire enduring spiritual death. When
Dante meets Francesca in the Second Circle of Hell, he explores a similar problem. The details are different but the
results are the same—death and damnation.[53]

If we remember Artegall's past actions in Book Four, we
will see that the implications of this kind of love extend to
his own character. After all, he entered Satyrane's tournament, indicating that he could be swayed by the illusions of
beauty. Since the problems of true and illusory beauty, true
and false love, are very much Artegall's own, Spenser is to
investigate them fully in the course of the book. Although
false lovers—Radigund, Burbon, Philterra, Clarin, Bragga-

---

[53] See the commentaries of Jacopo della Lana, Benvenuto Ram-
baldi, and Giovanni da Seravalle included in Guido Biagi's variorum
edition, *La Divina Commedia nella figurazione artistica e nel secolare
commento*, 3 vols. (Torino, 1924), I, 160ff.

docchio, and Amidas—abound, Spenser balances them with
the true—Florimell, Marinell, Lucy, Bracidas, and Arthur.
The problem of love is just one theme to be developed at
length in Book Five, and the other themes marked for later
treatment are embodied in the character of the recreant
knight.

The part of Faery Land through which Artegall is riding
westward has suffered long decay. From Spenser's Proem
to Book Five we learn that the imperceptible movement of
the sun along the ecliptic effects a shifting of the signs of
the Zodiac, where there is a progressive encroachment of all
the signs on one another. On the cosmic level Artegall's is
a journey through time to eternity. In this context any
reader of Plato's *Timaeus* and Chalcidius' commentaries
would recognize the problems to be encountered on such
a journey. Artegall's true movement in his quest is from
east to west, the movement of the sun, or reason, Plato's
motion of the *same*. If he perseveres in his quest, he will
restore Irena, or Peace,[54] to her rightful place.[55] In the
Golden Age man was governed by reason, and Astraea,
Artegall's teacher, lived among men because all men were
just. As such she was the physical embodiment of their perfected mental states. When the "wicked seede of vice/ Began to spring" among them, she departed, leaving behind
the idea of justice that heroic men in each succeeding age
could bring to reality. Whenever one of these chosen men
deviates from his symbolic westward course, he falls in nature—Plato's motion of the *other*, representing the pas-

[54] Alfred Gough first discovered Ἰερνη in Strabo but denies the
possibility that Spenser may be playing on Ἰερνη and εἰρήνη, peace
(*Variorum, Book Five*, 161).

[55] For a study of the relationship between celestial motion and the
movement of man's soul as related to the *Divine Comedy*, see John
Freccero's brilliant article, "Dante's Pilgrim in a Gyre," *PMLA*,
LXXVI (1961), 168-181.

sions.[56] Since Spenser has so sedulously drawn the character of his patron of justice, we can anticipate the struggles, both internal and external, he will have in a decadent society. In the fallen world, every just man undertakes the journey to the West, doing battle with his own nature to arrive at a state of peace. Because Artegall, as a type of Hercules, emblematically bears the burden of all just men, he achieves an inward state of peace at the end of his quest.

Since the intemperate lovers are mutually self-destroying, Artegall will have no success in rehabilitating them. His first real problem representing all the obstacles he is to encounter in his quest, is to be found in the character of the false knight, as the Squire's narrative of this knight's actions is an accurate portrayal of the physical evils of this part of Faery Land. This is a lawless country, where the weak are terrorized by the strong, and the downtrodden, sunk in the luxury of love, have neither the energy nor the will to resist. Some greater man must restore the natural order and establish justice, and subjugation of the outlaw knight is a primary requisite in the establishing of a just peace.

In describing his own actions, the love-longing Squire gives an accurate picture of the recreant knight. When the Squire tries to account for the knight's behavior ("He, whether mine seem'd fayrer in his eye,/ Or that he wexed weary of his owne,/ Would change with me"), he natural-

[56] "Which thyngs Plato perceyvyng by inspiracyon of god/ wrote in his booke called Timeus how the sones of goddes had forged in man to theyr owne lykenes two kyndes of soules/ the one kynde spirituall and immortall/ the other as it were mortall, in daunger to dyverse perturbacions or mocyons of unquietnes. Of whiche the fyrst is voluptuousnes (as he sayth) the bayte whereby men are allured and brought to ungracyousnes or mischefe": Erasmus, *Enchiridion militis Christiani* (London, 1533), sig. D.iii. This popular translation domesticated some of the major ideas of the Timaeus for general English readers.

ly puts it in terms demonstrating his habitude of thought, thinking that the vagaries of love must have prompted his boarish behavior. His analysis is only partially true, because we must distinguish here between the Squire's description of the event and his opinionated glosses upon it. As did Verdant in Book Two, the Squire is getting his solace in the arms of dalliance when the knight rides up with his lady. His lady's "gay clothes" mark her as worthy of her knight, since, but for a few questionable exceptions, Spenser always uses "gay" in a pejorative sense. Lucifera is "Adorned all with gold, and girlonds gay" (I.iv.17.2), and Philotime is a "woman gorgeous gay" (II.vii.44.6). Diana upbraids Venus for the actions of her "gay sonne," Cupid (III.vi.21.4). When all parties object to the transfer of the knight's gay lady for the Squire's, the knight, "whose spirit was with pride upblowne,/ Would not so rest contented with his right" (V.i.17.5-6), throws his own lady down from his horse and snatches the Squire's lady love from him. The knight's own lady races after him and begs to be taken back, or failing that, to die of his own hand: "With that his sword he drew all wrathfully,/ And at one stroke cropt off her head with scorne" (V.i.18.5-6) and he rides off with the Squire's lady.

We should recognize this familiar pattern of proud and intemperate behavior, because Spenser is deliberately eliciting a character who echoes his hero, who we have already observed has succumbed to these passions in the same order. This knight, of course, is Artegall's greatest enemy; for until he is subdued, Spenser's hero cannot begin his quest to restore peace by establishing justice. That this knight is the enemy of all true knights is boldly emblazoned on his shield.

> To hope (quoth he) him soone to overtake,
> That hence so long departed, is but vaine:
> But yet he pricked over yonder plaine,
> And as I marked, bore upon his shield,

By which it's easie him to know againe,
A broken sword within a bloodie field;
Expressing well his nature, which the same did wield.

(V.i.19.3-9)

The Squire has not yet regressed to the point where he does not know the importance of a knight's shield—these are the arms of a disenfranchised knight, an outlaw. When a knight is drummed out of the corps, his sword is taken from him and broken. Later while Braggadocchio is being degraded and stripped of his pretended knighthood, Talus breaks "his sword in twaine." The knight's identity established, Artegall sends Talus after him:

<blockquote>
who him pursew'd so light,
As that it seem'd above the ground he went:
For he was swift as swallow in her flight,
And strong as Lyon in his Lordly might.
It was not long, before he overtooke
Sir Sanglier; (so cleeped was that Knight)
Whom at the first he ghessed by his looke,
And by the other markes, which of his shield he tooke.
</blockquote>

(V.i.20.2-9)

Sir Sanglier, the wild boar, has been overtaken.

In retrospect, we can see Spenser's artistic technique at work and just how he is using the tools of his trade for maximum effect in building up to the climactic moment when he names Sanglier. First setting the scene in which he investigates the character of the recreant knight, Spenser describes the shield which marks him an outlaw. At exactly the right moment, he names him Sir Wild Boar. Just as he gradually invested his hero with details that in total effect unmistakably link him to Hercules, so has he gradually metamorphosed this knight into a boar. It is no coincidence that one of the famous labors of Hercules was to capture alive the Eurymanthean Boar. In keeping with the general pattern of imagery, Talus is "strong as [a] Lyon in his Lordly might," symbolizing not only the resistless power of justice but also the attributes of the conqueror of the Nemean Lion. Spenser underscores his identification of Sanglier by having Talus bring him back "Bound like a beast appointed to the stall" (V.i.22.6).

In the Renaissance the labors of Hercules were read allegorically.[57] Whenever he was not distracted by serious personality problems, Hercules employed his great strength and intelligence for the benefit of mankind. (See Plate II, following page 68.) The labors commanded him by Eurystheus (such as the capture of the Eurymanthean Boar) were so interpreted that they pointed to the development of the hero and simultaneously aided the welfare of society. They were both private and public labors, or to retain the common metaphor of justice, internal and external. That the restraining of the ravages of the boar aided society is undeniable, and for its effect upon the character of Hercules we are indebted to the commentators. In Diodorus' account the capture of the boar was an exacting assignment.

> The third command which he received was the bringing back alive of the Erymanthian boar which lived on Mount Lampeia in Arcadia. This Command was thought to be exceedingly difficult, since it required of the man who fought such a beast that he possess such superiority over it as to catch precisely the proper moment in very heat of the encounter. For should he let it loose while it still retained its strength he would be in danger from its tushes, and should he attack it

[57] Marcel Simon's little book, *Hercule et le christianisme* (Paris, 1959), shows how Hercules was read as a type of Christ, with some of his labors taken as illustrating Christ's ministry. He does not investigate the larger moral implications (both personal and public) these labors had for Renaissance readers.

more violently than was proper, then he would have killed it and so the Labour would remain unfulfilled. However, when it came to the struggle he kept so careful an eye on the proper balance that he brought back the boar alive to Eurystheus.[58]

Considering the perfect judgment required in restraining the boar, it seems inevitable that Heraclidis Ponticus should view the action as the quelling of intemperance.[59] From Spenser's elaborate investigation of intemperance in Book Two, the evils of the irascible and concupiscible passions should be clear. Boccaccio, who does not read Hercules' labors allegorically except for Admetus, Alcestis, the Lion, and the Boar, sees these particular labors as representing the whole man.[60] When the true nature of Sanglier is known, it is obvious how he is such a threat to society.[61]

In Spenser's time and in antiquity, boars had great talent and skill in disrupting civilized society, Sanglier terrorizing Faery Land, the Eurymanthean Boar laying waste to Arcadia, and the boar in the Psalms trampling underfoot the vineyard of the Lord.[62] Neither Valeriano[63] nor Aldrovandi[64] draws absolute distinctions between the biblical and mythological boars, since both beasts share the same characteristics and are linked to man. Singing of the

[58] *Library of History*, iv.xii.1-2.

[59] Quoted by Mignault in Alciati's *Emblemata*, p. 492.

[60] *Genealogie deorum gentilium libri*, ed. Vicenzo Romano, *Scrittori D'Italia*, 201 (Bari, 1950), 642.

[61] See also T. A. d'Aubigné's moralization, *L'Hercule Chrestien* in *Oeuvres*, ii, 228.

[62] And there is the boar that killed sweet Adonis. For an interpretation of Shakespeare's *Venus and Adonis* and the implications of hunting the boar, see D. C. Allen's "On Venus and Adonis," in *Elizabethan and Jacobean Studies Presented to Frank Percy Wilson* (Oxford, 1959), pp. 100-111.

[63] *Hieroglyphica*, pp. 65verso, 67verso.

[64] *Quadrupedum omnium bisulcorum historia* (Bonn, 1621), p. 1010.

miseries of the church, the Psalmist laments that the hedges of the vineyard brought safely out of Egypt are down, permitting foreigners to pluck its fruits: "The wilde bore out of the wood hath destroyed it, and the wilde beasts of the field have eten it up" (lxxx.13; Geneva version). In addition to political interpretations linking it with Vespasian or Assyrian tyrants, the commentators chiefly read this boar as a symbol of insuperable pride, an unpleasant trait also shared by Spenser's Sanglier.[65] The tributary streams of biblical exegesis and mythological moralizing empty smoothly into the river of the Renaissance, where, in the Middle Ages, they flowed side by side with underground seepage mingling the one's wine with the other's water, a discreet Alpheus to his timid Arethusa. Writers like Valeriano and Aldrovandi could freely draw parallels between the Word and the myth, and Spenser's Sanglier is an issue of this marriage. In the Renaissance the boar generally was a symbol of pride and intemperance, that is, the complete range of the passions—wrath and desire.

That Sir Sanglier is an aspect of Artegall's discordant character is obvious from the text, and the manner in which he handles this outlaw is central to Spenser's argument. When Artegall asks him whether or not he has killed the lady, Sanglier, "with sterne countenance and indignant pride/ Did aunswere, that of all he guiltlesse stood" (V.i. 23.4-5). Following George Craik,[66] who first propounded it, Hamilton asks why he did not question the Squire's lady herself; and he answers: "But Artegall knows that the lady might not tell the truth, and so frustrate the workings of justice."[67] Hamilton's is a misleading critical question. Al-

---

[65] See Hugh of St. Cher, *Opera*, II, 212 and Henry Ainsworth's *Annotations on the Five Books of Moses . . . Psalmes . . . Song of Songs* (London, 1639), "Psalmes," p. 124.

[66] See *Variorum, Book Five*, 168.

[67] *Structure*, p. 172.

though he has only practiced on beasts, Artegall at least learned the rudiments of judicial procedure from Astraea, and certainly the Faerie Queene chose Artegall for the quest because "to her he seem'd best skild in righteous lore" (V.i. 4.9). Artegall knows that in any criminal case the accused is brought to the bar and is asked whether he pleads guilty or not guilty—*before* the testimony of witnesses is heard. Knowledge that a man was innocent until proved guilty was a source of satisfaction to the British lawyers and judges who smugly proclaimed the superiority of the common law over the varieties of the civil law practiced on the Continent. The presumption of the defendant's innocence is reflected in actual legal procedure today, as in the sixteenth century. John Cowell, a contemporary of Spenser's at Cambridge, published in his declining years *The Interpreter: Or Booke Containing the Signification of Words* (first published, London, 1607). A legal dictionary, it is described by the author as "A worke not only profitable, but necessary for such as desire thoroughly to be instructed in the knowledge of our Lawes, Statutes, or other Antiquities." In the section treating of the jury, he outlines the possible responses to an indictment.

> In matters of life and death, the party indited is commanded to hold up his hand, and answer (guilty) or (not guilty); if (guilty) he standeth convicted by his owne confession: if (not guilty) he is farther referred to the Enquest of life and death: which consider upon the proofe brought against the prisoner, and accordingly bring in their verdict, (Guilty) or (not Guilty) so is he judged to die, or delivered by the Court.[68]

Spenser's training at Cambridge and his many litigious squabbles with the Irish would have taught him at least this much about legal procedure,[69] and from his elaborate

---

[68] *Interpreter* (1637), sigs. Xxx2v-Xxx3.

[69] For an account of general legal reading in the two universities,

analysis of justice in Book Five we are entitled to infer that he understood much more.

Consistent with the chivalric and the sixteenth-century legal code, the accused is entitled to confront his accuser upon the field of battle, an option Sanglier promptly takes (V.i.23.7). For his own part, the Squire, characteristically enough, is ready to perjure himself rather than risk trial by combat, and "guilty chose him selfe to yield" (V.i.24.5).

> But *Artegall* by signes perceiving plaine,
> That he was not, which that Lady kild,
> But that strange Knight, the fairer love to gaine,
> Did cast about by sleight the truth thereout to straine.
>
> (V.i.24.6-9)

Because Artegall knows who is the guilty party, he is not going to allow a trial by "Sacrament be tride,/ Or . . . by ordele, or by blooddy fight" (V.i.25.2-3). Considering the Squire's weakened state, all such trials would work to the advantage of the guilty Sanglier, who demonstrated his physical superiority when he carried away the Squire's lady.

Since he shows good judgment in ruling out the alternatives in this case that would surely thwart the workings of justice, Artegall has no choice but to get the defendant to incriminate himself by his own testimony. Thinking of another judge in another time, Artegall frames his strategy accordingly.

> Sith then (sayd he) ye both the dead deny,
> And both the living Lady claime your right,
> Let both the dead and living equally
> Devided be betwixt you here in sight,
> And each of either take his share aright.
> But looke who does dissent from this my read,

---

see Abraham Fraunce's *Lawiers Logic* (London, 1588). We know Spenser was appointed sheriff of Cork (A. C. Judson, *Life of Spenser* [Baltimore, 1945], p. 200).

He for twelve moneths day shall in despight
Beare for his penaunce that same Ladies head;
To witnesse to the world, that she by him is dead.

Well pleased with that doome was *Sangliere,*
And offred streight the Lady to be slaine.
But that same Squire, to whom she was more dere,
When as he saw she should be cut in twaine,
Did yield, she rather should with him remaine
Alive, then to him selfe be shared dead;
And rather than his love should suffer paine,
He chose with shame to beare that Ladies head.
True love despiseth shame, when life is cald in dread.

(V.i.26-27)

Sanglier convicts himself of the charge brought against him by the Squire, when he readily assents to a murder being committed under the show of equity. For centuries scholars have known that Spenser here is deliberately echoing the judgment of Solomon in 1 Kings (iii.16-27).[70] Hamilton thinks Spenser's is a "poor imitation" and indicative of the quality of the poetry of Book Five.[71] In the Renaissance the word imitation did not carry the pejorative connotations it has today, schoolboys learning Latin by imitating Cicero and Seneca, learning moral behavior by imitating parents and precepts. Roger Ascham devotes the Second Book of his *Scholemaster* to "Imitation" and Pope proves brilliantly the Renaissance theory that imitation inspires invention. Although Hamilton is silent about what comprises a "good imitation" of the judgment of Solomon, Spenser has provided one that is good enough for his artistic purposes, one richly suggestive of the hero's character and the personal trials he will face when undertaking his quest.

In the universally known biblical story, two harlots are

[70] *Variorum, Book Five,* 168. The numbering in the Vulgate is 3 Kings iii.
[71] *Structure,* p. 172.

contending for an infant son, both claiming to be his mother. Since the truth lies obscured by conflicting testimonies, Solomon sends for a sword to decide the issue.

> Devide ye the living childe in twaine, and give the one halfe the one, and the other halfe to the other. Then spake the woman, whose the living childe was, unto the King, for her compassion was kindled toward her sonne, and she said, Oh my lord, give her the living childe, and slay him not: but the other said, Let it be neither mine nor thine, but devide it. Then the King answered, and said Give her the living childe, and slay him not: this is his mother. And all Israel heard the judgment, which the King had judged: for they sawe that the wisdome of God was in him to do justice. (1 Kings iii.25-28; Geneva version)

The parallel of the biblical passage with Spenser's is rather obvious; and if we examine the details of this scriptural excerpt, we will discover just how closely it matches Spenser's rendering in intent. As the Fathers quickly noticed, the two harlots (*meretrices*) are unworthy women, just as Sanglier and the Squire are unworthy men. In his gloss on this passage, Gregory the Great knew their characteristics well, calling them greedy, lustful, impudent, irascible, and litigious.[72] Gregory's commentary would fit exactly as a characterization of Sanglier and, except for a few minor particulars, the Squire. In showing the similarities that exist between Spenser's portrayal of the unworthy complainant and the equally unworthy defendant and Gregory's account of the two harlots, I need not argue a one-for-one relationship, since the biblical text alone is sufficient.

In adapting the judgment of Solomon, Spenser, as he almost invariably does, has employed the image which

---

[72] Included in Cornelius a Lapide, *Commentarius in IV Libros Regum* (Antwerp, 1687), p. 116b.

exactly suits his theme. When Solomon decides the case between the two mothers, he makes his *first* judgment, and when Artegall handles the complaint of the Squire, he performs his *first* act as patron of justice. If anyone reads Martin Del Rio's *Disquisitionum Magicarum*, he will see that variations upon Solomon's judgment have been made many times in history.[73] In defending Susanna against the accusations of the lecherous elders, Daniel uses similar tactics.[74] Robert Aylett, who never made a point unless he made it obviously, draws the analogy in his verses, *"Susanna, Or the Arraignment of the Two Unjust Elders."*[75]

As Wisest Salomon when he could finde,
No certaine witnesse to resolve his minde,
When as two women did before him strive,
Whose was the dead, and whose the childe alive:
Well knowing one of them the truth did know,
Devis'd how by themselves it plaine to show:
So this yong Judge [Daniel] in heav'nly wisdome wise,
Doth with the Lords and people thus advise. (p. 36).[76]

Claudius Caesar's method of determining kinship also was likened to Solomon's decision. "There was a woman that would not acknowledge her own son. Now when by evidences and arguments alleged *pro et contra* on both sides, the question rested in equal balance doubtful, he awarded that she should be wedded to the young man, and so forced her to confess the truth and to take him for her child."[77]

[73] "De divinatione" (Venice, 1616), pp. 478-480.

[74] Parallels to Solomon are made by Del Rio *supra*; Lapide, *In Danielem Prophetam* (Antwerp, 1696), p. 1404; the *Glossa*, and many others.

[75] London, 1622.

[76] Although none of Aylett's poetry I have read rises above the obvious, yet in the passage given above, he sought to clarify the allusion to Solomon by citing "1 Kings 3.23" in the margin.

[77] Suetonius, *History of Twelve Caesars*, trans. P. Holland, ed. J. H. Freese (London, 1930), p. 235; for listing of Solomon

While the modern reader may twitch with the painful recognition of an image invoked tritely by present day judges in determining difficult cases of equity, his Renaissance counterpart would probably not experience such discomfort. Except for that which is to come after the final day, Solomon's judgment is the most eminent in the Bible. As such, it was to be taken as a model for all difficult cases, a point clearly made by Flavius Josephus in his famous history.

> . . . a verie difficult judgement [the case of the contending women] was brought him to decide, the resolution whereof, was very hard to bee discovered. And I have thought it necessarie to declare the occasions whereon at the present the debate was grounded, to the end that the readers may understand the difficultie of the cause in question, and that if they happen at any time to be assistant in such like affaires, they might draw as it were from the counterfeit of this kings wisdome, a perfect modle whereby they may directly shape an answere to such demaunds as shall be offered them.[78]

Given the theme of Book Five, it is difficult to see how Spenser could have done otherwise.

Artegall's reenacting the judgment of Solomon is in keeping with Spenser's theme that justice is divinely inspired, since the marginal gloss of the Geneva Bible reminds us that "by this example it appeareth that God kept promes with Salomon in granting him wisdome." Had Spenser gone no further, this episode would have been sufficient to pay his respects to the Judaeo-Christian tradi-

---

parallels see the edition of Maximilianus Ihn, 1 (Leipzig, 1907), 207 [xv.2].

[78] *The Famous and Memorable Workes of Josephus*, trans. Thomas Lodge (London, 1602), pp. 192-193 [vii.2]. Lodge's translation is very faithful to the Latin version, *Antiquitatum Judicarum libri xx* (Basel, 1534), p. 203.

tion which permits his hero to wrap about him the mantle of wisdom. With this perfectly achieved, the remaining cantos of Book Five would deserve Grierson's censure of being the "dullest of all," since all further action would, of necessity, assume a ritualistic cast and have a most perfunctory air. In Spenser's talented hands, however, the sword of Solomon cuts both ways, and the key to its use is to be found in the punishment of Sanglier—he is to wear his Lady's head about his neck for a year as penance for his crime.

> But *Sangliere* disdained much his doome,
> And sternly gan repine at his beheast;
> Ne would for ought obay, as did become,
> To beare that Ladies head before his breast.
> Untill that *Talus* had his pride represt,
> And forced him, maulgre, it up to reare.
> Who when he saw it bootlesse to resist,
> He tooke it up, and thence with him did beare,
> As rated Spaniell takes his burden up for feare.
>
> (V.i.29)

Artegall's having the head hung about Sanglier's neck is similar to Satyrane's putting Florimell's girdle about the Witch's Beast, and this method of controlling him, coupled with Artegall's sitting in Solomon's seat, indicates that although the judgment is good its execution is faulty. As the poetry shows, Sanglier is the symbolical embodiment of Artegall's problems of pride, wrath, and concupiscence. Although his punishment is supposed to force Sanglier into repentance, to a disenfranchised knight, a little more shame would be small punishment. The fact that Sanglier is to carry his emblem of shame for one year shows that Artegall's control over him is temporary. Since Artegall is trying to rehabilitate Sanglier's character (an error in judgment itself), he has mistaken force for moral suasion, external for internal reform, strength for reason.

When Spenser makes Artegall into a type of Solomon, the reader should be alive to the deliberate ambiguity involved. Although Solomon was widely celebrated as a wise judge, he was also luxurious and proud, and more important for Artegall, he was somewhat concupiscent: "But King Salomon loved many outlandish women. . . . And he had seven hundreth wives, that were princesses, and three hundreth concubines, and his wives turned away his heart. . . . Therefore the Lord was angrie with Salomon, because he had turned his hearte from the Lord God of Israel" (1 Kings xi.1-9; Geneva version). Solomon's dereliction caused the Fathers to dispute the eventual resting place of his soul, and when Saint Antoninus writes his *Chronicon* he is conscious of the antiquity of the problem.[79] It is not likely that Spenser was ignorant of the controversy; in any case his treatment of Artegall suggests that he would have voted affirmatively.

In having Artegall call upon the judgment of Solomon, Spenser is culminating a progress of character development begun in Book Three. There Britomart sees him in his full potential, learns of the coincidence of their destinies, and hears of his honorable exploits in Faery Land. In direct contrast, Book Four reveals all the flaws in his discordant temperament—his proud appearance at the Tournament of the Girdle, his wrathful search to avenge his defeat there, and his slavish courtship of Britomart. These differing treatments of character are potentially resolved by modes of presentation—both in art and nature, and his identification with Hercules implicitly mitigates these seemingly anomalous appearances.

In the Sanglier episode, Spenser fuses the elements of the narrative into a single poetic image which simultaneously shadows his noble theme and the character of his

[79] (Basel, 1491), folio xxia. The irascible Tertullian lifted his pen in damnation (*Adversus Marcionem*, PL, II, 311); and Isidore gave his consent ("De ortu et obitu patrum," PL, LXXXIII, 140).

hero. By unmistakably implicating the character of his hero with that of Solomon, Spenser clearly marks out his intentions. Solomon's long reign was a reign of peace and represented the fulfillment of God's prophecy: "but upon David, and upon his seede, and upon his house and upon his throne shall there be peace for ever from the Lord" (1 Kings ii.33). During his reign, Solomon "had peace round about him on every side" (1 Kings iv.24). Jerome's characterization of him as peacemaker preserves the image.[80] In this context, Erasmus is of similar mind in writing that "Salomon woulde beare his [Christ's] type and figure, the which unto us is called peasable."[81]

As the patron of justice, Artegall is a type of Eirenarcha, and his quest naturally is to restore Irena to her rightful place. When he dons Solomon's robes, he anticipates his becoming wise. This and the pervasive association with Hercules also anticipate his willing subjugation at the hands of Radigund.

The dense matrix of implications of the Sanglier episode should now be fairly clear. Although Artegall, as a type of Hercules, has had great success in subduing animals, this time he has let the biggest one of all get away—the *sanglier* within. Since Artegall, like Socrates' just man, must undertake a double journey, he must first free himself from crippling discords; and having established this interior peace, he can then effectively pursue the end of justice in society. As this is Artegall's task, his handling of Sanglier reveals that the course will be long and arduous. Only when he has succeeded in controlling his personal *sanglier* will he be able to free Irena and establish peace with justice.

---

[80] "Epistolae LIII, ad Paulinum," *PL*, XXII, 547. See also his "Commentarius in Ecclesiasten," *PL*, XXIII, 1063ff.

[81] *Complaint of Peace* (1559), sig. B.vii recto.

CHAPTER II

Humility and Wisdom

IN THE first four cantos of Book Five Artegall suffers no outward setbacks, since with the aid of the club of Talus he generally succeeds in imposing his judgments upon offenders, and thereby restores order to the people of Faery Land. The apparent ease with which Artegall implements his judgments has led scholars to overlook a disturbing uneasiness of mind that Spenser has taken great pains to reveal. To be sure, Artegall is not conscious of his personal failings and grows more and more confident with each successful decision. Spenser's plotting of his hero's character reveals a keen understanding of psychology, Renaissance or modern; for just as his estimation of his own abilities increases, his power of self-control declines. His ignorance of his own character rashly leads him to accept Radigund's terms for combat, the result of which is humiliating subjugation. The deterioration of his character is a slow process, a sad chronicle of a descent into a hellish discord of the passions.[1] Having sown the seeds of internal discord and watered them with self-esteem, he reaps a baleful harvest. This chapter will show how it is possible for Spenser to present Artegall both as an outward success and as an inward failure, a shell of a justice administering the laws by rote. And it will show that, stripped of authority and manhood and forced upon his inner resources, he gains

[1] It has been customary to equate Artegall's submission to Radigund with his submission to Britomart and thereby to overlook the subtle differences between these two acts. Artegall gradually becomes so weakened in his resolve that his surrender to Radigund is inevitable. His defeat by Britomart anticipates his defeat by Radigund but does not explain his so wilfully abandoning his quest.

wisdom through humility and learns to control his passions.

i

After the condemnation of Sanglier, Spenser quickly changes the nature of the obstacles confronting Artegall—both in manner and mode. Since in the boar episode the truth lay hidden, obscured by conflicting testimonies, Artegall first had to determine the guilt of Sanglier and then to devise a stratagem that would force him to convict himself. In Canto II the guilty parties could not be more obvious: Pollente's long, treacherous bridge of extortion, Munera's stately castle (built and sustained by bribery), and the Reforming Giant with his foolish crowd of admirers stand forth as monumental symbols of injustice. The problem here is not one of detection but of punishment. Since the discovery of the guilty is just one aspect of Artegall's duties, Spenser here presents him administering penalties and/or reform. In closely examining his attendant actions, Spenser probes a little more deeply into his hero's psyche to make manifest those discords so subtly suggested by the judgment of Sanglier.

Upon refusing the proffered services of the effeminate squire, Artegall intercepts a "Dwarfe in hasty course" and asks for the latest news. This is a typically effective narrative device used by Spenser; it enables him both to knit up the loose ends of the action (particularly those kept hanging for several cantos or so) and to implicate the questioner in its resolution. In this case, Dony, Florimell's dwarf, performs his function well. At Artegall's request he tells of the happy conclusion of Florimell's chase through the forest and subsequent submarine adventures, after which she was found and "spousde" to Marinell (V.ii.2). Dony is hurrying because he has but three days to get to Marinell's Castle of the Strand to be of service at Florimell's "bridale cheare." Unfortunately, he may not arrive on time since he must use the bridge of the extortionist Pollente.[2]

Making its influence felt in all estates, the father and daughter team of Pollente and Munera is a most efficient subverter of society. Pollente, powerful in battle, and his helper Guizor extort money from all levels of society (the latter "pols and pils the poore in piteous wize" [V.ii.6.8]). Those refusing to pay fight Pollente on his own terms, his bridge of "many trap fals pight" through which the un-wary rider falls and is overcome (V.ii.7-8).

> Then doth he take the spoile of them at will,
> And to his daughter brings, that dwels thereby:
> Who all that comes doth take, and therewith fill
> The coffers of her wicked threasury;
> Which she with wrongs hath heaped up so hy,
> That many Princes she in wealth exceedes,
> And purchast all the countrey lying ny
> With the revenue of her plenteous meedes,
> Her name is *Munera*, agreeing with her deedes.
>
> (V.ii.9)

Together, Pollente and Munera constitute a symbiosis of evil, a self-perpetuating malignancy in the heart of society, forming together an almost insuperable combination, power and wealth, which presents a dual challenge to Artegall. He must physically overcome Pollente, despite his strength and deceptions, and he must resist the attractions of bribery that the wealth of Munera would present. That he will succeed in both endeavors is fairly certain, because he has the strength of Hercules and would never debase himself by accepting bribes. The manner in which he presses execution is a test of his self-control, which we have had reason enough to doubt.

When he and his small company reach the bridge,

---

[2] This most heavily traveled bridge in Faery Land is of symbolical importance, as Britomart must also cross it in riding to rescue Artegall.

Guizor comes forward to demand the passage money. Artegall is not going to waste his time with this underling; "To whom he aunswerd wroth, Loe there thy hire;/ And with that word him strooke, that streight he did expire" (V.ii. 11.8-9). His angry act kindles a similar emotion in Pollente, who "wexed wroth,/ And streight him selfe unto the fight addrest" (V.ii.12.1-2). The verbal parallel between their separate but related actions is not fortuitous, for it is Spenser's way of precisely drawing the reader's attention to the temperamental similarities of the prospective combatants. After they rush together on the bridge and drop through the trap, Spenser completes the identification.

> There being both together in the floud,
> They each at other tyrannously flew;
> Ne ought the water cooled their whot bloud,
> But rather in them kindled choler new.
>
> (V.ii.13.1-4)

Apparently Artegall has forgotten his Seneca, and his noble intentions ("God to guide") are forgotten in the tide of anger. Since they are motivated by the same passion, the outcome is in doubt; "There they together strove and struggled long/ Either the other from his steede to cast" (V.ii.14.6-7). The degrading effect of the battle of anger is evident in Spenser's imagery:

> As when a Dolphin and a Sele are met,
> In the wide champian of the Ocean plaine:
> With cruell chaufe their courages they whet,
> The maysterdome of each by force to gaine,
> And dreadfull battaile twixt them do darraine:
> They snuf, they snort, they bounce, they rage, they rore,
> That all the sea disturbed with their traine,
> Doth frie with fome above the surges hore.
> Such was betwixt these two the troublesome uprore.
>
> (V.ii.15)

Artegall finally makes his superior strength felt, pursues Pollente "with bright Chrysaor in his cruel hand," and strikes off his head, thereby mastering his antagonist but failing to restrain himself. When he becomes wrathful, openly displaying his discordant temper, he violates a cardinal rule for the dispensing of justice in allowing his personal feelings to intrude upon the execution of the law. Cicero's *De Officiis*, a popular book in sixteenth-century England, leaves no doubt about what is to be avoided in exacting penalties upon offenders.

> And in ponnishing we must chiefly refrain from anger. For the angry man that goth about ponishment shal never keepe that measure, that is betweene too micle, and too little: the which measure liketh the Peripatetikes: and of good cause it liketh them, were it so, they would not commend angrines, and say, that it is profitably geven of nature. But in al cases, that affection is to be refused: and it to bee wished, that such as governe the common weale be lyke the lawes: which be moved to ponish offenders not upon any wrath, but upon equitie.[3]

As his action shows, this Artegall has failed to do. Even if we apply St. Thomas' analysis of Gregory's remark that "zealous anger troubles the eye of reason, whereas sinful anger blinds it,"[4] we still could not mitigate Artegall's

[3] *Ciceroes three bookes of dueties . . . turned out of latine into english, by Nicholas Grimalde* (London, 1568), folio 39 verso [1.xxv.89]. Grimalde's translation went through seven editions in Spenser's lifetime. In his edition, Aldus cites Plato, Plutarch, and Xenophon for confirmation (Lyons, 1582), pp. 39-40.

[4] "Anger may stand in a twofold relation to reason. First, antecedently; in this way it withdraws reason from its rectitude, and has therefore the character of evil. Secondly, consequently, inasmuch as the movement of the sensitive appetite is directed against vice and in accordance with reason, this anger is good, and is called *zealous anger*. Wherefore Gregory says (Moral.V.45): *We must beware*

shortcomings. In the handling of Pollente, he is neither the dispassionate judge nor the indifferent executioner.

With Munera the case is quite different. No longer secure in the protection of her father, she barricades herself in her castle, where Artegall must call upon Talus to beat down the door to prepare for his entrance. Talus himself must also resist the temptations of Munera, since bribery can subvert all aspects of justice.[5] When her warders fail to stop him with a rain of stones, Munera, thinking to avoid expense, prays to him for mercy.

> But when as yet she saw him to proceede,
> Unmov'd with praiers or with piteous thought,
> She ment him to corrupt with goodly meede;
> And causde great sackes with endlesse riches fraught,
> Unto the battilment to be upbrought,
> And powred forth over the Castle wall,
> That she might win some time, though dearly bought
> Whilest he to gathering of the gold did fall.
> But he was nothing mov'd, nor tempted therewithall.
>
> (V.ii.23)

Having breached the gate, Talus makes "way for his maister to assaile" (V.ii.24.4), and once in the castle

---

lest when we use anger as an instrument of virtue, it overrule the mind, and go before it as its mistress, instead of following in reason's train, ever ready, as its handmaid, to obey. The latter anger, although it hinders somewhat the judgment of reason in the execution of the act, does not destroy the rectitude of reason. Hence Gregory says (*ibid.*) that *zealous anger troubles the eye of reason, whereas sinful anger blinds it.*" *Summa Theologica*, II.ii.Q.158.a.1.

[5] Critics have remained silent about Talus' role here, even though his indifference to the blandishments of Munera and his part in her total destruction suggest a closer relationship between him and Artegall than has heretofore been granted. His potential, of course, is inferior to that of his master's, and his one weakness (generally true) is of omission not of commission.

Artegall and his iron groom form a relentless pair, effort-
lessly scattering her warders.

While the ease with which they proceed symbolizes the
effective working of justice, they have yet to meet the
hardest test of all, Munera herself, whose "wicked
charmes" and not-so-subtle beauty have long seduced men
away from the arduous road of public good to the well-
beaten pathway of profit and delight. Talus finds her
hiding, appropriately enough, under a pile of gold.

> Thence he her drew
> By the faire lockes, and fowly did array,
> Withouten pitty of her goodly hew,
> That *Artegall* him selfe her seemelesse plight did rew.
> (V.ii.25.6-9)

Through narrative structure and imagistic scheme, Spenser
is focusing upon the differing responses of Talus and
Artegall. Although both have resisted her first entreaties
and have ignored the proffered gold, Artegall reveals another deep-seated weakness of character in feeling pity for
the disfeaturing of fair Munera. When he entered Satyrane's Tournament of Beauty and when he surrendered to
Britomart's charms, his behavior seemingly had only local
implications. Now in proper character as a patron of justice,
Artegall with his brief nod of pity for Munera raises considerable doubt about the successful completion of his
quest.[6] Spenser properly distinguishes here between Artegall's personal regard and his knowledge of the enormity
of her crimes, since "for no pitty would he change the
course/ Of Justice, which in Talus hand did lye" (V.ii.
26.1-2). Bodin knew that any form of pity was inimical to
the law.

Now nothing is more contrarie unto true justice, than

---

[6] It also prepares us for his feeling pity for the beauty of the fallen
Radigund.

pitie; neither anything more repugnant unto the office and dutie of an upright judge, than mercie; he not only by the civill law, but even by the law of God also being forbidden to have pitie (even of the poore) in judgment: which we said to be so proper unto majestie,[7] as that it cannot be therefrom divided or separated. So that a prince sitting in judgment must take upon him two contrarie persons, that is to say of a merciful father, and of an upright magistrat; of a most gentle prince, and of an inflexible judge. And if the prince be mild and pitiful, there shall be none so evil or wicked, who by force of teares and prayers shall not escape the punishment by the law appointed, even the most cruel man being oftentimes by them overcome.[8]

Under the circumstances Artegall's lapse is inexcusable. That he has violated the rule of justice after hearing from Dony of Munera's great wrongs and experiencing her methods first hand only reinforces the knowledge of his uncertain commitment—to himself and to his quest.

Outwardly, however, the inexorable course of justice makes its way, with Talus mutilating Munera by striking off her golden hands and silver feet. Having symbolically and actually deprived her of her strength, he drowns her and burns the gold.

> And lastly all that Castle quite he raced,
> Even from the sole of his foundation,
> And all the hewen stones thereof defaced,
> That there mote be no hope of reparation,
> Nor memory thereof to any nation.
>
> (V.ii.28.1-5)

[7] Artegall is not acting here as the king he is to become but as the justiciar he is.

[8] *The Six Books of a Commonweal*, trans. Richard Knolles (London, 1606), iv.vi. [p. 509].

Talus' remorseless destruction of Munera, the gold, and the castle is of universal significance, as it is to be an exemplum of the fate of all who would blind the eyes of the judge with gifts.[9] In physically obliterating this symbol of bribery, Talus "races" it from the memory of all men, an action reminiscent of a prophecy made by Eliphaz to Job: "For the congregacion of the hypocrite shal be desolate, and fyre shal devoure the houses of bribes" (xv.34).[10] Artegall himself reforms the customs of the bridge and then resumes the quest for Irena.

Drawing near the sea after much weary travel, they are attracted by a great concourse of people from many nations.

> There they beheld a mighty Gyant stand
> Upon a rocke, and holding forth on hie
> An huge great paire of ballance in his hand,
> With which he boasted in his surquedrie,
> That all the world he would weigh equallie,
> If ought he had the same to counterpoys.
> For want whereof he weighed vanity,
> And fild his ballaunce full of idle toys:
> Yet was admired much of fooles, women, and boys.
>
> (V.ii.30)

In one sense the Gyant is a subverter of the natural order of society. By emphasizing his claims that he "all things would reduce unto equality" (32.9) and that he would "Lordings curbe, that commons over-aw;/ And all the

[9] "Rewardes and giftes blinde the eyes of the wise, and makes them domme, that they can not reprove fautes" (Deut. xvi.19). See also Exodus xxiii.8.

[10] The Geneva gloss identifies these "houses" as those "which were buylt or maintained by powling and briberie"—a perfect description of Pollente's and Munera's actions. Jerome's translation differs slightly, by placing emphasis upon those who receive bribes ("and fire will devour the tabernacles of those who freely receive bribes"). Regardless of the text used, the commentators were pleased to include both bribers and the bribed in the general conflagration.

wealth of rich men to the poore will draw" (38.8-9), earlier critics have largely read the giant as a social reformer, showing how cleverly Spenser anticipated the evils of the French Revolution and the schemes of Marx. But insofar as this episode needs to be read as a social tract, Spenser's clairvoyance proves upon examination to be hindsight, since his strictures are commonplaces drawn from the writings of political philosophers, beginning with Aristotle.[11]

[11] Gough (*Variorum, Book Five*, 177) thinks that Spenser takes his material from the *Nichomachean Ethics*, v.iii. *The Politics*, vi.1-5, outlining the structures of democracies, would be more valid, as Aristotle presents here the complete workings of such societies, not just aspects of distribution. But no such direct source is needed here, since the evils of democracies were staple wares of both greater and lesser political thinkers of the sixteenth century. Jean Bodin's influential *Six livres de la république* (1576) tells of the dangers of commutative distribution (Knolles translation, p. 570h) and thinks the end of "Popular estates is to banish vertue" (p. 703e). Charles Merbury's simplistic account parrots the common line (*A Brief Discourse of Royall Monarchy* [London, 1581], pp. 9-12). More importantly, mainstream Protestant theologians agreed with these strictures and were vehement in denouncing what we now call democratic reform. Crucial to their arguments for the status quo was a nice interpretation of the passage in Exodus xvi.16-18, where the manna, gathered variously, is shared in common. Calvin's reading is typical:

> But I thus paraphrase the passage, that, when they had applied themselves to the gathering of it, the whole amount was found sufficient to fill an omer for every individual. For they did not each of them collect a private store; but, when all had assisted, at length they took their prescribed portion from the common heap. Thus, as each was more especially diligent, the more he benefitted his slower and less industrious neighbor, without any loss to himself. This is aptly applied by Paul to almsgiving (2 Cor. vii.14) wherein every one bestows of that he possess on his poor brethren, only let us remember that this is done figuratively [per anagogen]; for though there be some likeness between the manna and our daily food, yet there is a distinction between them to be observed, on which we shall elsewhere remark. Since, then, the manna was a food differing from what we commonly use, and was

Although tendencies relating to social reform seemingly can be gleaned from the giant's speeches, an emphasis upon these elements is misleading. These few promised reforms, after all, are just sops thrown to please the crowd in order to conceal the giant's larger intentions, but should not fool the readers. In depicting the giant standing on a rock holding a balance, Spenser has created a figure who parodies his hero, providing on the literal level an episode which depicts a confrontation of false with true justice. Not only is the giant a monstrous figure of injustice, he also is—and more importantly—a colossal image of pride; for when Artegall approaches the crowd, he hears the giant boasting in "his surquedrie." That such a figure should now test Artegall is rather obvious, in view of the fact that he has recently encountered his other two personality problems in the characters of Pollente and Munera. This episode, like the other two, has transcended the immediate and particular and has become of universal significance, as gathered here are "so many nations" (V.ii.29.9), who listen to a debate upon heaven and hell, earth and creation, the elements and mutability.

Even if we accept the widely held thesis that Spenser is

---

given daily without tillage or labour almost unto their hands, it is not to be wondered that God should have called each one of the people to partake of it equally, and forbade any one to take more than another. The case of ordinary food is different; for it is necessary for the preservation of human society [pour nourrir les hommes en amitie et paix] that each should possess what is his own; that some should acquire property by purchase, that to others it should come by hereditary right, to others by the title of presentation, that each should increase his means in proportion to his diligence, or bodily strength, or other qualifications. In fine political government requires, that each should enjoy what belongs to him: and hence it would be absurd to prescribe, as to our common food, the law which is here laid down as to the manna (*Last Four Books of Moses*, trans. C. W. Bingham [Edinburgh, 1852], I, 278-279).

arraigning the Anabaptists in the episode of the reforming giant (which is highly probable), we need not also commit ourselves *a priori* to the social issues involved and in that way overlook the poetic center of the debate. Those scholars who say the giant has the better of the argument have certainly not drawn their conclusions from the poetry, relying instead perhaps upon their own sympathies for democratizing reform. Although the giant's descendants are slowly winning the day in the twentieth century, we would do well to remember for critical purposes that the ordering cosmos of Faery Land is divine not secular, monarchistic not democratic, conservative not progressive. It seems critically inconsistent to praise the beauty and order of the Garden of Adonis and then to belittle the efforts of Artegall, Spenser's chosen defender of its principles. Since this is a debate upon "heavenly justice," the arguments pro and con are not about social issues, which are the effect, but upon God's order, which is the cause—hence the thoroughly theological bent of the arguments. On the grounds they have pitched their battle, Artegall easily defeats the giant, both intellectually and physically. The casting of the debate in theological, rather than political or social, terms shows plainly that the giant's proposals are counter to divine—thereby natural—law. Although critics have remarked for some time about the prevalence of scriptural imagery in Artegall's meeting with the giant, other than noticing obvious parallels, they have not attempted to divine Spenser's purpose.[12] The initial extent of the giant's presumption should give us an idea of his character. Speaking to the assembled throng, he claims "That all the world he would weigh equallie,/ If ought he had the same to counterpoys" (V.ii.30.5-6), a boast which reveals not only his character but also his limitations. In the apocryphal Esdras is found

[12] See *Variorum, Book Five* (175-179) for a list of scriptural echoes more or less relevant to the text.

a similar assaying:[13] "And upon this [question of final things] Jeremial the Archangel answered, and said, When the nomber of the sedes is filled in you: for he has weighed the worlde in the balance" (2 Esdras iv.36). The giant exhibits his most damning flaw by presuming godhead in his great pride; and the manner in which the giant deceives the crowd only adds to his great sin, because we know from Proverbs that "False balances are an abomination unto the Lord: but a perfite weight pleaseth him" (xi.1). In acknowledging only himself and trumpeting his own strength, the giant is ignorant of the fact that "A true weight and balance are of the Lord: all the weights of the bagge are his worke" (Proverbs xvi.11). The gloss on this passage in the Geneva Bible identifies Artegall's adversary and is consistent with Spenser's imagery: "If they [the weight and balance] be true and juste, they are Gods worke, and he deliteth therin, but otherwise if they be false, they are the worke of the devil, and to their condemnation that use them." The commentators upon these two passages in Proverbs invariably draw attention to the opening of the third seal in Revelations: "And when he had opened the thirde seale, I heard the thirde beast say, Come and se, Then I behelde, and lo, a blacke horse, and he that sate on him had balances in his hand" (vi.5). The rider of course is anti-Christ, truly the devil who uses God's word for perverse and deceptive purposes.[14] That Spenser intended the

---

[13] The anonymous correspondent who drew Craik's attention to Esdras was certainly correct (*Variorum, Book Five,* 177). Neither Craik nor Gough (who uses the information) tries to relate it to the poetry.

[14] Hugh of St. Cher, *Opera,* VII, 385 verso. Cornelius a Lapide confirms the identification and shows the dangers of weighing God's word and works by hand (the scales) rather than pondering them in the mind (*Commentaria in Apocalypsin* [Antwerp, 1681], 122a). Spenser's giant certainly fits the description. He quotes scripture for his own purposes, uses the balance instead of the mind, and questions the validity of God's work. The glossators also thought the balances

giant to be a type of false Messiah is everywhere present in the text of the episode, his claims to weigh the world fixing his diabolical character and his deliberately distorted interpretation of Scripture shadowing his eventual fall.

Since the giant represents a direct challenge to orthodox Christian doctrine, his overthrow differs from that of Pollente or Munera. The battle is a contest of words as Artegall assumes the role of an orator in refuting the arguments of the giant. Having shown Artegall's wisdom, strength, and seeming resistance to the blandishments of beauty in the previous encounters, Spenser now delineates the eloquence and learning of his hero, two other important attributes necessary for the justiciar. Although Plutarch tells us that Hercules, Artegall's mythological counterpart, was associated with the Muses because he taught Evander writing,[15] the best known example of his erudition and eloquence is to be found in Lucian's famous "introduction."[16] There Lucian reports viewing a painting of Hercules as an old man drawing after him a crowd of admirers, their ears fastened with delicate chains which originate from his tongue. Upon seeing him puzzling over the painting, a nearby Celt explains to him that his people identify Hercules, not Mercury, with eloquence and that in the main they think he was a learned man who conquered by persuasion.[17] Lucian's image found a comfortable home in Renaissance emblem books and Alciati uses it to illustrate

---

were a sign of famine. If it is applicable here as a submerged reference, it serves to double the irony; for instead of increasing the lot of the common people by despoiling the rich, the giant will bring chaos and want.

[15] *Quaestiones Romanae,* LIX.

[16] "Hercules Gallicus," *Opera quae extant . . . cum Gilberti Cognati Nozereni, et Joannis Sambuci annotationibus* (Basle, 1563), I, 784-791. In this edition Erasmus' Latin translation faces the Greek original.

[17] See Cognatus' note, *ibid.,* 791.

the motto *eloquentia fortitudine praestantior*.[18] The eloquence of Hercules belongs also to Artegall, and what
arises from the encounter with the giant is an elaborately
symmetrical debate in which points advanced by the giant
are refuted with rhetorical skill by the hero. Inasmuch as
Artegall's victories in past battles subtly unfolded painful
weaknesses, his behavior at the beginning of the debate and
his apparent disregard for his own arguments after the
giant is humbled, mark another flaw of character, as Spenser further elaborates the design of outward success and
inward shortcomings previously established in the canto.

The intricate pattern Spenser has provided for the debate
itself follows the standard schema for forensic oratory fa-
vored by the rhetoricians, whose precepts formed the ubiq-
uitous thongs with which Cambridge students laced up
their academic disputations.[19] When Artegall and Talus
approach, the giant is finishing his *exordium*, which obviously has succeeded in its primary purpose of gaining the
goodwill of the audience. Continuing his speech, the giant
in his *narratio* sets forth his general intentions and prospects
for reform (30-32), which Artegall counters with an affirmative restatement of divine order (34-36). In his *con-
firmatio* the giant first slights (*reprehensio*) Artegall's evidence, enumerates supposed injustices in nature, and then
offers specific reforms (37-38); and Artegall uses similar

[18] Emblem CLXXX. Mignault's commentary surveys writers on the
subject from antiquity to Budé. In this regard, see Robert E. Hallo-
well's essay showing the relevance of the myth to Ronsard ("Ronsard
and the Gallic Hercules Myth," *Studies in the Renaissance*, ix
[1962], 242-255).

[19] For a brief, but thorough, account of the techniques of the
orator see Cicero's *De partitione oratoria*. Or for a more detailed
analysis of the divisions, types of evidence, refutation, and other matters central to Spenser's managing of the debate, see Quintilian's
Institutio oratoria, especially III.ix-x (structure of forensic oratory,
controversial causes); IV.i-ii (*exordium, narratio*); V.xi-xiii (*con-
firmatio, refutatio*); VI.iv (*altercatio*).

techniques with which to deny seriatim the validity of his
opponent's case (39-42). At this formal point the pattern
shifts. Instead of simply meeting the giant's arguments with
better ones defending the status quo, Artegall takes the
initiative by asking questions (*altercatio*)[20] which directly
challenges the efficacy of the balances and by setting a series
of measurement tests, which the giant fails (43-46). Having easily won the debate, Artegall offers to teach the
giant the limits of his mechanical scales and to instruct
him in its proper use; but when the giant refuses the advice and persists in his error, Talus shoulders him from the
rock (47-50).[21]

Although the giant's original presumption of godhead
identifies his diabolical nature, he is no mere blasphemer,
as his deceptive plans for equality fully reveal his insidious
character.

> He sayd that he would all the earth uptake,
> And all the sea, devided each from either:
> So would he of the fire one ballaunce make,
> And one of th'ayre, without or wind, or wether:
> Then would he ballaunce heaven and hell together,
> And all that did within them all containe;
> Of all whose weight, he would not miss a fether.
> And looke what surplus did of each remaine,
> He would to his owne part restore the same againe.
>
> For why, he sayd they all unequall were,
> And had encroched uppon others share,
> Like as the sea (which plaine he shewed there)
> Had worne the earth, so did the fire the aire,
> So all the rest did others parts empaire.

[20] For the important role of *altercatio* in forensic oratory after the
prepared speech, see Quintilian, vi.iv.

[21] If we read the giant's (30-32, 37-38) and Artegall's (34-36,
39-42) presentations separately, we will see they are consistent with
formal oratorical demands.

And so were realmes and nations run awry,
All which he undertooke for to repaire.
In sort as they were formed aunciently;
And all things would reduce unto equality.

(V.ii.31-32)

In promising to recreate creation he implicitly refuses to acknowledge that "The Lord by wisdom hath layd the foundation of the earth, and hath stablished the heavens through
understanding" (Proverbs iii.19); his claims to divide the
waters and the earth anew, mock the work of God in Genesis. His greatest threat to God (however small in absolute
terms) is the desire to "ballaunce heaven and hell together," since if he succeeds in this, he will force God to
repudiate his creation—man. According to Jeremiah, "Thus
saith the Lorde, If the heavens can be measured or the foundations of the earth be searched out beneath, then will I
cast off all the sede of Israel, for all that they have done"
(xxxi.37). From the complexities of Hugh of St. Cher[22]
to the simple comment in the Geneva Bible (*The one and
the other is impossible*), generations have learned that God
would not betray their faith. By attempting to tamper with
the elemental stuff of the universe, the giant feigns that he
"would reduce [all things] unto equality," as they "were
formed aunciently." But what was the condition of things
before God arranged the elements in their proper order,
leading upward from the cesspool of the universe (earth)
to the purifying empyrean (fire)? The elements were equal
then, and their equality produced chaos. Following Du
Bellay, Spenser wrote of this primordial conflict:

So when the compass course of the universe
In sixe and thirtie thousand yeares is ronne,
The bands of th'elements shall back reverse
To their first discord, and be quite undonne:

---

[22] "In libros Prophetarum," *Opera*, IV, 250,

The seedes, of which all things at first were bred,
Shall in great *Chaos* wombe againe be hid.[23]
(*Ruines of Rome*, ll.303-308)

From the giant's first speech, we can see that under the guise of reform he promises destruction, arrogating to himself the role of creator; had he but the power, his would be the *uncreating* word. The scope of his intentions and his blatant ignorance of God's work make it appear obvious that he is the greatest figure of pride, a type of anti-Christ.

The giant, of course, becomes the current favorite of the vulgar, and they flock about him to gain favors and to obtain "uncontrolled freedome,"

All which when *Artegall* did see, and heare,
How he mis-led the simple peoples train,
In sdeignfull wize he drew unto him neare.
(V.ii.33.6-8)

The manner in which Artegall has entered the controversy exposes his most unpleasant character trait—his pride—although, to be sure, disdain is only *gradus superbiae* which indicates tendencies toward arrogance. As the Common-Place books were fond of saying, "Arrogance is the daughter of pride . . . because anyone appraising himself highly disdains others whom he sees below him."[24] The expression occurs frequently in Spenser's poetry, the Ape in "Mother Hubberd's Tale" ruling with "sdeignfull pride, and wilfull arrogaunce" (l.1135), brothers being "pricked with proud disdaine" and seas puffing up with "proude disdayne." Artegall's initial reaction is most important because it sets the tone of his rebuttal and explains his later embarrassment when confronted by the rabble.

Although Artegall is overmuch given to pontificating in

[23] This Du Bellay has adapted from the *Timaeus*.
[24] In Lawrens Beyerlinck's *Theatrum vitae humanae* (Leyden, 1678), I, 521.

the debate, his arguments are quite sound, since in all cases his most telling points are derived from Scripture. He rightly challenges the giant's authority from the outset and twits him on presuming far above his "forces pitch to sore" (V.ii.34.4).

> For ere thou limit what is lesse or more
> In every thing, thou oughtest first to know,
> What was the poyse of every part of yore:
> And looke then how much it doth overflow,
> Or faile thereof, so much is more than just to trow.
>
> (V.ii.34.5-9)

Artegall's is an approved rhetorical tactic—an appeal to tradition which subtly undermines the giant's case. This approach points up the difference between the two debaters that is to become more pronounced as the argument increases in intensity with charge and countercharge. On the one hand, Artegall bases his argument upon biblical authority and precedent, because, as he later points out, the senses can be deceiving. Artegall's cautionary statement here is deliberately reminiscent of a question God put to Job. After thirty-seven chapters of misfortune, Job begins to have serious doubts about Divine Providence when suddenly God appears out of the whirlwind, asking a series of questions. One question demands: "Where wast thou when I layed the foundations of the earth? declare if thou hast understanding" (xxxviii.4). The commentators knew that this question fixed Job's limitations; "Seeing he could not judge of those things, which were done so long before he was borne, he was not able to comprehende all God's workes: much lesse the secrete causes of his judgments" (Geneva gloss). That Artegall's opening statement carries similar force is shown by subsequent demonstration.

> For at the first they all created were
> In goodly measure, by their Makers might,

And weighed out in ballaunces so nere,
That not a dram was missing of their right.
(V.ii.35.1-4)

It is part of Spenser's technique here that these verses
answer the next question put to Job: "Who hath layed the
measures thereof, if thou knowest, or who hath stretched
the line over it?" (xxxviii.5). The purpose of Artegall's
opening remarks is to establish the provenance of his authority, since with this accomplished he can show the cor-
rectness of the natural order of the elements (35.5-9) and
warn against the perils of innovation (36). The burden of
proof for the desirability of change now rests in the giant's
balance.

Angry to be so confronted, the giant rebukes Artegall as
a "foolishe Elfe" and disregards his arguments from authority. Because the giant has been reading the Book of
Nature by the flickering light of his own senses, he only
sees what he apparently sees, and asks Artegall to look at
nature in the same way. Each estate is going out of order,
the sea is eating away the land, and the land is daily in
creased by the burden of the dead (37.2-6). The basis for
his argument, as Artegall quickly discovers, is a syllogism
with the faulty major premise that the divine order of
things is wrong.

Therefore I will throw downe these mountaines hie,
And make them levell with the lowly plaine:
These towring rocks, which reach unto the skie,
I will thrust downe into the deepest maine,
And as they were, them equalize againe.
Tyrants that make men subject to their law,
I will surpresse, that they no more may raine:
And Lordings curbe, that commons over-aw;
And the wealth of rich men to the poore will draw.
(V.ii.38)

As this passage evidences, the giant is not above using Scripture for his own purposes, his initial reform coming from the Messianic fortieth chapter of Isaiah: "Every valley shalbe exalted, and every mountaine and hill shalbe made lowe: and the crooked shalbe streight, and the rough places plaine" (xl.4). It is not unexpected from what we already know of the giant's nature to see him directly assuming the role of the Savior.

Having determined the degree of the giant's spiritual blindness, Artegall can undermine his argument at its strongest point: "Of things unseene how canst thou deeme aright. . . . Sith thou misdeem'st so much of things in sight?" The earth is not destroyed by being washed into the sea, since it comes to land at another place (39.4-9).

> Likewise the earth is not augmented more,
> By all that dying into it doe fade.
> For of the earth they formed were of yore,
> However gay their blossome or their blade
> Do flourish now, they into dust shall vade.
>   (V.ii.40.1-5)

When Adam prepares to leave the Garden, the Lord reminds him of his state: "In the sweate of thy face shalt thou eat bread, till thou return to the earth: for out of it wast thou taken, because thou art dust, and to dust thou returne" (Genesis iii.19), and David sings of man, the flourishing flower of the field, soon to be gathered into the dust (Psalm CIII.14-16).[25] With undeniable logic derived from the word of God, Artegall has destroyed the bases of the giant's arguments for change.[26]

At this point Artegall seizes the initiative in the debate by cross-examining his adversary. Since the giant has boasted

[25] Osgood first noticed the relevance of these verses to Artegall's argument (*Variorum, Book Five*, 178).

[26] Stanzas 41 and 42 are practically literal paraphrases from Old Testament texts; see especially 1 Samuel xi and Daniel iv.35.

of the accuracy of his scales, Artegall wants him to prove their accuracy.

> For take thy ballaunce, if thou be so wise,
> And weigh the winde, that under heaven doth blow;
> Or weigh the light, that in the East doth rise;
> Or weigh the thought, that from mans mind doth flow.
> But if the weight of these thou canst not show,
> Weigh but one word which from thy lips doth fall.
> For how canst thou those greater secrets know,
> That doest not know the least thing of them all?
> Ill can he rule the great, that cannot reach the small.
>
> (V.ii.43)

Artegall is here using a common rhetorical stratagem, the dilemma,[27] to force the giant to admit his limitations and tacitly to confess his subservience to his Maker. Being the *non in mente sed in manu* giant of the commentators, he, of course, fails all the tests, and implicitly admits defeat when he becomes furious with his balance for his failure.

Since for all intents and purposes the giant has been shorn of his pretensions, Artegall in the last part of the debate no longer finds it necessary to treat him as a serious opponent. Instead he offers to teach him to use his balance correctly. Right is not to be weighed with wrong (45-46), because the mind must determine, just as the "eare must be the ballance" to judge the truth or falsehood of the spoken word (47). When the giant persists in thrusting the right away and attempting to weigh extremities, Talus "shouldered him from off the higher ground,/ And downe the rock him throwing, in the sea him dround" (V.ii.49.8-9).

With this one violent act the underlying pattern of the debate stands revealed. We are entitled to infer from the beginning of the giant's speech that he is of the devil's party, although the extent of his involvement is not known. In the highly stylized debate upon first and last things

---

[27] Quintilian, VI.iv.18-19.

that follows, the degree of the giant's complicity becomes greater and greater until he has clearly identified himself. At that very moment Talus pushes him from the cliff and he drowns in the sea below. The giant's fate symbolically links him to the Old Testament giants, who lived before the Flood.[28] From Genesis we learn, "There were gyantes in the earth in thos days: yea, and after that the sonnes of God came unto the daughters of men, and they had borne them children, these were mighty men, which in olde time were men of renoune" (vi.4). Unfortunately, these giants "usurped authoritie over others, and did degenerate from that simplicitie, wherein their fathers lived" (Geneva gloss). Their hybrid natures fostered great pride which in turn led them to rely upon their own strengths, for they were of the brood of Cain and the fallen angels.[29] Spenser's giant is of the same diabolical family,[30] and the progress of the debate shows clearly just how little he knows and how far he has turned from the right, an especial ignorance to be expected from one who challenges godhead: "There were the gyants, famous from the beginning, that were of so great stature and so expert in warre. Those did not the Lord chuse, neither gave he the way of knowledge unto them. But they were destroyed, because they had no wisdome, and perished through their owne foolishnesse" (Baruch iii.26-28; Geneva version). At every point Spenser's giant agrees with his counterpart in the Old Testament: he is proud, challenges God's authority, and betrays a fundamental ignorance. It is poetically consistent and logically inevitable that he dies as they died—by drowning: "the

[28] It would be more profitable to consider all of Spenser's giants as part of biblical tradition rather than the necessary baggage of Romance.

[29] Hugh of St. Cher, "In libros Genesis," *Opera*, I, 9.

[30] For an account of accepted meanings of the giants see Hugh of St. Cher's analysis of Psalm xxxii (*Opera*, II, 81) and also Philo Judaeus' *De gigantibus*.

giants groan under the waters, and they that dwell with them" (Job xxvi. 5; Douay version).[31] With this fate the identification is complete, and it is significant that the humbling of the giant's pride is accompanied by a literal fall.

> So downe the cliffe the wretched Gyant tumbled;
> His battred ballances in peeces lay,
> His timbered bones all broken rudely rumbled,
> So was the high aspyring with huge ruine humbled.
> (V.ii.50.6-9)[32]

The debate with the giant pits Artegall against one who is symbolic of his greatest enemy—his pride. When he first confronts his adversary, Artegall is motivated by disdain, a minor species of pride, a momentary lapse soon forgotten in the course of the debate. The ensuing argument proves beyond doubt that Spenser's hero is an accomplished orator and theologian; and although his manner is a bit pompous, his knowledge of Scripture nevertheless is impressive. His initial disdain and his debating style are not sufficient evidence for showing a definite weakness of character, and are no more than strategically dropped poetic hints. Exactly at the moment of Artegall's success, however, Spenser has contrived to present him in a compromising light, in which consideration of self obtrudes once again upon judicial procedure. When the giant falls, the people he has misled naturally are disappointed at the "certaine losse of so great expectation" (51.5) and arm themselves to confront Artegall.

> Which lawlesse multitude him comming too
> In warlike wise, when *Artegall* did view,
> He much was troubled, ne wist what to doo.

---

[31] See also Wisdom xiv.6; Geneva version: "for in the old time also when the proud giants perished, the hope of the world went into a ship which was governed by thy hand, and so left the seede of generation to the world."

[32] Calvin's interpretation of Genesis (vi.4-7) is to the same point.

For loth he was his noble hands t'embrew
In the base blood of such a rascall crew;
And otherwise, if that he should retire,
He fear'd least they with shame would him pursew.
Therefore he *Talus* to them sent, t'inquire
The cause of their array, and truce for to desire.
(V.ii.52)

Artegall, who had all the answers for the giant on the tip
of his tongue, now knows not "what to doo," a dilemma of
his own making which reflects his pride. Symbolically, his
pride produces a stasis, in which the proper working of
justice has come to a standstill. Artegall is "loth" to soil
"his noble hands" on the common people, thereby forget-
ting that justice is to be given impartially both to the high
and the low. It is even more ironic that he should take such
a stand, considering the fact that he had previously lectured
the giant on the point that "The hils doe not the lowly
dales disdaine" (41.3).

In this episode, Spenser has skillfully called the reader's
attention to the protean vagaries of the mob, showing the
metamorphosis of the giant's audience from a "simple
people's traine" (33.7) into a "lawlesse multitude" (52.1).
The mutinous rabble must of course be dispersed, dispersed
quickly before its contagion infects the core of law-abiding
citizens; but according to Elizabethan law, the first attempt
to bring order must be peaceful. Artegall perhaps for-
feited an opportunity when he spent all his time making
"legal" points with the giant and none whatsoever in attempting to win over the crowd. Such an omission simply
may have been a tactical error. It is no great matter.
Nevertheless in his official capacity as justiciar in Faery
Land and as Gloriana's "instrument" (Proem V.xi.9),
Artegall should know his legal duties. In cases of unlawful
assembly, "routs," or riot, responsibility first rests with the
Queen's ranking lieutenant, whoever he may be. He was

required by statute to address the group threatening the peace. Regardless of whatever preliminary remarks the Queen's officer made, he always read the standard proclamation for such disturbances: "The Queene our Soveraigne Ladie chargeth and commandeth all persons beeing assembled, immediately to disperse themselves, and peaceablie to depart to their habitations, or to their lawfull businesse, upon the paines contained in the Acte lately made against unlawfull and rebellious assemblies. And God save the Queene."[33] If the order did not effect compliance within an hour, the Queen's officer used all necessary force, employing his own men and deputizing citizens when needed.

Instead of taking a positive step himself in an effort to lessen the possibility of violence, Artegall sends Talus to enquire the "cause of their array," an irrelevant question, because unlawful assembly, not their motivation, is the issue. When the crowd attacks Talus, he scatters them relentlessly.

> As when a Faulcon hath with nimble flight
> Flowne at a flush of Ducks, foreby the brooke,
> The trembling foule dismayed with dreadfull sight
> Of death, the which them almost overtooke,
> Doe hide themselves, from her astonying looke,
> Amongst the flags and covert round about.
>   (V.ii.54.1-6)[34]

Artegall's reasons for dispatching Talus seem contradictory. He does not want to "embrew" his noble hands in the

---

[33] Statutes against unlawful assembly are part of the long history of the Common Law. For the law in force during Elizabeth's reign, see John Rastell's *A Collection in English, of the Statutes Now in Force. . .* (1621), pp. 346-350 [Riots, Routes, etc.]. See also Lambarde's *Eirenarcha* (1588), pp. 185-194.

[34] The references to the scattered mob as hiding ducks is Spenser's way of delineating the inherent stupidity of the giant's erstwhile followers. See Mignault's commentaries in Alciati's *Emblemata*.

"base blood of such a rascall crew," yet he had no similar compunction when shortly before he struck off the head of that base "villaine," Guizor. Nor should Artegall fear their pursuit when he has Talus as his agent. This is the first time Artegall has confronted the mob; and the vain reasons he gives himself for not fulfilling his responsibilities offer further evidence of internal discords.[35] In all cases he has handled thus far, Artegall manages to get justice done—but at a price. Although he saves his "reputation," he has demonstrated again, as he did with Pollente and Munera, essential flaws marring his personality. His outward successes are Pyrrhic victories; and when his character has been sufficiently weakened by them, he will fall.

ii

With the defeat of the giant's admirers, the scene abruptly changes to the tournament celebrating the wedding of Florimell and Marinell, a transition not wholly unexpected, since Artegall told Dony at the beginning of Canto II that he would attend and pay his respects if he had time. Spenser anticipates his readers' questioning the propriety of having the patron of justice attend a social function, especially when Irena, the Pearl White of *The Faerie Queene*, is in imminent peril. Accordingly, after setting the scene in the briefest possible way, the "poet" declines to add further detail, claiming that such things "Were worke fit for an Herauld, not for me" (V.iii.3.6).

> But for so much as to my lot here lights,
> That with this present treatise doth agree,
> True vertue to advance, shall here recounted bee.
> (V.iii.3.7-9)

Professor Hamilton thinks that Spenser's didacticism is

[35] At the end of his quest Artegall becomes indifferent to the mob and quietly pursues the course of justice.

showing through here,[36] but it is the poet's purpose in these lines to apprise his readers of a subtle change in emphasis in the conduct of the tournament itself. This is the Tournament of Virtue, where no rewards are offered except the high regard of fellow knights. Since this is a test of the highest knightly principles, "Ne any Knight was absent, that brave courage bore" (V.iii.2.9). As such, the tournament invites comparison with the one that Satyrane staged for the false Florimell. It also lasts for three days, and in terms of narrative structure it closely resembles the other. By drawing obvious parallels between the two tournaments, Spenser has established a poetic construct in which the ennobling qualities of the pursuit of virtue contrast sharply with the brutalizing character of the pursuit of beauty.

When the marriage tournament begins with "all men" addressing themselves "To deedes of armes and proofs of chevalrie" (4.3), Spenser wants us to remember that for beauty "all men threw out vowes and wishes vaine" (IV. iv.16.6). The latter contest is a contest of men not of beasts, as Marinell's six companions (V.iii.5) are soldiers. Gough speculates that their names, "like many in *The Faerie Queene* were probably chosen or invented by Spenser for the sake of sound rather than for any significance."[37] Yet in almost every case, these same names serve as an etymological link that proclaims them to be men: Brunell (Brunello); Ecastor (*équestre*); Armeddan (fighting noble); Lansack (*lansquiner*). To make sure that his readers grasp his meaning, he provides Marinell's companions with descriptive tags: *noble knight*; *skild in lovely layes*; *a redoubted knight* (5). With one fatal exception, all the battles are indicative of the high moral purpose to which all these noble contestants have addressed themselves, and

---

[36] *Structure*, p. 170.
[37] *Variorum, Book Five*, 186.

the first two days of the tournament have a ritualistic cast.

> And them against came all that list to giust,
> From every coast and countrie under sunne:
> None was debard, but all had leave that lust.
> The trompets sound; then all together ronne.
> Full many deedes of armes that day were done,
> And many knights unhorst, and many wounded,
> As fortune fell; yet litle lost or wonne:
> But all that day the greatest prayse redounded
> To *Marinell*, whose name the Heralds loud resounded.

> The second day, so soone as morrow light
> Appear'd in heaven, into the field they came,
> And there all day continew'd cruel fight,
> With divers fortune fit for such a game,
> In which all strove with perill to winne fame.
> Yet whether side was victor, note be ghest:
> But at the last the trompets did proclame
> That *Marinell* that day deserved best.
> So they disparted were, and all men went to rest.
>
> $\qquad\qquad\qquad\qquad\qquad\qquad\qquad$ (V.iii.6-7)

Unlike the earlier tournament where each of the contestants revealed his animalistic nature, here during the first two days the individual feats of valor are submerged in the common display of knightly virtue. In the general excellence of the "many deedes of armes" no completely overpowering victory is won by a single knight. Since each side is striving "with perill to win fame," there is little difference between contestants. Although Marinell wins the first two days' fighting, he has won by the narrowest of margins. Exuberant from these past successes and apparently not satisfied with being acclaimed a little better than his peers, Marinell overreaches himself on the last day, during which he fights furiously and "through the thickest like a Lyon flew" (V.iii.8.5). This change anticipates his fall; and characteristically he fights like an animal (the first chivalric lapse in the whole tourney), heedlessly pressing on, leaving his fellows behind, and eventually falling captive. Since Artegall was similarly defeated at the Tournament of Beauty, Spenser's point could not be more obvious. In this case Marinell has violated the rules and must pay the penalty.

At this moment Artegall comes to the lists, just as he also appeared at Satyrane's tournament on the third day. This time he is not alone but is accompanied by Braggadocchio and the snowy Florimell, two unfit traveling companions he has met along the way. When he hears of Marinell's plight, he determines to rescue him: "And streight that boaster prayd, with whom he rid,/ To change his shield with him, to be the better hid" (V.iii.10.8 9). With this exchange the pattern of relationships between the tournaments is completed: just as he fought in disguise for the false Florimell, Artegall now fights incognito for the true. He frees Marinell, and together they renew the battle against "all the other crew."

> Whom with sore havocke soon they overthrew,
> And chaced quite out of the field, that none
> Against them durst his head to perill shew.
> So were they left Lords of the field alone:
> So *Marinell* by him was rescu'd from his fone.
>
> (V.iii.12.5-9)

Something is greatly wrong here; the whole style of battle has reverted to that of Satyrane's tournament. When Artegall and Marinell become "Lords of the field," they emulate Satyrane, who earlier achieved similar distinction (IV.iv.28.1). With abrupt change the indifferent pursuit of virtue has been replaced by an uncompromising desire for vengeance.

Since virtue has both metaphorically and actually left the field, the way is prepared for the entrance of Braggadocchio.

When Artegall restores his shield to him, Braggadocchio moves into the vacuum created by the dispersal of the knights. Proclaimed the victor of the day, he receives the thanks of the true Florimell for proving her excellence.

> To whom the boaster, that all knights did blot,
> With proud disdaine did scornefull answere make;
> That what he did that day, he did it not
> For her, but for his owne deare Ladies sake,
> Whom on his perill he did undertake,
> Both her and eke all others to excell:
> And further did uncomely speaches crake.
> Much did his words the gentle Ladie quell,
> And turn'd aside for shame to heare, what he did tell.
>
> (V.iii.16)

The tournament which began in Florimell's honor now causes her to feel shame, a sudden turn of events which reflects and revives the imagistic scheme begun at Satyrane's parody of virtue. Florimell's manifesting shame because of the disgraceful behavior of Braggadocchio is an example of her perfect exercise of temperance. Under the circumstances, her delicacy and reserve result in the praiseworthy passion of shame which mitigates the ultimate effect of Braggadocchio's obscenities upon her (see Aquinas, *Summa Theologica*, II.ii, Q.144). Braggadocchio succeeds in confusing Marinell, however. When the snowy Florimell comes forth and Marinell himself cannot tell the false from the true (V.iii.18), Spenser underscores the results of the final battle.

Having indignantly shown Braggadocchio's claim of earning the victory to be incapable of proof, Artegall calls for the true Florimell; and when he places "her by that snowy one/ Like the true saint beside the image set," the snowy Florimell vanishes. This aspect of the problem of illusion and reality, artifice and art, false and true love, originated at the earlier tournament, at which the false Florimell was revealed as illusion, the product of insidious artifice:[38]

> As guilefull Goldsmith, that by secret skill,
> With golden foyle doth finely over spread
> Some baser metall, which commend he will
> Unto the vulgar for good gold insted,
> He much more goodly glosse thereon doth shed,
> To hide his falshood, than if it were trew:
> So hard, this Idole was to be ared,
> That *Florimell* her selfe in all mens vew
> She seem'd to passe: so forged things do fairest shew.
>
> (IV.v.15)

She also succeeds in deluding the people at the wedding tournament: "That Florimell her selfe she then did pas" (V.iii.17.8). As she chooses Braggadocchio, completing the parody of love, Spenser sets them up as false emulators of virtue. For when the snowy Florimell, who shines as "Phebes light" (IV.v.14.3), and Braggadocchio, who carries a shield bearing "the Sunne brode blazed in a golden field" (V.iii.14.9), link themselves together in unholy band, they mock the chaste Diana and virtuous Apollo. After the false Florimell is put to the test of proving the validity of her character, she melts to nothingness, symbolically and actually returning to the artificial and illusory world whence she originated.

Although it is tempting to commend Artegall for his actions at the tournament and to applaud his judgment which results in the "uncasing" of Braggadocchio and the vaporizing of his consort, it will be seen upon closer examination that he merits little praise. He is the one who is ultimately responsible for the chaos at the tournament

[38] For the insubstantial, but diabolical, origin of the false Florimell see III.viii.5-9.

which results in the extreme embarrassment of the gentle Florimell.[39] When he exchanges his shield with Braggadocchio, he violates a cardinal rule of chivalry, a foolish act which enables the mock knight falsely to claim the victory for his lady and to undermine the whole basis of the Tournament of Virtue. Artegall, who is able to intuit the guilt of the unworthy Sanglier in the opening episode, cannot determine Braggadocchio's character, even though he has traveled with him and even despite the fact that almost everyone else in Faery Land knows of his unworthiness (IV.iv.10-14). When Artegall fought in Satyrane's Tournament of the Girdle, he wanted to win the fairest lady—the false Florimell. At the wedding celebration, although he thinks he is fighting for Marinell in order to bring honor to Florimell, he is, ironically, fighting once again for the snowy lady. When he willingly exchanges shields, he demonstrates once again a basic lack of discretion, so necessary for the pursuit of justice. This unthinking consideration of his "honours stile" anticipates his willful abandonment of his shield to the Amazon Radigund.

Spenser is not content to let Artegall's failure remain understated, trusting the judicious reader to make the logical inferences. Instead he seizes the opportunity to knit up a long-hanging strand of narrative and to present an unmistakable emblem of his hero's shortcomings. While the crowd is defaming Braggadocchio, Guyon steps forward to claim his horse Brigadore, which marks the denouement of one of the most famous of Spenser's narrative suspensions: Braggadocchio stole Guyon's horse and spear in Book Two (ii.11-12). Some critics have thought this an awkward interpolation, a rather arbitrary attempt to round out an uneven narrative. Yet Guyon has every right to be present at the wedding tournament. Aside from the fact that this is the most publicized event in *The Faerie Queene* ("The

[39] Marinell's one rash act initiates the change of tone, but Artegall's indiscretion leads to chaos.

time and place was blazed farre and wide") and it attracts
noble men from "every coast and countrie under sunne,"
we should expect to see Guyon here. He, with Arthur,
undertook to rescue the fleeing Florimell a long time ago
(III.i.18). Guyon's presence here is most natural and
should be taken for granted.

As Guyon wants to prove his claim by combat (V.iii.
30.5) when Braggadocchio refuses to relinquish the horse,
Artegall, assuming the role of peacemaker, stays his intentions and asks the circumstances of the theft. This gives
Guyon an opportunity to tell of the "wofull couple" and
the "yong bloodie babe" to whom he was administering
when the horse was stolen. Even though he knows Braggadocchio to be a liar, a disrupter of the peace, and a thief
whose guilt stands forth in his every act, Artegall is un-
decided and desires more evidence in proof of the claim.
Guyon tells him of an identifying mark in the horse's
mouth; and before he can reach the horse, two men are
badly hurt attempting to see the tell-tale mark.

> Ne he his mouth would open unto wight,
> Untill that *Guyon* selfe unto him spake,
> And called *Brigadore* (so was he hight)
> Whose voice so soone as he did undertake,
> Eftsoones he stood still as any stake,
> And suffred all his secret marke to see:
> And when as he him nam'd, for joy he brake
> His bands, and follow'd him with gladfull glee,
> And friskt, and flong aloft, and louted low on knee.
>
> (V.iii.34)

Nature itself has supported Guyon's claim, as the horse
knows his own master. The "secret marke" is simply final
confirmation. Finally satisfied with the validity of Guyon's
claim, Artegall awards him the horse. Braggadocchio ob-
jects to the decision and he reviles, berates, and disdains
Artegall (35.7-9).

Much was the knight incenst with his lewd word,
To have revenged that his villeny;
And thrise did lay his hand upon his sword,
To have him slaine, or dearely doen aby.
But *Guyon* did his choler pacify,
Saying, Sir knight, it would dishonour bee
To you, that are our judge of equity,
To wreake your wrath on such a carle as hee:
It's punishment enough, that all his shame doe see.

(V.iii.36)

Artegall's temper tantrum here epitomizes his discordant character, since a good judge knows that anger is not answered with anger and that he should never interpose his personal feelings in the deposition of a case. It is ironic that the man who assumed the role of peacemaker must himself be *pacified* (V.iii.36.5), an irony which is heightened when Guyon, the patron of temperance, must read him a lecture on the proper performance of his duties. It is difficult for the reader to escape the unpleasant feeling that Artegall is deviating widely from the course of true justice and becoming less and less qualified to rescue Irena from Grantorto. In this canto he has succeeded in creating chaos at the Tournament of Virtue, has provided Braggadocchio with the opportunity to discomfit the fair Florimell, and has lost his temper. In the Sanglier episode we learned that when Hercules captured the Eurymanthean Boar, he gained temperance. Artegall's handling of Sanglier indicates that his self-control was, at least, unsteady. Here we have an emblem which shows just how slender is his control over his passions, indicating anew the hero's shortcomings. The work of justice is peace but is first of all contingent upon inner harmony.

iii

As an artistic device which enables him to provide a link between cantos, Spenser often has the "poet" add remarks by way of summary which either give point to the action just concluded or anticipate new problems. Spenser has used this narrative technique in the two preceding cantos but for slightly different reasons. In this case they are not simply clear-cut statements of intentions or purpose, because in truth they are ambiguous and qualified and, when read in context, quite ironic. At the beginning of Canto II Spenser uses the "poet" to remind his readers of the divine calling of justice and of the nobility of his hero. In defending the weak, "those great Heroes got thereby/ Their greatest glory, for their rightfull deeds,/ And place deserved with the Gods on hy" (V.ii.1.5-7), a flattering comparison of Artegall with "those great Heroes" which implicitly inspires the image of Hercules. Spenser's outline of the toils of justice is cliché; but he is in good company, as Cicero makes a similar point.

> And in like manner, more accordinge to nature yt is, for the saving and ayding of nations (if it may possibly be done) to undertake great travailes, and pains folowinge that notable Hercules whom mens report (the recorder of descrts) hath placed in the companye of them above: than to live in solitarynesse, not only without any paines, but also in great pleasures, flowing ful of all richesse: yea though more over you mai excell all other, in beautye and strength.[40]

Artegall's first act as the patron of justice, the defense of the squalid squire, is anything but heroic, results from a minimum of effort (Talus does all the work), and hangs upon the doubtful efficacy of a thin cord of shame. We infer these weaknesses from the decision of the hero as Solomon-Hercules, and we find they prove true as he errs in handling Pollente, Munera, and the giant. When Artegall stands flat-footed (disdaining to soil his noble hands in dealing with the common people and fearing lest he

[40] *De officiis*, Grimalde's trans. (1568), folio 122 verso [III.v.25].

draw shame upon himself by running away) and has Talus wreak havoc among them, he is not defending "the feeble in their right" nor is he redressing wrong "in such as wend awry" (V.ii.1.2-4). Rather he is defending his noble reputation.

Continuing this subtle pattern in the next canto, Spenser begins with a beautiful statement of virtue rewarded.

> After long stormes and tempests overblowne,
> The sunne at length his joyous face doth cleare:
> So when as fortune all her spight hath showne,
> Some blisful houres at last must needes appeare;
> Else should afflicted wights oftimes despeire.
> So comes it now to *Florimell* by tourne,
> After long sorrowes suffred whyleare,
> In which captiv'd she many moneths did mourne,
> To taste of joy, and to wont pleasures to retourne.
>
> (V.iii.1)

The "tempests overblowne" in line one provides a verbal parallel with the "cruel tempest" which drives the diabolical giant to perdition. In the former, divine justice (i.e., King Neptune) releases her from the sea tortures of Proteus (IV.xii.29-33); in the latter, the giant is overwhelmed in the flood. Poor unfortunate Florimell deserves to "taste of joy," since this pure soul has been frightened, pursued, and imprisoned in turn. The tournament which is to bring her deserved honor becomes a turmoil and instead of experiencing great joy she feels deep shame in order to protect her honor. The artistic pattern of these two stanzas in which a seemingly innocuous statement has most ironic implications properly prepares the reader for the greatest irony of all, the characterization of the patron of justice that opens Canto IV.

> Who so upon him selfe will take the skill
> True Justice unto people to divide,

Had neede have mightie hands, for to fulfill
That, which he doth with righteous doome decide,
And for to maister wrong and puissant pride.
For vaine it is to deeme of things aright,
And makes wrong doers justice to deride,
Unlesse it be perform'd with dreadlesse might.
For powre is the right hand of Justice truely hight.

Wherefore whylome to knights of great emprise
The charge of Justice given was in trust,
That they might execute her judgements wise,
And with their might beat downe licentious lust,
Which proudly did impugne her sentence just.
Whereof no braver president this day
Remaines on earth, preserv'd from yron rust
Of rude oblivion, and long times decay,
Then this of *Artegall*, which here we have to say.

(V.iv.1-2)

As a straightforward statement of the duties and toils of a
man pursuing the cause of justice, these verses should remain unchallenged. When Spenser adds the name of Arte
gall as the sterling representative of such principles, he is
being deliberately ambiguous. Artegall, as the "bravest
president this day," is to master "puissant pride." Ad-
mittedly, he has mastered by force Sanglier, the giant, and
Braggadocchio, all examples of pride; but in dealing with
these offenders, he has not mastered his own. And while
"licentious lust" is perhaps too harsh a term to describe
Artegall's concupiscence, his appearance at Satyrane's Tournament of the Girdle, his submission to Britomart (providential as it is), and his nod of pity for Munera, indicate
that he must curb his own weakness for feminine beauty
before he is able to control lust's extreme perversions.
These opening stanzas outline the principles that a true
justiciar must follow, the reference to Artegall setting in
perspective all the personal obstacles that stand in the way

of the successful undertaking of the quest to establish peace. From Artegall's past behavior we know that he acts as if he has mastered himself while in reality his internal discords are there for all to see, and point inevitably to his fall and total submission which are soon to come.

Up to this point, the pressure of events has led Artegall to consider criminal cases ranging from homicide to horse theft. Shortly after his "triumphs" at the Tournament of Virtue, however, he has an opportunity to try his hand as a judge of equity, in which he assumes the role of a civilian in disposing of the rival claims of the warring brothers Amidas and Bracidas.[41] Although each brother has inherited an island of equal size from his father, the "devouring Sea" has washed away part of Bracidas' island only to deposit the alluvium upon Amidas' shores. Bracidas also was betrothed to "Philtera the faire" (a Graeco-Roman lady whose name betrays her heart) who soon elopes with Amidas when she finds that Bracidas' substance has gone to the other island. Unfortunately, Amidas first has to abandon his own betrothed Lucy, a girl of great virtue but little dowry. In great despair, Lucy tries to commit suicide by drowning, soon repents of her rashness, and seizes upon a chest which washes ashore on the smaller island. Bracidas finds Lucy and they find love. The chest that saves Lucy contains great treasure, which Philtera claims is rightfully hers as part of her dowry for Amidas. When Artegall arrives he finds the brothers fighting for possession of the treasure and manages to get them to call a truce to their "greedy bickerment," while he arbitrates the dispute. When Artegall asks Ami-

---

[41] The legal implications of equity in the case of the contending brothers have been carefully examined in the complementary essays of Herbert B. Nelson ("Amidas v. Bracidas," *MLQ*, 1 [1940], 393-399) and Roland M. Smith ("Spenser's Tale of the Two Sons of Milesio," *MLQ*, iii [1942], 547-557). Smith argues suggestively for the compatibility of the story of the two brothers with Irish legend and Irish legal tradition.

das what right he has to his brother's property that has washed over to his island, he answers: "What other right . . . should you esteeme,/ But that the sea it to my share did lay?" (V.iv.17.6-7). The same question put to Bracidas concerning the ownership of the sea chest elicits a similar response (V.iv.18.6-7). Artegall allows both claims, the one retaining the land, the other keeping the treasure.

On the literal level, the circumstances of the Amidas-Bracidas episode furnish an explicit tie-in with the debate of Artegall and the giant in Canto II, where the giant's chief argument for reform was based upon his claim that the sea washes away the land and the land encroaches upon the sea. In rebuttal Artegall maintained that whatever was washed away at one place was brought "with the tide unto another" (V.ii.39), and the fable of the two islands provides the final validity of his argument. It follows that the disposition of the conflicting claims of the two brothers is in accord with the principles of natural law, which Artegall affirmed earlier. Within this legal and divine framework Spenser plays yet another variation upon the theme of false and true love. In contrasting the grossness of Philtera with the radiance of Lucy, he establishes a polarity very much like that of the two Florimells, a polarity in which the false always proves the true. In the struggle for the treasure that breaks the natural ties of fraternal love, Artegall's judgment mitigating their strife is only partly successful. Even though he has established peace when he ceases "their sharpe contention" (V.iv.20.7), the inner discords that remain in Amidas and Philtera (20.2) are symptomatic of Artegall's own problems. With a subtle shift in emphasis, Spenser has presented his hero with a situation that mirrors his own character. Artegall passes on unmindful of the discord that remains in them and in himself.

Artegall is soon attracted by a crowd of people milling about in the distance, where he sees a group of warlike women preparing a knight for the gallows. As this unfortunate knight bemoans his plight at the hands of the Amazons, they taunt him and rejoice "at his miserable case." When Artegall asks the reason for such vile treatment (hanging is the worst ignominy of knighthood), the Amazons "swarme" in upon him intending to get another victim. Artegall withdraws, because he is ashamed to raise his arm against "womankinde" (V.iv.24.1-4); instead, he again dispatches Talus, who "sent them hom to tell a piteous tale,/ Of their vaine prowesse, turned to their proper bale" (V.iv.24.8-9). After watching Talus disperse the lawless women, Artegall turns his attention to the unfortunate knight whom he knows.

> Sir *Terpine*, haplesse man, what make you here?
> Or have you lost your selfe, and your discretion,
> That ever in this wretched case ye were?
> Or have ye yeelded you to proude oppression
> Of womens powre, that boast of mens subjection?
> Or else what other deadly dismall day
> Is falne on you, by heavens hard direction,
> That ye were runne so fondly far astray,
> As for to lead your selfe unto your owne decay?
>
> (V.iv.26)

Artegall's pompous criticism of Terpine is another example of his equivocal personality, since every woman he has met thus far has mastered him in one way or another. Even though he has disdained to help in his rescue and has persisted in offering patronizing advice, Artegall unknowingly makes Terpine reenact his recent humiliation in forcing him to tell the story of his sad state.

Terpine's narrative exposes the exact nature of the obstacles soon to confront Artegall. As a true knight "errant," Terpine had challenged a "proud Amazon [who] did late defy/ All the brave Knights that hold of Maidenhead" (V.iv.29.5-6), killing or putting to shame all who challenge her.

The cause, they say, of this her cruell hate,
Is for the sake of *Bellodant* the bold,
To whom she bore most fervent love of late,
And wooed him by all the waies she could:
But when she saw at last, that he ne would
For ought or nought be wonne unto her will,
She turned her love to hatred manifold,
And for his sake vow'd to doe all the ill
Which she could doe to Knights, which now she
doth fulfill.
(V.iv.30)

Subduing all who oppose her by "force or guile," she despoils them of their arms and compels them to wear women's clothes and do women's work (V.iv.31), those refusing to obey her orders being "hang'd up out of hand." Rather than lead what he considered a "shamefull life, unworthy of a Knight," Terpine chose the latter fate, and was to be executed by the troop of Amazons when Artegall appeared with Talus.

Reluctant as he was to battle the other Amazons, Artegall promises to avenge the Knights of Maidenhead by trying the might of their leader, Radigund. With Terpine as a doubtful guide, Artegall and Talus reach her city and at first are denied entrance but succeed in enraging Radigund, who orders her troops to prepare for battle. At the unbarring of the gates, a shower of arrows forces Artegall and his companions to retreat.

But *Radigund* her selfe, when she espide
Sir *Terpin*, from her direfull doome acquit,
So cruel doale amongst her maides divide,
T'avenge that shame, they did on him commit,
All sodainely enflam'd with furious fit,
Like a fell Lionesse at him she flew,
And on his head-peece him so fiercely smit,

That to the ground him quite she overthrew,
Dismayd so with the stroke, that he no colours knew.

                                                    (V.iv.39)

As she is savoring her triumph, Artegall drives her away.
"Through vengeful wrath and sdeignfull pride half mad,"
Radigund rushes at Artegall, only to be separated from him
by her followers. Continuing the battle until nightfall,
Radigund leaves the field after she first guides the
"wounded, and the weake in state" to the safety of the city.
To gain revenge and to save her women from further
harm, Radigund wishes to engage Artegall in single combat and orders her trusted maid, Clarin, to act as the
intermediary in arranging the test for the following
morning.

> But these conditions doe to him propound,
> That if I vanquishe him, he shall obay
> My law, and ever to my lore be bound,
> And so will I, if me he vanquishe may;
> What ever he shall like to doe or say.
>
>   (V.iv.49.1-5)

Radigund is the logical and most vicious example of the
predatory woman whose love has turned to hatred, a Malecasta, armed and able, with a hideous army of willing followers. Where before, Britomart unwittingly entered Castle
Joyeous to "reape the dew reward" for her chivalric efforts only to feel Gardante's barbed shaft; Artegall now
carelessly assumes Clarin's mission to be a chivalric enter-
prise only to be offered ungallant terms for battle. When
Artegall hears of the commission, he foolishly agrees to
Radigund's terms, and like any chivalrous knight, he entertains Clarin and her company and sends them home-
ward with "gifts and things of deare delight" (V.iv.51.6).
Having had both a report and a sample of Radigund's vile
behavior, Artegall's performance is mindless in the extreme.

From the elaborate description of Radigund's character, we know that she will be Artegall's greatest enemy, and since he agrees to fight on her own terms, we know that he will fail.[42] Through the imagistic pattern of the necessarily involved preliminaries, discussed above, Spenser has shown the true terms of the proposed duel, terms which are identical with Radigund's character. She is proud,[43] irascible,[44] and concupiscent.[45] It is not coincidental that Spenser has pitted his hero against someone embodying the very qualities of character which have hindered him in his quest for Irena. Since his fight with Radigund will determine whether or not he has succeeded in controlling his wayward temperament, the duel will be a true test of the patron of justice, a test in which the thoughtful reader cannot share Artegall's confidence in the outcome.

iv

Artegall's battle with Radigund is a magnificently staged affair. Since each contestant foolishly thinks he is fighting for a noble purpose, the atmosphere created by the extending and accepting of the challenge is one of high chivalric resolve. Ostensibly, Radigund wants to limit the fight-

---

[42] Hamilton makes the obvious point, as others have done, but thinks that this is just another sexual battle in which the hero loses the "maistrie" (*Structure*, pp. 183-184).

[43] Her pride generally can be inferred from her having assumed as many masculine prerogatives as she can; but it is manifest in all her other actions. Terms like "proud Amazon," "proud observance," "Greater pride," "Womans pride" leave little doubt about Spenser's characterization.

[44] When she hears of Artegall's coming, "Her heart for rage did grate, and teeth did grin" (37.7). Rushing at him after his first attack, she is moved by "vengeful wrath and sdeignfull pride half mad" (43.3). See also 39.6 and 40.4.

[45] The psychological basis of her unseemly character is her thwarted love for Bellodant (v.v.30). The degree of her concupiscence is shown in her "fervent love" which leads her to take the initiative in courtship. Bellodant was perhaps wise to leave.

ing to single combat, because she wishes to spare her own people further harm (V.iv.47.6-9), and for his part, Artegall is fulfilling his obligation as a Knight of Maidenhead to "venge the shame, that she to knights doth show" (V.iv.34.1-4). Radigund's entrance destroys these illusions, and puts their duel in proper perspective.

All in a Camis light of purple silke
Woven uppon with silver, subtly wrought,
And quilted uppon satin white as milke,
Trayled with ribbands diversly distraught
Like as the workeman had their courses taught;
Which was short tucked for light motion
Up to her ham, but when she list, it raught
Downe to her lowest heele, and thereuppon
She wore for her defense a mayled habergeon.

And on her legs she painted buskins wore,
Basted with bends of gold on every side,
And mailes betweene, and laced close afore:
Uppon her thigh her Cemitare was tide,
With an embroidered belt of mickell pride;
And on her shoulder hung her shield, bedeckt
Uppon the bosse with stones, that shined wide,
As the faire Moone in her most full aspect,
That to the Moone it mote be like in each respect.
(V.v.2-3)

Her costume reveals her ambiguous sexuality and confirms her to be "halfe like a man" (V.iv.36.8), her "camis" being a dual purpose garment which serves either as military kilt or an evening gown. The equivocal subtlety of her "camis" contrasts sharply with the deliberate artifice portraying her as a type of Diana.[46] We remember that the snowy Florimell also masquerades as Diana and is sustained by a diabolical artificer, and the "workeman" who created this il-

---

[46] See Kathleen Williams, "Venus and Diana," 107.

lusionary aspect of Radigund's character had in mind a
true model, the chaste Belphoebe (II.iii.25-27). Upon
closer examination, it will be seen that Spenser has made a
precise distinction between the two; for while Belphoebe's
chemise is "lylly white," Radigund's is "purple," a presumption of sovereignty which links her with Lucifera and
Duessa. Belphoebe herself is graced by nature, bears no
traces of artificiality, and has no pretensions. Radigund proclaims hers boldly with her "belt of mickell pride." Everything pure in Belphoebe's character is perverted in Radigund's, since she is the infernal Diana.

In terms of the narrative structure, however, Radigund
does not exist simply as an insidious parody, only to vanish
into nothingness like the snowy Florimell. As queen of the
Amazons, she has a character of her own, the full force
of that character symbolized by her belt of pride which
places her challenge to Artegall in proper perspective. For
one of the labors of Hercules ordered by Eurystheus was
to obtain the belt of Hippolyte, queen of the Amazons,
which was read by the commentators as the assertion of
masculine authority by the conquering of libidinous desire.

At the beginning of the battle, it appears that Artegall
will subdue the proud Amazon. Although Radigund, true
to her nature, attacks him in a "furious rage," Artegall is
quite composed ("having like tempests tride") and lets
her spend her strength. After she weakens he becomes very
workmanlike, a smith beating on an anvil (V.v.7-8), and
cuts away part of her shield. "Halfe enrag'd," Radigund
wounds him on the thigh and begins to revile him as if she
had already won the battle.

> That his great hart gan inwardly to swell
> With indignation at her vaunting vaine,
> And at her strooke with puissance fearefull fell;
> Yet with her shield she warded it againe,
> That shattered all to peeces round about the plaine.
>
> (V.v.10.5-9)

Artegall's fall to pride echoes his reaction to Braggadocchio's taunts; but this time there is no knight of temperance
to quell his anger. Once again Artegall has demonstrated
that the intemperate man cannot effectively pursue the ends
of justice, for what happens when he has unlaced her hel-
met is foreordained.

But when as he discovered had her face,
He saw his senses straunge astonishment,
A miracle of natures goodly grace,
In her faire visage voide of ornament,
But bath'd in bloud and sweat together ment;
Which in the rudeness of that evill plight,
Bewrayd the signes of feature excellent:
Like as the Moone in foggie winters night,
Doth seeme to be her selfe, though darkned be her light.

At sight thereof his cruell minded hart
Empierced was with pittifull regard,
That his sharpe sword he threw from him apart,
Cursing his hand that had that visage mard:
No hand so cruell, nor no hart so hard,
But ruth of beautie will it mollifie.
                                    (V.v.12-13.1-6)

In describing the battle with Radigund, Spenser is deliberately recalling Artegall's earlier fight with Britomart, in
which the pattern of defeat is similar, Artegall falling to
pride, wrath, and concupiscence. It is not, as Hamilton
thinks, a repeat performance. We have seen that although
Radigund's dress is modeled after the chaste Belphoebe's,
subtle shadings and differences clearly mark the illusion
from the reality. Since Spenser knows Britomart and Radigund are as unlike as day and night, he first shows Artegall
the one's angel face "like to the ruddie morne" (IV.vi.19.6)
and then the other's natural beauty "as the Moone in foggie
winters night" (V.v.12.8). Artegall's capitulation to Brito-

mart is involuntary, his sword falling from his hand (IV.-vi.21). By extension, his act manifests the workings of Providence of which Merlin spoke, because the divine destinies of Britomart and Artegall require two reasonably healthy people. In the case of Radigund, his submission is patently a willful act: "his sharpe sword he threw from him apart,/ Cursing his hand that had that visage mard" (V.v.13.3-4), which of course anticipates the surrender of his shield, the emblem of justice and the banner of Hercules. We were also prepared for this final and utterly complete defection by the alacrity with which he exchanged shields with Braggadocchio, and brought chaos to the Tournament of Virtue.

The intricate variations Spenser has played upon the theme of Artegall's shortcomings are designed to alert even the most casual reader. The first few notes of doubt were played when Britomart looked in Merlin's artful glass, and through pressure of the narrative, these few subdued sounds are amplified to greater volume until they reach maximum crescendo in the battle with Radigund. Artegall has simply contracted to fight and is defeated by his greatest enemy—himself. When he permits Sanglier to go free with a minimum of restraint (that thin cord of dishonor), he telegraphs his fall, which Radigund confirms. The intent of Spenser's imagery is to remind the reader (if he has not already sensed it) that Artegall is the sole agent of his own fall. Although Terpine tells him that Radigund subdues her opponents "by force or guile," Artegall nevertheless consents to meet on her terms, conditions under which he could not possibly win. And Spenser was not one to miss an opportunity to drop the obvious poetic footnote, "yet was he justly damned by the doome/ Of his own mouth, that spake so warelesse word" (V.v.17.3-4). Artegall has fallen through ignorance, more precisely, an ignorance of self; and the reason for his fall establishes the criteria for his redemption.

When Radigund receives his shield, she metaphorically

deprives him of his knighthood, "his honours stile," and
his total humiliation comes when she dubs him her vassal
and orders him to be dressed in "womans weedes" which
literally strip him of manhood.[47] He then joins the ranks
of Radigund's other victims.

> Amongst them all she placed him most low,
> And in his hand a distaffe to him gave,
> That he thereon should spin both flax and tow;
> A sordid office for a mind so brave.
> So hard it is to be a womans slave.
> Yet he it tooke in his owne selfes despight,
> And thereto did himselfe right well behave,
> Her to obay, sith he his faith had plight,
> Her vassall to become, if she him wonne in fight.

> Who had him seene, imagine mote thereby,
> That whylome hath of *Hercules* bene told,
> How for fair *Iolas* sake he did apply
> His mightie hands, the distaffe vile to hold,
> For his huge club, which had subdew'd of old
> So many monsters, which the world annoyed;
> His Lyons skin chaunged to a pall of gold,
> In which forgetting warres, he only joyed
> In combats of sweet love, and with his mistress toyed.
> (V.v.23-24)

Spenser here confirms what the reader has known about
Artegall for a long time, making explicit that his hero is
a type of Hercules. Hercules' submission to *Iolas* (and
Omphale) was an enduring object lesson for men of the
Middle Ages and the Renaissance. Fulgentius writes that
the Omphale fable shows that even invincible virtue can
be conquered by libidinousness.[48] The anonymous anti-

---

[47] Another irony is that Artegall now is once again costumed in
"squallid weed," as were the lovelorn squire and the late, un-
lamented Terpine—and Britomart when she visited Merlin's cave.

[48] *Mythologiae* (Basel, 1536), pp. 39-40 [II.v].

feminist who wrote *The Deceyte of Women* recites the sad litany of men beguiled by women, among whom are such stock types as Adam, Samson, and Hercules.

> The strong and worthye Hercules was overcome in all his power and strength through the love of a yonge mayde, the fayre Yole. . . . [Yole] under a colour of false love and with subtle meanes smylynge and with flatteryng wordes hath drawen Hercules to such great love that she caused him for to lay away his iron staffe, wherewith he was wont for to rule the stronge monsters, and beastes withall. She caused him to lay away the lyons skynne, and caused him to be clothed with soft clothes of silke, she caused him for to wear a crowne of rosemary upon his head and gold rynges upon hys fingers. . . . She caused hym for to give himselfe to womens besynes and ydlenes, in so much that he went and sat among the women and told ryddles and fortunes as the chyldren dyd and sat and spon yarne at the distaffe as the women dyd.
>
> Now behold how the worthy Hercules is brought to femynyne workes through the decyte of Yole to his utter confusion, the which was wont to be so manly in all his feates. Now behold what myschiefe, what marvayles and folyshnes that the false and subtil woman bring to pass, yea that seemeth unpossyble for to be that they can doo and brynge to passe.[49]

Artegall is the newest member of the club. But Spenser is going to pivot the myth of Hercules-Omphale neatly about and make it reveal his inner strength instead of emphasizing his weaknesses. Since his physical humiliation is complete, nothing remains to remind Artegall of his former glories—his armor hangs high in disgrace, Talus is gone, and his very clothes and present occupation deny his masculinity. The only thing he has is himself, a person he

[49] (London, 1560?), sigs. K,i-ii.

has never learned to know. Yet the moment he is forced upon his inner resources he begins a process of discovery, a growing self-awareness that leads to wisdom.

This understanding grows out of a self-imposed intellectual humiliation, which begins exactly when he receives the ultimate symbol of his effeminacy, the distaff, which he takes "in his owne selfes despight" (23.6), and determines to abide by the bargain. Although his resigned acceptance of woman's rule has been read as another symbol of weakness, the logic of the narrative will not support such an interpretation. Rather, Artegall's willing acceptance of his state is an extreme form of intellectual humility; or to put it in Marvell's terms, he has made destiny his choice.

> Thus there long while continu'd *Artegall*,
> Serving proud *Radigund* with true subjection;
> How ever it his noble hart did gall,
> T'obay a womans tyrannous direction,
> That might have had of life or death election:
> But having chosen, now he might not change.
>
> (V.v.26.1-6)

Up to this point Artegall has demonstrated his humility; and to still any doubts that remain in the reader's mind about its validity, Spenser has prepared to put it to the test.

Developing a "secret liking to this captive straunge" (V.v.26.9) during his imprisonment, Radigund confides her desires to Clarin and asks her to act as intermediary in order to bend him to her will. Radigund, who once wooed Bellodant "by all the waies she could" now attempts similarly to win a subject's love, this time by proxy. The manner in which Clarin pursues her commission offers the greatest imaginable temptation to Artegall, since her methods confirm her lineal descent from Eve. After several days of calculated pleasantries, Clarin instinctively probes for the flaws in his character.

Unhappie Knight, upon whose hopelesse state
Fortune envying good, hath felly frowned,
And cruel heavens have heapt an heavy fate;
I rue that thus thy better dayes are drowned
In sad despaire, and all thy senses swowned
In stupid sorrow, sith thy juster merit
Might else have with felicitie bene crowned:
Looke up at last, and wake thy dulled spirit,
To thinke how this long death thou mightest disinherit.

(V.v.36)

Hers is a clever deception. Not having committed herself in any way, she nevertheless has created a situation in which any affirmative move on Artegall's part would end in eternal damnation. Phrases like *hopelesse state*, *cruel heavens*, and *heavy fate* lead with relentless logic to an image of *sad despaire*. Thomas Aquinas has taught us that despair is the greatest of sins because it denies the possibility of redemption.

> If, however, despair be compared to [unbelief and hatred of God] from our point of view, then despair is more dangerous, since hope withdraws us from evils and induces us to seek for good things, so that when hope is given up, men rush headlong into sin, and are drawn from good works. Wherefore the gloss on Prov. xxiv. 10, *If thou lose hope being weary in the day of distress, thy strength shall be diminished*, says: *Nothing is more hateful than despair, for the man that has it loses his constancy both in the every day toils of this life and, what is worse, in the battle of faith.* And Isidore says (*De. Sum. Bono* ii.14); *To commit a crime is to kill the soul, but to despair is to fall into hell.*[50]

[50] *Summa Theologica*, ii.ii.Q.20. This also was good Protestant doctrine; see Calvin, *Institutes*, iii.viii.10 and iv.xv.3.

Having suggestively described what she wants Artegall to acknowledge his state to be, Clarin tells him that his "juster merit" should have "with felicitie been crowned," a rhetorical subterfuge which represents the ultimate temptation of pride through which he fell originally. The theological framework of this temptation scene is truly revealed when she speaks of his deliverance from bondage (and despair) in Christian terms (36.8-9). The whole drift of her rhetorical tactic is to set up her mistress as the redeemer, as Radigund is to be the one who delivers Artegall from "this long death."

Artegall, newly wrapped in the mantle of physical and intellectual humility, is equal to the test. Although he does not completely discern the "hidden drift" of Clarin's speech, he rightly begins to doubt her good intentions (37.-1-4) but answers her in even-tempered, courteous, and closely reasoned terms. After thanking her for her kind regard and compassion, he proceeds to destroy her argument in a deferential tone which contrasts markedly with the lordly manner in which he defeated the giant with the scales.

> Yet weet ye well, that to a courage great
> It is no lesse beseeming well, to beare
> The storme of fortunes frowne, or heavens threat,
> Then in the sunshine of her countenance cleare
> Timely to joy, and carrie comely cheare.
> For though this cloud have now me overcast,
> Yet doe I not of better times despeyre;
> And, though unlike, they should for ever last,
> Yet in my truthes assurance I rest fixed fast.
>
> (V.v.38)

Just as he did in the controversy with the giant, Artegall completely undermines Clarin's argument by revealing the flaw in her original premise. As Clarin has built her case upon the sands of his supposed despair, his simple denial effectively disposes of her brief. When he has Artegall declare that he will remain true to himself even if his present state "should for ever last," Spenser further exhibits the degree of his humility and the measure of his hope. For all intents and purposes, Artegall has redeemed his past failings and has shown himself to be equal to any temptation.

Through her many conversations with Artegall in the line of duty, Clarin falls in love with him, an irony which Spenser fully exploits (43). Clarin's infatuation adds yet another link in the growing chain of Hercules parallels: Omphale's handmaid, Malis, also succumbed to his charms.[51] Spenser is going to use this conflict of interest between Radigund-Omphale and Clarin-Malis to present yet another form of trial to Artegall. Since it is now contrary to Clarin's interest to present good reports of his admirable behavior, she misrepresents his character, calling him *obstinate*, *sterne*, and *scornful* (46), traits which he clearly shows he no longer has. Enraged by the news, Radigund orders other tactics.

> Some of his diet doe from him withdraw;
> For I him find to be too proudly fed.
> Give him more labour, and with streighter law,
> That he with worke may be forwearied.
> Let him lodge hard, and lie in strawen bed,
> That may pull downe the courage of his pride;
> And lay upon him for his greater dread,
> Cold yron chaines, with which let him be tide;
> And let, what ever he desires, be him denide.
>
> (V.v.50)

As we learned from the Sanglier episode, the use of force to change men's minds is not successful, and this effort too is doomed from the beginning to failure. In *Paradise*

[51] See Estienne's *Dictionary* (Acela), Diodorus Siculus (iv.xxxi.5-8), and Stephanus Byzantinus.

Regained, Satan, after offering various temptations, uses force as a last desperate resort to tempt the Son of God. Artegall, of course, remains steadfast, and "never meant he in his noble mind,/ To his owne absent love to be untrew" (V.v.56.2-3). For Artegall has remembered and has taken to heart a Proverb of Solomon, whose judgment he imitated in the Sanglier episode and whose footsteps he has followed too well: "Where pride is, there also shall be reproach: but where humility is, there also is wisdom" (xi.2).[52] Since all of Artegall's failures (both internal and external) resulted from failures of character, the course of his redemption is a kind of growing into wisdom, an exemplification of that dog-eared maxim with which so many Renaissance emblem books began—*Nosce te ipsum*. Under the most severe conditions, Artegall has proved his worth to undertake the quest to free Irena from Grantorto, for having resolved his inner discords, he is fully qualified to pursue the end of justice—peace.

[52] Douay version. See Calvin's commentary on this passage and also Michel Cope's *Exposition uppon Proverbs* (London, 1580), p. 164. The Geneva version reads, "When pride commeth, then commeth shame: but with the lowly is wisdome."

CHAPTER III

Desire and Love

Throughout the long humiliating servitude during which one word on his part would have brought ease and accompanying damnation, Artegall has demonstrated his steadfast love for Britomart. "That no new loves impression ever could / Bereave it thence" (V.vi.2.8-9). Having given his "Warelesse word" to Radigund, he may make no effort to escape even though opportunity is at hand. He may perhaps take advantage of Clarin's sympathies as Theseus once took advantage of Ariadne's, only to leave her pregnant on an unfortunate isle. Spenser's narrator, however, has assured us that Artegall's "owne true love" will free him from bondage, and when she does, her rescue of him will complete an interior design of deliberately balanced thematic opposites. On the one hand, Radigund's "wandring fancie after lust" leads her to employ Clarin as her surrogate to win Artegall by enticing him away from his "truthes assurance," in the course of which Clarin establishes her mistress as his redeemer from despair. In contrast to a lustful Radigund, whose schemes would remove Artegall's galling chains only to wrap him securely in the toils of endless despair, Spenser has created a loving Britomart, whose heroic efforts would free him from enslavement in order to tie him to happy matrimony. Unfortunately, this neatly patterned image is somewhat out of focus, because Britomart is not now the trusting and understanding woman Artegall deserves. Although we must ultimately agree with Kathleen Williams that Britomart is superior to other women and represents the ideal of womanhood, we should also be aware of the obstacles she must overcome before she achieves such distinction. Britomart is the only one of Spenser's knights who does not complete her quest in the book specifically treating of her virtue. The reason for this is partly related to the nature of her search, the sole object of which is the winning of Artegall. In Spenser's poetic structure, she cannot complete her mission as exemplar of "magnificke chastity" by marrying Artegall until she has purged herself of all the fickle vagaries that complete the caricature of ordinary woman. This chapter will explain how all of Britomart's difficulties stem from her brief visit to *Castle Joyeous*: for, beset with doubt and sorrow as she rides closer and closer to Artegall, she is less and less able to rescue him since she must spend all her time extricating herself from unnecessary predicaments. Once Britomart submits herself to Divine Providence in the Church of Isis, she discovers the true nature of her mission and is able to free her lover from woman's slavery.

i

At the beginning of Canto VI Spenser is deliberately playing the character of the "new" Artegall against that of Britomart. He disarms those readers who would censure his hero by reminding them that "never yet was wight so well aware,/ But he first or last was trapt in womens snare" (V.vi.1.8-9). Lest we think this a lame apology, we should remind ourselves that the script of this perennial tragicomedy was written by Eve and has never lacked a plentiful supply of leading ladies. In the truest possible sense, Artegall's was a happy fall; for by it he grows in wisdom and understanding and proves his love for Britomart.

Yet his owne love, the noble *Britomart*,
Scarse so conceived in her jealous thought,
What time sad tydings of his balefull smart
In womans bondage, *Talus* to her brought;
Brought in untimely houre, ere it was sought.
For after that the utmost date, assynde
For his returne, she waited had for nought,
She gan to cast in her misdoubtfull mynde
A thousand feares, that love-sicke fancies faine to fynde.

Sometime she feared, least some hard mishap
Had him misfalne in his adventurous quest;
Sometime least his false foe did him entrap
In traytrous traine, or had unwares opprest:
But most she did her troubled mynd molest,
And secretly afflict with jealous feare,
Least some new love had him from her possest;
Yet loth she was, since she no ill did heare,
To thinke of him so ill: yet would she not forbeare.

(V.vi.3-4)

The vacillating qualities of Britomart's mind serve the poet
as a contrast to the "Adamantine mould" of Artegall's resolve. Although perfectly grounded in psychology, her
jealousy and her doubts of his constancy are inappropriate
to a woman whose mission is to help continue the British
nation. Were she an ordinary woman destined to wear
out her life in some rural croft, we could excuse her fears
more readily. But she is to be the exemplar of "magnificke
chastity," or married love. Love above all things implies
trust.

Britomart's grief, occasioned by Artegall's failure to return within the stipulated time, is an error (vi.5), by which
she readily assumes her lover has betrayed his trust and she
indulges in self-pity. Since her mind is now directed upon
herself, she lightly dismisses any thought that he may be
in difficulty. Instead, she construes his absence as a direct
insult to her and imagines him in all sorts of compromising
situations.

Now she deviz'd amongst the warlike rout
Of errant Knights, to seeke her errant Knight;
And then againe resolv'd to hunt him out
Amongst loose Ladies, lapped in delight:
And then both Knights envide, and Ladies eke did spight.

(V.vi.6.5-9)

Her fantasy bears no relationship to the realities of Artegall's plight but reveals clearly her current state of mind, the unflattering picture of Artegall confirming how little faith she has in him. As envy is a species of sorrow,[1] sorrow for oneself at another person's good fortune, her envying of unworthy knights and ladies indicates a lack of perspective.

One day while troubling her heart with these "vaine fancies," she sees Talus rapidly approaching from the West, whither her love had departed. Meeting him at the door, and questioning him about Artegall (vi.9), she elicits the information from the laconic Talus that her lover lies "in wretched bondage, wofully bestad." When she asks if he was vanquished by Grantorto (vi.10.9), he replies simply that a "tyrannesse" has reduced his master to "haplesse woe" (vi.11.1-3). At this point Britomart cuts short the exchange, accuses Talus of duplicity, and berates her lover. Wrongly thinking that all her vain imaginings are verified, she flies into a rage because she considers it a deliberate affront to her honor.

And then she in her wrathfull will did cast,
How to revenge that blot of honour blent;
To fight with him, and goodly die her last:
And then againe she did her selfe torment,
Inflicting on her selfe his punishment.
A while she walkt, and chauft; a while she threw
Her self uppon her bed, and did lament:
Yet did she not lament with loude alew,
As women wont, but with deepe sighes, and singulfs few.

Like as a wayward childe, whose sounder sleepe
Is broken with some fearefull dreames affright,
With froward will doth set him selfe to weepe;
Ne can be stild for all his nurses might,
But kicks, and squals, and shriekes for fell despight:

---

[1] Psalm LXXIII.3; Thomas Aquinas, *Summa Theologica*, II.ii.Q.36.-a.1; Aristotle, *Rhetoric*, II.ix-x.

Now scratching her, and her loose locks misusing:
Now seeking darknesse, and now seeking light;
Then craving sucke, and then the sucke refusing.
Such was this Ladies fit, in her loves fond accusing.

(V.vi.13-14)

Hamilton thinks that this scene points up the poetic defects of Book Five because the noble Britomart "who has overwhelmed all who look upon her with awe and dread of her royal presence, throws herself upon a bed . . . and weeps 'like a wayward childe.' "[2] Hamilton misses Spenser's point; for this passage, instead of revealing his weaknesses[3] and the poetic inferiority of Book Five, demonstrates his absolute control of his materials and theme. Although Britomart is a magnificent example of womanhood, she is far from perfect. Spenser has dropped enough hints along the way to apprise his readers of this fact: her dissembling speeches to Red Cross, her willingness to follow Glauce's lead, her sleepy neglect of Amoret even though she is directly responsible for her rescue from the House of Busyrane, her surrender to Artegall. These are just general indications, sporadic and inconclusive symptoms of a serious malaise. By making an explicit comparison between Artegall's and Britomart's attitudes at the beginning of Canto VI, Spenser sets her problems in sharp relief. Britomart's doubting mind spins a web of fancies that entraps all her noble motives. Her unfounded doubts lead to jealousy from which comes sorrow and her sister envy. This demeaning progression succeeds in drawing her attention from her lover and fastening it upon herself, a descent into selfishness paralleled by a retreat in time through which Britomart returns metaphorically to childhood. The child-

---

[2] *Structure*, p. 171.

[3] B.E.C. Davis uses the phrase "waning power" (*Edmund Spenser* [Cambridge, 1933], p. 124).

ish Britomart here is an emblem of complete selfishness
brought about by the lover's folly—jealousy.

Since "such unquiet fits" bring no relief, she returns to
Talus in order to hear the particulars of her lover's imprisonment, whether "he did woo, or whether he were
woo'd" (vi.15.9). It is characteristic of Britomart at this
point that she comes to Talus again "seeking to ease her
paine" (vi.15.5). After he recites the sad chronicle of his
master's unwitting defeat and "wretched thraldome," she
is overcome with grief, dons her armor, and orders Talus
to lead her to her lover. Although this marks a positive
step, literally a turning away from herself, it is accompanied by an ambiguous intellectual commitment.

> So forth she rode uppon her ready way,
> To seeke her Knight, as Talus her did guide;
> Sadly she rode, and never word did say,
> Nor good nor bad, ne ever lookt aside,
> But still right downe, and in her thought did hide
> The felnesse of her heart, right fully bent
> To fierce avengement of that womans pride,
> That had her Lord in her base prison pent,
> And so great honour with so fowle reproch had blent.
>
> So as thus she melancholicke did ride,
> Chawing the cud of griefe and inwarde paine,
> She chaunst to meete toward th'even-tide
> A Knight, that softly paced on the plaine,
> As if him selfe to solace he were faine.
> Well shot in yeares he seem'd, and rather bent
> To peace, then needlesse trouble to constraine,
> As well by view of that his vestiment,
> As by his modest semblant, that no evill ment.
>
> (V.vi.18-19)

By the use of the words *sadly, melancholicke, griefe,* and
inwarde paine, Spenser not only has examined the present

cast of Britomart's mind but also has created what might be called standard atmosphere for temptation. The biblical text for this is, of course, the Book of Job. Deprived of children, goods, and health, Job naturally feels extreme sorrow. In the midst of his grief, being met by people who seem to be his friends but who instead turn out to be his temptors, he displays great patience but eventually weakens. Since sorrow is a species of *accidia*,[4] the temptation usually is effective; for "tristitia inducit hominem ad desperationem." We should remember that Clarin tries to trick Artegall into admitting sorrow or despair *before* she tempts him.[5] When Britomart herself reaches such a melancholic state, she has fulfilled the necessary requisites. Just at that moment, it is rather inevitable that she should meet the old knight, who seems harmless, but the reader should have honest doubts.

When the aged knight greets her, Britomart is reluctant to talk; but rather than repay his "kindness" with anger, she answers him courteously. He tries to draw her into further conversation, but is unsuccessful, since "Her minde was whole possessed of one thought,/ That gave none other place" (V.vi.21.3-4), a description of Britomart's purpose of mind which is subtly equivocal. It may either mean she is so determined to win back her love she is unwilling to let other matters obtrude upon her consciousness, or it may mean she wishes to be left alone to savor the full extent of her sorrow. Apparently an old hand, the knight immediately changes the subject when he senses her mood. Instead of trying to draw her out by innuendo and suggestion, he changes tactics and tries a direct approach, telling her to be of good cheer now that night is approaching and inviting

---

[4] *Summa Theologica*, ii.ii.Q.35.a.1. See also Hugh of St. Cher's gloss on Isaiah xxix.2 (*Opera*, iv, 61).

[5] In this regard, Britomart's and Artegall's actions are complementary and fit nicely into the providential design of their love.

her "To lodge with him that night, unles good cause empeach" (V.vi.21.9).

> The Championesse, now seeing night at dore,
> Was glad to yeeld unto his good request:
> And with him went without gaine-saying more.
> Not farre away, but little wide by West,
> His dwelling was, to which he him addrest;
> Where soone arriving they received were
> In seemely wise, as them beseemed best:
> For he their host them goodly well did cheare,
> And talk't of pleasant things, the night away to weare.
>
> (V.vi.22)

The course of Britomart's journey, so elaborately plotted by Spenser, is now seen in its fullest implications. To rescue Artegall she must travel due westward (V.vi.7.4-5), whither her lover has already gone. When she falls into *tristitia*, she succumbs to the temptations of the knight of "modest semblant" and deviates from her quest, going "little wide by West." That this is a completely voluntary act is shown by the fact Britomart "Was glad to yeeld unto his good request:/ And with him went without gaine-saying more" (vi.22.2-3). Just as *tristitia* provides the rationale for the knight's success, abandoning the way is a common metaphor for falling into sin. When Job wishes to affirm his faith, he uses the language of man the wayfarer: "My foote hath followed his steps: his way have I kept, and have not declined" (xxiii.11).[6] Britomart has declined, however; and her tergiversation is potentially of a most serious kind, since she not only jeopardizes her

---

[6] The metaphor of the way and the path of righteousness was industriously repeated by writers of the Old and New Testaments; see Deut. xi.28; Prov. xxi.16; Mal. ii.8; Wisdom v.6; Rom. ii.12; Heb. v.2; etc.

chances of freeing her lover but also casts doubt on the future of the British nation.[7]

When the time comes for retiring, the knight escorts Britomart to a "bowre," where his grooms are waiting to undress the guest, services Britomart refuses by pleading she has vowed never to remove her armor until she has exacted revenge upon a mortal enemy. Upon hearing this, the knight becomes discontented "for feare least by that art/ He should his purpose misse, which close he ment" (V.vi.-24.2-3). Up to this point in the narrative, Spenser has given his readers a sufficient number of reasons to doubt the good offices of the host. His is a world where nothing is but all things seem, where even his own makeup is quite indefinite

[7] Just as Artegall's individual actions have cosmic implications, Britomart's transcend the immediate and particular, magnifying slight faults into gross error, precisely because she is of such importance to the providential plan. In Chapter I, I alluded to the fact that the true movement of the soul (or reason) was from east to west, Plato's motion of the *same*. The contrary is the movement of the passions, Plato's motion of the *other*. As Spenser's great example of the decay of the world is couched in an elaborate astronomical metaphor, we learn from the Proem to Book Five that the imperceptible drift of the sun along the ecliptic leads to the precession of the equinox. And sin rides the ecliptic. In this context it is sufficient to remember the direction Satan takes in *Paradise Lost* after he is shown the way to earth by the angel Uriel.

> Thus said, [Uriel] turnd, and Satan bowing low,
> As to superior spirits is wont in Heav'n,
> Where honour due and reverence none neglects,
> Took leave, and toward the coast of Earth beneath,
> Down from th'Ecliptic, sped with hop'd success,
> Throws his steep flight in many an Aerie wheele,
> Nor staid, till on Niphates top he lights.
>
> (III.736-742)

To complete the metaphor, Milton has Sin and Death build their causeway from hell to earth, following their creator's path along the ecliptic. Both Britomart and Artegall are journeying westward and each has deviated from his quest. Artegall has gained knowledge to correct his error; and Britomart will soon see her true mission.

(V.vi.19.4-9). Revealing his treacherous character by his reaction to Britomart's wish to remain in armor, the knight nevertheless disguises his intent and takes his leave of her.

There all that night remained *Britomart*,
Restlesse, recomfortlesse, with heart deepe grieved,
Not suffering the least twinckling sleepe to start
Into her eye, which th'heart mote have relieved,
But if the least appear'd, her eyes she streight reprieved.

Ye guilty eyes (sayd she) the which with guyle
My heart at first betrayd, will ye betray
My life now to, for which a little whyle
Ye will not watch? false watches, wellaway,
I wote when ye did watch both night and day
Unto your losse: and now needes will ye sleepe?
How ye have made my heart to wake alway,
Now will ye sleepe? ah wake, and rather weepe,
To thinke of your nights want, that should yee waking
    keepe.
                                    (V.vi.24-25)

Although Britomart's interior monologue has been read as illustrative of the typical love complaint,[8] an emphasis upon the tradition will distort Spenser's meaning. This passage is the key to Britomart's character, and explains her ready suspicions of her betrothed and her wayward behavior, traits certainly unbecoming an exemplar of "magnificke chastity." When Britomart accuses her eyes of betraying her, Spenser is spelling out for us the cause of all her troubles. Basically, her problem is a problem of perception; for she has never truly learned to see. Mr. Joseph Dallett's recent provocative essay has demonstrated conclusively that images of sight operate on many different levels in *The Faerie Queene* and that Spenser consciously uses them as

[8] Dorothy Buchanan, "The Love Complaint in *The Faerie Queene*" (quoted in *Variorum, Book Five*, 210).

an artistic device which helps him unify theme and narrative.[9] To my knowledge, no one has suggested that Britomart's problems arise from the fact that from first to last she is almost solely motivated by what she has seen. And since *The Faerie Queene* is as full of illusion as it is of truth, he who sees with the eye alone may wander from the way.

ii

It is customary to regard Book Three of *The Faerie Queene* as radically differing in structure from the two that precede it. In Books One and Two each hero begins his quest and shortly faces what is to be his greatest obstacle. Red Cross meets Errour; Guyon is incited to wrath by Archimago and almost engages his predecessor in senseless battle. Eventually, Red Cross falls into error; Guyon succumbs to the passions. The parallelism extends to their both being rescued by Prince Arthur, both then attending rest homes which confirm each in his particular virtue, and both successfully achieving their quests. On the other hand, Book Three seems to have no such straightforward development. Part of the willingness to consider it a structural mutation probably is the result of after-effects stemming from drinking too deeply of Mrs. Bennett's well. Even critics who deny Mrs. Bennett's basic premise in her book *The Evolution of* THE FAERIE QUEENE that Spenser's is a patchwork poem, nevertheless have cast about for other ways of explaining Book Three and its thematic counterpart, Book Four. Accordingly, the critics in question, Miss Williams and Mr. Hamilton, have affirmed that a system of classical myth provides the structural order and determines the meaning.[10] As each postulates a different myth-

[9] "Ideas of Sight in *The Faerie Queene*," *ELH*, xxvii (1960), 87-121.

[10] "Venus and Diana," 101-120; *Structure*, pp. 138-169. These essays, when read with Thomas P. Roche's thoughtful examination of the structure of Books Three and Four (*The Kindly Flame*,

ological sequence (Hamilton proposes Cupid and Psyche; Williams suggests Venus and Diana), their interpretations seem to differ radically. Since in the Renaissance these particular myths were highly susceptible to syncretic readings by commentators and mythographers alike, the differences between the two are more apparent than real. Both essays add significantly to our understanding of these two books. Through a strict adherence to such a rigid archetypal reading, Miss Williams is logically led to conclude that Britomart *(Diana Mammosa)* is superior to Artegall; but owing to the ineluctable workings of *concordia discors*, their marriage will be a success. The narrative will not support such a reading, since in any last analysis, Britomart and Artegall become *equal* partners.[11] At the end of Canto V, Artegall has demonstrated he is worthy of Britomart's love; yet blown by doubt and sorrow, she has drifted from her proper course and remains staring at the darkness in unfamiliar surroundings. Since her uncertain journey to free Artegall literally leads her into the darkness, her monologue is symbolical of an acute case of spiritual glaucoma. Her blindness does not come suddenly as it did to the men be-

---

Princeton, 1964), should help to exorcise the shades of Spenser's uncertainty of purpose and his unsure architectonic ability. Sister Mary Adelaide Grellner will shortly publish in *SEL* a paper, written for my Spenser class at the University of Wisconsin, on the Masque of Cupid at the House of Busyrane. This paper complements Roche's careful analysis and fits in precisely with the interpretation of Britomart's character offered here. In its own right, the Florimell-Marinell story now merits further serious study, particularly in regard to its relationship to Renaissance theories of love.

[11] But compare Miss Williams' analysis: "Artegall lives as the warrior who must either subjugate or be subjugated, who is either all pride or 'humblesse meek.' The vision in Isis Church shows what the final harmony is to be. The fierce and at first inimical beast Osiris/Artegall, now tyrannically wrathful, now fawning, is to become with Britomart complete justice, the union of opposed principles operating as the instrument of destiny" ("Venus and Diana," 108).

fore Lot's house but is the inevitable result of a long process which originated in Malecasta's Castle, where her specific problem and its solution are foreshadowed. It is not simply fortuitous that this element of structure is similar to that of the two preceding books.

Britomart's overnight stay at Malecasta's Castle is the ironic consequence of her thinking that she "Would not so lightly follow beauties chace" (III.i.19.2). Although critics have unhesitatingly complimented Britomart for such a display of "virtuous resolve," her actions when read in the light of her own quest are not so commendable as they seem. The reason Florimell's quest for Marinell is a unifying motif of Books Three and Four is simply that her pursuit is the true pattern and course of virtuous love in Faery Land. After all, Britomart herself came expressly to Faery Land as an entry in "beauties chace" to gain Artegall for a husband. Having refused to aid Guyon and Prince Arthur in their endeavors to help Florimell and thereby help herself, Britomart pushes on through the forest after waiting a short while for their return.

Coming to a spacious plain, she sees a castle before which an uneven battle is taking place: six knights are attacking one. When the knights pay no heed to her entreaties, she rides into their midst forcing a truce and learns from the lone defender that the others are attempting to force him to abandon his own lady for their mistress if he cannot defend his right. Although the six knights propose the same terms to Britomart, she forces them to surrender, after which the defeated knights flatter her strength and promise to be her servants.

> So underneath her feet their swords they mard,
> And after her besought, well as they might,
> To enter in, and reape the dew reward:
> She graunted, and then in they all together far'd.
>
> (III.i.30.6-9)

The "dew reward" which tempts Britomart into the castle should have served instead as a due warning; for the prize is to be the qualified favors of Malecasta, the "Lady of Delight" (III.i.27.6-9). When the six knights tell Britomart that "yours be the Damozel,/ Which by her owne law to your lot doth light" (30.3-4), they affirm a world in which the natural order is reversed, a world in which the woman takes the initiative in love. In the short space of a trip through the forest, Britomart metaphorically and actually has seen the extreme effects of lust's perversions. At one pole the Foster, "Breathing out beastly lust," relentlessly pursues the fair Florimell. At the other, Malecasta uses all the means she has to entrap unwary knights.

Once in the castle Britomart is actually physically surrounded by the most notorious example of an aggressive woman: the walls are "round about apparelled" with costly tapestries depicting the "love of *Venus* and her Paramoure/ The fair *Adonis*, turned to a flowre" (III.i.34.4-5). In another context, Professor Allen has firmly established the tradition of Venus as huntress.

> We know that Love is a hunter, that the seduction of the beloved is a kind of chase, and that it is all the soft hunt, which is essentially improper. On the other hand, the hard hunt, the work of the sacred hunters, is the honest training of those who would be heroes. But there are hunts available to some and not to others, and the best that one can do is to see, as Bruno suggests, that all of life is a hunt and to hope that one has the implements helpful in its conduct. [Shakespeare's *Venus and Adonis*] fits this doctrine as well as any poem fits any doctrine. Venus hunts Adonis; Adonis hunts the boar. The first hunt is the soft hunt of love; the second is the hard hunt of life.[12]

Spenser's pictorial representation of the tragedy of

[12] "On Venus and Adonis," 106.

Adonis is largely to the same point. In the tapestry, Venus, stricken with love at the sight of Adonis' beauty, begins her inexorable hunt.

> Then with what sleights and sweet allurements she
> Entyst the Boy, as well that art she knew,
> And wooed him her Paramoure to be;
> Now making girlonds of each flowre that grew,
> To crowne his golden lockes with honour dew;
> Now leading him into a secret shade
> From his Beauperes, and from bright heavens vew,
> Where him to sleepe she gently would perswade,
> Or bathe him in a fountaine by some covert glade.
> (III.i.35)

Here the "honour dew" of Adonis is of the same value as Britomart's "dew reward." By seducing him away from his peers, Venus has drawn him away from his noble pursuits. The "secret shade" and "covert glade" effectively seal him off "from bright heavens vew," which might have given him a sense of purpose. Since Venus has drawn her lover into a shadowy world where the round of activities consists of sleeping and bathing, she, like Acrasia, has contrived through her art to provide a simulacrum of nature.

> And whilst he slept, she over him would spred
> Her mantle, colour'd like the starry skyes,
> And her soft arme lay underneath his hed,
> And with ambrosiall kisses bathe his eyes.
> (III.i.36.1-4)

Under the malignant influence of her starry mantle which serves as a substitute for the long lost "bright heavens vew," Venus confirms his spiritual blindness "with ambrosiall kisses." On the other hand, Venus is very much the *seeing* huntress: "And whilest he bath'd, with her two crafty spyes,/ She secretly would search each daintie lim" (III.i.36.5 6). Hers is the lust of the eyes against which

St. John has given sufficient alarm (I.ii.16).[13] Despite her strenuous efforts to control his environment, Venus sees in Adonis an overpowering desire "To hunt the salvage beast in forrest wyde"—in Professor Allen's terms, "the hard hunt of life." He dies, pursuing his destiny in the world, and the goddess who once made "girlonds of each flowre that grew,/ To crowne his golden lockes with honour dew" now fashions a "daintie flowre" as a memorial of his death and the shortness of his span.[14]

Within this luxurious design of seduction and death exists the world of Malecasta, a world of "many beds."

> And all was full of Damzels, and of Squires,
> Dauncing and reveling both day and night,
> And swimming deepe in sensual desires,
> And *Cupid* still amongst them kindled lustfull fires.
> (III.i.39.6-9)

On the lowest possible level, the Damzels and Squires parody the drama of the tapestry—that which was so delicately expressed in art becomes gross in nature. Although the tapestry treats of lust's dominion, it also bears an implicit moral for those who wish to see. Through the efforts of Venus' sightless son, who provides the specific

---

[13] In the *Fowre Hymnes*, Spenser has given a most detailed analysis of Renaissance love. The *Fowre Hymnes* illustrates a process that leads from beauty in nature to the essence of beauty—in grace. In the case of Britomart it is helpful to remember that these two aspects of beauty are apprehended with the eye—natural beauty with the outward, the essence of beauty with the inward. If we were to schematize the course of Britomart's journey in *The Faerie Queene*, it would consist of three stages: 1) the love of Artegall's natural beauty which leads to 2) jealousy, sorrow, and the spiritual dark of Dolon's Castle, and to 3) the purgation of the soul in Isis Church, the true vision of her lover, and her rescue of him from Radigund.

[14] Miss Williams, however, considers the tapestry only a "trivialized" version of the Adonis story (*Spenser's World of Glass* [Berkeley, 1966], p. 112).

link between the tragedy and the travesty, the revelers are blinded by lust.

With fine precision Spenser has established the source of Malecasta's strength even before she appears in the narrative. She is a type of *Venus lascivia* who employs the complete arsenal of the weapons of seduction with the dexterity which comes from long practice. But the one weapon upon which all success depends is the double-edged dart of sight/blindness. Its awesome efficacy is manifest both in the tapestry and the tireless rounds of the Squires and Damzels. A blind Adonis complements a spying Venus. Sightless Cupid flits among the sight-drunk revelers. Since virtuous love also enters through the eyes, Britomart must be able to distinguish between the sight which begins and ends in natural beauty and that which begins in nature and ends in grace.

If Britomart's vision were perfectly developed at this stage, she would not have accepted the flattering invitation to enter Malecasta's Castle to get her "dew reward." Nor would she have failed to see the true significance of the tapestry in which is woven the legend of Venus and Adonis. The behavior of the Squires and Damzels cannot be ignored, however, by Britomart and her companion.

> Which when those knights beheld, with scornefull eye,
> They sdeigned such lascivious disport,
> And loath'd the loose demeanure of that wanton sort.
> (III.i.40.7-9)

Certainly theirs is a proper response to such deportment and indicates their noble bearing; *yet* Britomart permits herself to be drawn to the person under whose aegis the Squires and Damzels follow their carnal desires, the wellspring of wantonness, Malecasta herself. She naturally holds court "sitting on a sumptuous bed," which serves as a symbol both of her sovereignty and of her enslavement.

> She seemd a woman of great bountihed,
> And of rare beautie, saving that askaunce
> Her wanton eyes, ill signes of womanhed
> Did roll too lightly, and too often glaunce
> Without regard of grace, or comely amenaunce.
>
> (III.i.41.5-9)

The emphasis upon *eyes* confirms Malecasta's strength and signals her weakness and also points up the type of challenge Britomart will face, since she has already shown her aversion to the "lascivious disport" of the revelers.

As Malecasta's "goodly entertainment" of her guests serves as a prelude to seduction, she causes them to be led to a "bowre" and cheers them with "wine and spiceree," two mild aphrodisiacs.[15] When Britomart's companion disarms himself, we discover he is the Red Cross Knight. Britomart refuses to follow his example and simply lifts up her visor.

> As when faire *Cynthia*, in darkesome night,
> Is in a noyous cloud enveloped,
> Where she may find the substance thin and light,
> Breakes forth her silver beames, and her bright hed
> Discovers to the world discomfited;
> Of the poore traveller, that went astray,
> With thousand blessings she is heried;
> Such was the beautie and the shining ray,
> With which faire *Britomart* gave light unto the day.
>
> (III.i.43)

This is an innocent enough statement of Britomart's beauty and it initiates the Venus-Diana dialectic that Miss Williams has developed in detail. It is not without its attendant ambiguities, however. Britomart's beauty shines forth as a light to the "poore traveller, that went astray," at the same

---

[15] Alain Chartier, *Delectable Demaundes* (London, 1566), folios 64-65.

time that she, like the wandering moon, has bent her course to *Castle Joyeous*. The final irony rests in the fact that Malecasta, the *Errant Damzell*, is the only one to be "guided" by her *silver beames*.

With these preliminaries over, the seduction proper begins when the six knights who swore fealty to Britomart before the castle are disarmed. Their "company unsoght," they present themselves to her "vew" (III.i.44), their names identifying their specific services to Malecasta—Gardante, Parlante, Jocante, Basciante, Bacchante, and Noctante. Together, they form the well-known "ladder of lechery" and in terms of the basic images developed at length in the tapestry and in the scene of the revelers and their guide, we should notice that Britomart's new "liegemen" symbolize a process that begins in sight and ends in night. They seem to have no effect upon Britomart as they are "all but shadowes" to her when they present themselves to her service. Although their insubstantial appearance indicates Britomart's basic purity, it also suggests her innocence may be the result of culpable ignorance as well.

Although we have had sufficient hints in the narrative to suspect the steadiness of Britomart's intellectual commitment, the subsequent course of events demonstrates fully her culpable naïveté. Since the six knights of seduction are ostensibly working for Britomart, the primary target of their skills is Malecasta. When this *Errant Damzell* first sees Britomart's beauty, she immediately becomes enamored of her, being, of course "ignoraunt of her contrary sex" (III.i.47.2). The inevitable love fit follows, and Malecasta proves true to her name. Given to "fleshly lust" and "sensual delight," her "shamelesse beauty soone becomes a loathly sight" (III.i.48.9).

> Nought so of love this looser Dame did skill,
> But as a coale to kindle fleshly flame,
> Giving the bridle to her wanton will,

And treading under foote her honest name:
Such love is hate, and such desire is shame.
Still did she rove at her with crafty glaunce
Of her false eyes, that at her hart did ayme,
And told her meaning in her countenaunce:
But *Britomart* dissembled it with ignoraunce.

(III.i.50)

Malecasta is emulating the behavior of the Venus in the
tapestry, both in technique and style, which is to be expected since the tapestry truly establishes her *raison d'être*.
These darts fall harmlessly upon Britomart not because of
her vigilance but because of her "ignoraunce," a pattern
further elaborated upon at supper. Then the devious hostess
plies Britomart with rare foods and overflowing cups of
wine, which we need not add surpasses Spenser's "mean
degree." Between servings of wine, Malecasta continues
her dart game, but with no success; for "Britomart would
not such guilfull message know" (III.i.51.9).

After failing to get Britomart to disarm herself after
supper, Malecasta tries a direct approach, sighing, sobbing,
and finally telling Britomart if she will not comfort her
she will die (III.i.53.1-6).

But the chaste damzell, that had never priefe
Of such malengine and fine forgerie,
Did easily beleeve her strong extremitie.

(III.i.53.7-9)

Since it seems Malecasta is also suffering from the pains of
"imperious love," Britomart feels sympathy for her (54.
1-5).[16] This passage marks the turning point in Malecasta's
pursuit of her own desires. Where heretofore Britomart
feigned ignorance of her efforts, she now has identified
Malecasta's pains with her own, not knowing her predatory

[16] In Miss Williams' eyes this is Britomart's "only mistake"
(*Spenser's World of Glass*, p. 212).

design. Spenser uses a metaphor of the hunt to describe Britomart's heedless mind: "The bird, that knowes not the false fowlers call,/ Into his hidden net full easily doth fall" (III.i.54.8-9). She, of course, is partially ignorant of Malecasta's intentions; and rather than scorn her offer of goodwill and disdain a "gentle harts request," Britomart cheerfully entertains her temptress (III.i.55.1-5). The slightest flicker of doubt begins to come to Britomart's mind, only to be extinguished before it grows into the flame of understanding. Although this uncertain light fails to illuminate her, it serves the reader as a perfect characterization of her current state of mind. She responds sympathetically to Malecasta's lament of love; *nevertheless* "she inly deemd/ Her love too light, to wooe a wandring guest" (III.i.55.6-7). Of all the warnings she has seen—the six knights before the castle, the sad moral of the tapestry, the wanton revels of the Squires and Damzels—the only thing she has questioned is the propriety of Malecasta's love. Britomart's characterization of herself as a "wandring guest" is nice irony; and by it Spenser is able to pinpoint his heroine's difficulty as he could in no other way. The only true "wanderers" in *The Faerie Queene* are Knights of Maidenhead who have temporarily lost their sense of purpose or the genuinely evil characters whose very natures lead them astray.[17] Technically, Britomart is an errant knight, an opprobrious term to Spenser; and it is fitting that she meets the *Errant Damzell*, Malecasta.

Britomart's kind demeanor and her courteous behavior naturally are misconstrued by her hostess to mean that her

[17] We should remember Florimell, whom Britomart has refused to follow, is a purposeful traveler (III.vii.4). On the other hand, the Squire of Dames, who must "wander" at the service of young women (III.vii.50), seduces Paridell and Satyrane from the pursuit of Florimell (III.vii.51-52). Ironically, Paridell, Satyrane, and Britomart ultimately meet at the home of that reluctant host, the "halfe blinde" Malbecco.

guest feels a similar passion for her: "That from like inward fire that outward smoke had steemd" (III.i.55.9). Malecasta contents herself with the thought her endeavors will be rewarded and waits impatiently for night to come. For at midnight (57.5-9) all the revelers are led to their "bowres" (III.i.58.1-4).

> Tho when the Britonesse saw all the rest
> Avoided quite, she gan her selfe despoile,
> And safe commit to her soft fethered nest,
> Where through long watch, and late dayes weary toile,
> She soundly slept, and carefull thoughts did quite assoile.
>   (III.i.58.5-9)

Since Malecasta's knights set the pattern of seduction and since the evidence of their actions is apparent in the behavior of their mistress and the revelers, we should naturally be most apprehensive about Britomart at the time when Noctante begins his rounds. "Soft fethered nest" is a comfortable phrase for her bed; but it also confirms the identification of Britomart as "The bird, that knowes not the false fowlers call" (III.i.54.8). Since "her soft fethered nest" is nothing more than Malecasta's "hidden net," Britomart completes the pattern when she puts away her "carefull thoughts." Now it remains for the "bird" to fall into the false fowler's net.

Performing the elaborate ritual of lust's dominion, Malecasta dresses herself in a scarlet mantle, slips softly into Britomart's bed, and lies sighing by her side (III.i.59-61. 1-7). Britomart soon discovers the would-be seductress, leaps out of the bed, snatches up her sword, and intends to avenge herself on the "loathed leachour." Malecasta's shrieks awaken everybody. When Red Cross and Malecasta's six champions arrive "halfe armed and halfe unarmed," they see the scarlet lady senseless on the floor and Britomart in a white smock threatening her with a sword. After Gardante and his brothers revive their mistress, they

try to "stirre up strife, and troublous contecke broch" (III.
i.64.5). They remember the results of their last encounter
with her, however, and wisely keep their distance.[18]

> But one of those sixe knights, *Gardante* hight,
> Drew out a deadly bow and arrow keene,
> Which forth he sent with felonous despight,
> And fell intent against the virgin sheene:
> The mortall steele stayd not, till it was seene
> To gore her side, yet was the wound not deepe,
> But lightly rased her soft silken skin,
> That drops of purple bloud thereout did weepe,
> Which did her lilly smock with staines of vermeil steepe.
>
> (III.i.65)

Enraged by the wound, Britomart, with the help of Red
Cross, disperses Gardante and his brothers. After they are
put to flight, Britomart dons her armor, and she and Red
Cross leave the castle before dawn.

The slight wound that Britomart receives from Gardante's arrow symbolizes her basic weakness and anticipates
her spiritual blindness in Dolon's Castle. For the test presented to Britomart in *Castle Joyeous* is a test of true vision.
It certainly is not a test of her chastity, except perhaps in-
directly, since the very nature of the two encounters elim-
inates it as a major factor. When Britomart finds someone
in her bed, she thinks it is a "loathed leachour." Malecasta,
on the other hand, would not have wasted so many of her
darts had she known "so faire a wight" (47.1) to be a
woman.

In a sense, a double visual deception is the basis for
Spenser's poetic construct and points his meaning. Malecasta, seeing only her guest's beautiful face, is blinded by
lust, and from the very beginning, fruitlessly pursues her
carnal desires. Britomart's blindness is of another kind.

---

[18] Their hesitancy confirms her chastity and anticipates the riddle
of the doors in the House of Busyrane.

While we may be tempted to ascribe her lack of perception to innocence, the narrative will not support such a reading. She should never have gone into *Castle Joyeous* in the first place, since she had seen and heard in detail from Red Cross the work of Malecasta's servants. Once in the castle, she has ample opportunity to learn of the true nature of her prospective hostess. She enters and "sees" an "image of superfluous riotize,/ Exceeding much the state of meane degree" (III.i.33.6-7). Developing this image in great detail, Spenser logically moves from the tapestry depicting Venus and Adonis to the lust-blind revelers and the machinations of Cupid, and finally to the "wanton eyes" of Malecasta. Spenser's technique is a kind of poetic "zeroing in" on target. Even though Britomart, the "wandring guest," has all these examples before her, she only beholds the ceaseless activities of Squire and Damzell "with scornefull eye" and deems Malecasta's "love too light." What should have been a series of progressive illuminations turns out to be a gradual loss of perspective. Spenser's analysis of Britomart's success in handling the devious designs of her hostess points up the negative aspects of her intellectual commitment. When Malecasta throws the first dart in the game of lust, Britomart feigns "ignoraunce" (50.9). The second assault is likewise repulsed (51.9). But after Malecasta unburdens herself of her love-longing, Britomart can "easily beleeve her strong extremitie" (53.9) and then metaphorically becomes an unwary bird that is the prey of false fowlers (54.8-9). Spenser has Britomart lie in a "soft fethered nest," where she "soundly slept and carefull thoughts did quite assoile" (58.9); he culminates a process which began when he had his heroine think she would "not so lightly follow beauties chace" (III.i.19.2). Her "wandrings" have taken her from light into darkness, from a sense of commitment (19.2) to a loss of understanding. Since she could have avoided the rather distasteful scene with Malecasta and her subsequent wounding, however slight, by Gardante if she had taken time to understand what she had seen, Britomart's lack of perception is a culpable ignorance or naïveté. John Calvin has carefully established the criteria for such ignorance.

> But although we want natural power, whereby wee cannot climbe up unto the pure and clear knowledge of God, yet because the fault of our dullnesse is in our selves, therefore all colour of excuse is cut away from us. For we cannot pretend ignorance, but that even our conscience doth stil condemne us of slouthfulnesse and unthankfulnesse. It is a defense forsooth right worthie, if a man will allege that he wanted eares to heare the truth, for the publishing whereof the verie dumb creatures have lowde voices: if man shall say that he cannot see those things with his eyes, which the creatures without eyes do showe him: if man shall lay for his excuse the feebleness of his wit, where all creatures without reason doe instruct him: Wherefore sith all things do show us the right way, we are worthily put from all excuse of our wandering and straying out of the way.[19]

Britomart's ignorance truly is neither blameless nor excusable. As the patroness of chastity she should know her duty well enough not to become a "wandring guest" of her greatest enemy, Malecasta. Britomart's problem however is more subtle. Since both lust and love enter through the eyes and have as their object beauty in nature, it is difficult to distinguish one from another in the first stages. Britomart truly thinks Malecasta is suffering from the pangs of love (53.7-9). Lust begins and ends in nature, but love always leads to higher things. Or as Spenser puts it when

---

[19] *Institution of Christian Religion*, trans. Thomas Norton (London, 1587), p. 11 verso [1.v.15]; Thomas Aquinas' discussion of "invincible" ignorance is to the same point (*Summa Theologica*, 1. ii.Q.76.a.2).

he compares Malecasta's lust to love, "For love does alwaies bring forth bounteous deeds,/ And in each gentle hart desire of honour breeds" (III.i.49.8-9). It is important to remember that Britomart's inviolate chastity is never an issue in *The Faerie Queene*. It is assumed. Although Malecasta comes as close as anyone to seducing her, her attempt is thwarted by the very nature of things. Gardante's limited success, however, clearly underscores Britomart's problem. Her one weakness eventually leads her into the spiritual darkness of Dolon's Castle, but also promises a glorious vision in the Church of Isis.

iii

In depicting Britomart's wanderings in search of Artegall, from the relatively harmless snares of *Castle Joyeous* to the more dangerous entanglements of Dolon's Castle, Spenser has marked her path with a sufficient number of signs indicating that her basic problem is one of perception. Despite all the contrary evidence of her lover's virtues given by Merlin and Red Cross, she is still fondly led by the vision of his natural beauty. When he does not return within the stipulated time, she falls prey to jealous fears which eventually lead to sorrow. In the depths of melancholy, she is tempted from the true way, the one way which leads to her lover. Not only is her errant journey one from light into darkness; but it leads ironically from *Castle Joyeous* to the house of sorrow. There in the darkness of her room, she remains "Restlesse, recomfortlesse, with heart deepe grieved/ Not suffering the least twinckling sleepe to start/ Into her eye" (V.vi.24.6-8).

It will be useful to our purpose to catalogue here some of Britomart's visual responses between Book Three and her appearance in Book Five. They fall into three categories: 1) ordinary symptoms of love originating in natural beauty; 2) dereliction of duty caused by faulty vision; 3) choice of guide:

1) *Symptoms, pains induced by the false archer*: the most obvious of course is Gardante's literal wounding of her, which is symbolic of her whole problem; when she sees Artegall in the mirror, III.ii.26; her own analysis of the problem, III.ii.37-39; after hearing Red Cross's favorable description of Artegall, III.iv.6; after the battle with her lover, IV.vi.26-27; his courting of her, IV.vi.40.

2) *Dereliction of duty*: refusing to aid Florimell who is being chased by the "griesly foster," III.i.19; entering *Castle Joyeous*, III.i.30; her careless watch of Amoret, IV.vii.3; resting in Dolon's Castle, V.vi.22.

3) *Choice of guide*: it is important to remember that her close friend and confidante is named Glauce.[20] In Chapter I, I developed the idea that Glauce works exclusively in nature and in many ways lives up to her name, because essentially she is blind. Britomart leans upon her "foolhardy wit" for advice, III.iii.51-62; she then admits love is her pilot, III.iv.9; she makes "blind love" her guide, IV.v.29.

Although her ensuing "debate with her eyes" has been read as another chapter in the book written by that cliché expert, Cupid, the inexorable pressure of the narrative demands another more meaningful explanation. When she accuses her "guilty eyes" of being "false watches" that first "betrayd" her heart, she has sunk to the lowest possible level of spiritual despondency. Her concern is only for herself and she has lost sight of the providential plan and Artegall's plight. Of course, her eyes are the necessary agents whereby she first becomes attracted to Artegall and begins her quest. The circumstances of her pursuit leading to her present despair clearly show she has not progressed beyond this initial phase. Although she has traveled much, she has made little progress as her journey has brought

[20] It is appropriate that she be thus named, since Glauce was the mother of the third Diana (Cicero, *De natura deorum*, iii.xxii.58).

her back to the fears, doubts, and sorrows she experienced when she first saw her lover in Merlin's magic glass. That her present distress is the result of confusion, embarrassment, and doubt is clear. While these emotions are perfectly understandable in the context of the love quest, they lead, in Britomart's case, to a kind of spiritual denial—first implicit, then explicit. Both Britomart and the reader should know the full import of her journey, since both have visited Merlin's cave and have heard the prophetic voice that ranged across the centuries, telling of the glories of the British nation and praising the noble deeds of the worthy couple who continue its fame. Before Merlin begins to recite the litany of Britain, he makes clear the power underlying the future evolution of the nation.

> It was not, *Britomart*, thy wandring eye,
> Glauncing unwares in charmed looking glas,
> But the streight course of heavenly destiny,
> Led with eternall providence, that has
> Guided thy glaunce, to bring his will to pas:
> Ne is thy fate, ne is thy fortune ill,
> To love the prowest knight that ever was.
> Therefore submit thy wayes unto his will,
> And do by all dew meanes thy destiny fulfill.
>
> (III.iii.24)

Nothing could be clearer than Merlin's text; and to make sure that she does not miss the point, he appends an elaborate gloss consisting of twenty-three stanzas (26-49), which describe the time when "universall peace [will] compound civill jarre." Yet Britomart strays into *Castle Joyeous* and when "heavie sleepe" surprises her, she abandons Amoret to "greedie lust" (IV.vii.3-6), and she doubts the faith of her lover when he does not return within three months. Upon "seeing night at dore," she accepts Dolon's invitation, knowing full well that any delay on her part will prolong Artegall's miseries. And in her debate with her eyes she implicitly denies the "streight course of heavenly destiny." Her spiritual malaise is of the kind that her lover has already rejected. Obviously she will be unable to rescue Artegall until she, like him, has put away sorrow.

If I have drawn up a sad indictment of Britomart out of the same materials that have caused others to admire her, or to laugh at the foibles of love, or to postulate some subtly arcane working of *concordia discors,* I plead guilty. But my indictment is not so severe as Spenser's. He has spent a long time gathering evidence for his case against Britomart, gathering it with such consummate skill, patience, and artistry that we should not be surprised when it is presented. It has the ring of divine authority. For at the exact moment when Britomart implicitly denies her "hcavcnly destiny," admitting her sorrow is such "that none was to appease," Spenser makes his accusation in such a way that it is unmistakable.

> What time the native Belman of the night,
> The bird, that warned *Peter* of his fall,
> First rings his silver bell t'each sleepy wight,
> 'That should their mindcs up to devotion call,
> She heard a wondrous noise below the hall.
> All sodainely the bed, where she should lie,
> By a false trap was let adowne to fall
> Into a lower roome, and by and by
> The loft was raysd againe, that no man could it spie.
>
> (V.vi.27)

Through the metaphor of the "native Belman of the night," Spenser has implicated Britomart's with Peter's spiritual defection. It was the commonest of commonplaces that the cry of the cock reminded all of the sin of St. Peter. De Lancre's remarks may be taken as representative of this tradition: "C'est (dit-on) pour faire resouvenir du chant du Coq, qui fit sonner la retraicte a Saint Pierre, et luy donna advis de retourner a son Createur."²¹ It was also an accepted fact that the cock's crow marked the hours of the night. Since the biblical exegetes spent considerable energy determining the time of the cock's first crow in the Gospel accounts of Peter's denial, we now know that this occurred at midnight,²² which also marks the time when Malecasta slipped into Britomart's bed, and the temporal simultaneity serves as another link between the two temptations. The irony of Britomart's denial of her mission is reinforced by the fact that just at the time that she should her mind "up to devotion call," the trap is sprung that would cast her down to perdition. Just as the crowing cock and the analogy with Peter's fall confirm Britomart's spiritual vagrancy, they also anticipate her eventual redemption. As did the early commentators,²³ Renaissance theologians held Peter's faith to be the kind whose very defection shows "the stouteste Champion in the worlde" will fall.²⁴ Psychologically, Britomart's fall into despair is as understandable as Peter's. Moved solely by Artegall's natural beauty, she has lost faith in him and in their heavenly destinies. When she discovers his true beauty, she will

²¹ *Tableau de L'inconstance des mauvais anges et demons* (Paris, 1612), p. 154. For a full discussion of the significance of the cock in the Renaissance and a reading of Vaughan's "Cock-Crowing," see D. C. Allen's *Image and Meaning* (Baltimore, 1960), pp. 154-169.

²² "First after midnight; second, and more strong before dawn, when it senses the coming of the sun. Whence this time properly is called cockcrowing. And before this second cock crow Peter denied Christ thrice" (Lapide, *Commentarius in Quatuor Evangelia* [Antwerp, 1695], Matt. xxvi.34, p. 488).

²³ See Hugh of St. Cher, "Evangelium Secundum Matthaeum," *Opera*, vi, 82.

²⁴ The phrase is from John Udall's *Two Sermons on Peter* (1584), sig. C.1. These sermons develop at length Calvin's thesis advanced in *An Harmonie upon the Three Evangelists* that "The fall of Peter . . . is a notable example of our infirmity." Later Peter Broxup relieved himself of a tedious versification of the moral issues involved in his *Saint Peters Path* (London, 1598).

know her mission and "bring his will to pas" (III.iii.24.5).

Meanwhile, after seeing the treachery of Dolon's trap, she hears the footsteps of armed men in the hall coming toward her chamber. Equally alert, Talus drives them away with his iron flail and reports to Britomart, who becomes enraged and burns to "be avenged for so fowle a deede" (V.vi.31.2). Unknown to her is the fact that Dolon, the master of the house, thinks she is Artegall, since she is similarly dressed and is accompanied by Talus. Dolon was the father of Guizor, whom Artegall killed before Pollente's bridge of extortion. To Britomart, Dolon seems as if he "no evill ment" (V.vi.19.9). Here again, as in *Castle Joyeous*, a double visual deception establishes the poetic framework in which temptation occurs.

Now since danger of attack is ever present, Britomart remains alert, watching away the night, "Ne suffred slothfull sleepe her eyelids to oppresse" (V.vi.34.9). At dawn she searches throughout the house but finds everyone gone.

> She saw it vaine to make there lenger stay,
> But tooke her steede, and thereon mounting light,
> Gan her addresse unto her former way.
>
> (V.vi.36.1-3)

This marks a subtle change in Britomart's character, for instead of the slow and sorrowful way in which she began her journey, she now lightly resumes her former way. She does not travel far before she meets Guizor's two brothers waiting for her at the same bridge on which Artegall fought Pollente. Although Talus wants to prepare the way for her, she defeats them herself and passes on. Following this victory, as Britomart moves nearer to Artegall, she becomes more closely identified with him and his mission. In her vision in Isis Church, where she sees Artegall in his true light, she discovers that she will share his work.

iv

So long as Britomart is guided in her search by her lover's natural beauty, she is incapable of rising above herself. Since love in nature is essentially a selfish passion, based solely upon the physical beauty of the lover, it soon degenerates into jealousy and sorrow when the lover is gone. Britomart's behavior when Artegall is away and fails to return within a stated time is a classic example of the effects of this kind of love. The increasingly heavy burden of her spiritual lethargy results in her acceptance of Dolon's offer of comfort and cheer and in her going a "little wide by West." Dolon's subsequent treachery, however, forces her to direct her attention to the immediate danger and away from her own problems. Her eagerness to resume her quest is reinforced by the episode at the bridge. Where before she rode "sadly" behind Talus, she now declines his help, a refusal which anticipates her willing acceptance of her responsibilities to Artegall. Britomart's conversion is by no means complete, and the reader has no definite assurances that she will not once again wander from the way. Accordingly, Spenser has provided in the episode at the Church of Isis a means whereby she atones for her past errors and becomes worthy of her lover.

The paean to justice with which Spenser opens Canto VII serves once more to link Britomart's quest for Artegall to a higher purpose. For although Merlin's prophecy ranges through the course of history, he does not outline Britomart's specific duties—other than procreation. When Spenser has her come to the Church of Isis, representing "that part of Justice, which is Equity," he leaves little doubt as to her especial function in helping to bring about "universall peace."

> Unto whose temple when as *Britomart*
> Arrived, shee with great humility

Did enter in, ne would that night depart;
But *Talus* mote not be admitted to her part.
(V.vii.3.7-9)

The great humility she feels at the entrance of the church
is in direct contrast to the deep sorrow she expresses when
she hears of her lover's capture. If we remember that
Artegall gained wisdom through humility, we can hopefully expect Britomart's similar awakening. After she is
well received by the priests, they conduct her to the statue
of their goddess, who "had powre in things divine" (V.vii.
6.7). Dressed in white linen and holding a wand, the goddess is depicted standing with one foot on a crocodile whose
"taile her middle did enfold" (V.vii.6.9).

Such was the Goddesse; whom when *Britomart*
Had long beheld, her selfe upon the land
She did prostrate, and with right humble hart,
Unto her selfe her silent prayers did impart.
(V.vii.7.6-9)

Britomart's actions reveal the depths of her humility, in
recognition of which the statue inclines toward her and
shakes its wand. Britomart sees this as a "token of good
fortune"; and since night has fallen she prepares to go to
sleep on the earth beside the altar, as was the custom of the
place.[25]

Up to this point in the narrative, Spenser has frequently
used Britomart's many "sleeping scenes" to emphasize her
unwariness or her uncertain sense of purpose. When she
lies in her "fethered nest" in Malecasta's Castle, where she
"soundly slept, and carefull thoughts did quite assoile"
(III.vii.3-6), she symbolizes her degree of blindness. Her

[25] For the importance of *humilitas* in this context see Isidore,
Etymologiarum libri, x.115; Thomas Aquinas' discussion of Bene-
dict's twelve degrees of humility (*Summa Theologica*, ii.ii.Q.161.-
a.6); and Calvin, *Institutes* ii.ii.11.

midday nap results in her ward Amoret's being seized by
"greedie lust" (IV.vii.3-6).[26] In Isis Church it is a different matter, since with great humility Britomart has paid
her respects to the goddess and has received a favorable
sign from her.

> There did the warlike Maide her selfe repose,
> Under the wings of *Isis* all that night,
> And with sweete rest her heavy eyes did close,
> After that long daies toile and weary plight.
> And whilest her earthly parts with soft delight
> Of sencelesse sleepe did deeply drowned lie,
> There did appeare unto her heavenly spright
> A wondrous vision, which did close implie
> The course of all her fortune and posteritie.
>
> (V.vii.12)

Because Britomart's major problem is one of seeing, it is
fitting that its solution be presented to her in a vision. The
process by which Spenser achieves this effect follows a regu-
lar pattern that corresponds to the tripartite soul of man,
the vegetative, sensitive, and intellective: Britomart's
"earthly parts," senses, and "spright."[27]

In her vision Britomart is doing sacrifice to Isis when
suddenly her white stole is transfigured into a "robe of
scarlet red" and her moon-like mitre into a "crowne of

---

[26] Both Amoret and Britomart are in error here. Amoret, who has
just escaped the fears of the House of Busyrane, wanders off "daisy-
ing" only to endure the terrors of Lust. Britomart, the guardian
surprised, suffers physical and moral exhaustion after participating in
the Tournament of Beauty.

[27] For the specific functions of these "three" souls see Thomas
Aquinas, *Summa Theologica*, 1.Q.78.a.1; and Bartolomaeus An-
glicus (*Batman on Bartholomew* [London, 1582], pp. 12-16 verso).
Spenser has already employed the principles of the "three" souls in
organizing the House of Alma and in depicting the characters of
Priamond, Diamond, and Triamond.

gold." A tempest arises which scatters the embers of the
holy fire on the ground and puts the temple in "jeopardy."

With that the Crocodile, which sleeping lay
Under the Idols feete in fearlesse bowre,
Seem'd to awake in horrible dismay,
As being troubled with that stormy stowre;
And gaping greedy wide, did streight devoure
Both flames and tempest: with which growen great,
And swolne with pride of his owne peerelesse powre,
He gan to threaten her likewise to eat;
But that the Goddesse with her rod him backe did beat.

Tho turning all his pride to humblesse meeke,[28]
Him selfe before her feete he lowly threw,
And gan for grace and love of her to seeke:
Which she accepting, he so neare her drew,
That of his game she soone enwombed grew,
And forth did bring a Lion of great might;
That shortly did all other beasts subdew.
With that she waked, full of fearefull fright,
And doubtfully dismayd through that so uncouth sight.

(V.vii.15-16)

At daybreak after wandering about passive and melancholy, pondering the meaning of her vision, Britomart
sadly greets the priests preparing for "morrow Mas." After
she tells about her vision to a priest who offers to help her,
she asks him to guide her "out of errour blind" (V.vii.19.5),

---

[28] Miss Williams thinks this line is indicative of Artegall, the
warrior who must subjugate or be subjugated. Although it is true
Artegall's pride leads to humility, this humility, as we have seen in
the Radigund episode, is a supreme act of the will. Artegall's humility
is the humility that leads to wisdom. In the cantos following his
release, not one scrap of poetic evidence can be found to show Artegall
is proud, or for that matter, wrathful, or concupiscent.

a request which doubly underscores her problem. In a "heavenly fury" deliberately reminiscent of Merlin's poetic frenzy, the priest penetrates her disguise and interprets her vision—Artegall, her "faithfull lover," is the Crocodile Osiris and she is Isis. Together they represent justice and equity and will continue the British nation.

When Britomart hears again of her lover's devotion and of her divine destiny, she is much "eased in her troublous thought" (V.vii.24.2) and rewards the priests by leaving an offering of gold and silver to the Goddess Isis.

> Then taking leave of them, she forward went,
> To seeke her love, where he was to be sought;
> Ne rested till she came without relent
> Unto the land of Amazons, as she was bent.
>
> (V.vii.24.6-9)

This stanza signals Britomart's complete change of character. In a very real sense, she has purged herself of those doubts and sorrows she had when she first rode out to rescue her lover, only to be tempted into the profound spiritual darkness of Dolon's Castle. Where before she went a "little wide by West" to take her doubtful "ease" she now goes forward "without relent" and takes no rest until she succeeds in her mission. In retrospect we know that Britomart's course in the narrative of *The Faerie Queene* is a metaphorical journey between two visions. In the first, she sees Artegall's natural beauty in Merlin's mirror of the world. Then led by blind nature, Glauce, she wanders from place to place, stopping from time to time at some enticing way station, like *Castle Joyeous*. At each of these voluntary deviations from her quest, Britomart's blindness is rewarded with appropriate misadventure: Gardante's wound, Dolon's trap. Even when she is most successful, she eventually fails; for after braving the flames of the House of Busyrane and resisting the threats of its enchanter to rescue Amoret, she relaxes her vigil in broad daylight and loses her ward to "lust." When she enters the Church of Isis, prostrates herself, and prays with humble heart to the goddess, Britomart is, in effect, finally carrying out Merlin's admonition to "submit thy wayes unto his will,/ And do by all dew meanes thy destiny fulfill" (III.iii.24.8-9). Then she has her second vision; and it differs from the first in that it is not given to the outward eye of nature but to the inward eye of the spirit, the intellective soul. This vision has nothing whatever to do with Artegall's physical beauty and is almost completely nonrepresentational. It is patently symbolic and requires the divine inspiration of one of God's servants to reduce it to intelligible terms for Britomart. This vision marks the end of her spiritual search, for she now truly sees; and making destiny her choice, as did Artegall, she begins anew her quest for her lover.

The inevitable battle that ensues between Britomart and Radigund is the bitterest to be fought in *The Faerie Queene*. It is the only true physical clash between two women in the poem; and it pits upholders of different principles against one another—love against lust. In the logic of the poem's structure, it is Britomart's final confrontation of the forces of Malecasta, who, we remember, lures knights with her seductive wiles, as Venus did poor Adonis. Radigund woos "by all the waies she could"; and failing in her efforts, she has the strength to reduce men to servitude. Since Britomart is fully confirmed in her love for Artegall and refuses Radigund's terms, fighting instead under those that "prescribed were by lawes of chevalrie," the outcome of the battle is never in doubt. Her eventual defeat of Radigund anticipates her ruling over the city of the Amazons, where she changes "all that forme of common weale/ [and] The liberty of women did repeale,/ Which they had long usurpt" (V.vii.42.4-6). Britomart's reign symbolizes the final defeat of Malecasta.

This overriding theme of her quest, finely woven into

the texture of the poem, serves also as a vehicle for her own metamorphosis. After defeating Radigund and staying Talus' retributive slaughter of the fleeing Amazons, Britomart searches throughout the city for her lover. When she finally finds him and sees his humble estate, she turns her head aside, "abasht with secrete shame" (V.vii.38.3). The "secrete shame" initiates a ruthless self-searching which reveals Britomart's new perspective.[29]

> And then too well beleev'd, that which tofore
> Jealous suspect as true untruely drad,
> Which vaine concept now nourishing no more,
>   She sought with ruth to salve his sad misfortunes sore.
>
> (V.vii.38.6-9)

In these lines, which mark (and it cannot be emphasized too strongly) the *first time* she shows compassion for her betrothed, Spenser affirms Britomart's newly achieved maturity in her love for Artegall. For now she sees her jealous fears were unfounded and goes to comfort her lover. Spenser, who has built up to this scene of her self-revelation with the overpowering logic of the narrative, is not going to risk the possibility that his readers may miss the full import of his message. Accordingly, he adds an elegant stanza consisting of a single sentence that not only confirms Britomart's transformation but her lover's as well.

> Not so great wonder and astonishment,
> Did the most chast *Penelope* possesse,
> To see her Lord, that was reported drent,
> And dead long since in dolorous distress,

---

[29] But compare Blakeney: "Britomart has been the fierce fighter till recently; but at the sight of her love spinning and in woman's garb her instinctive womanhood at once asserts itself: 'abasht she turned her head aside.' This is a delicate touch, worthy of the tender-hearted poet" (quoted in *Variorum, Book Five*, 222).

Come home to her in piteous wretchednesse,
After long travell of full twenty yeares,
That she knew not his favours liklynesse,
For many scarres and many hoary heares,
But stood long staring on him, mongst uncertaine feares.

(V.vii.39)

Spenser is alluding here, of course, to the most famous recognition scene in Western literature, occasioned by Ulysses' return home at the end of his journey. Through comparison, Britomart is put in the same category as the chaste Penelope, who was in the Renaissance the finest symbol of the faithful wife. Conti's analysis of her exemplary character will serve as a representative example of the tradition which gave as much importance to the triumph of virtue as it did to the victories of heroes.

> The virtues of other women were awakened by Penelope's example—continence, patience in difficulties, home management, and lastly prudence in all things—as they depicted the wife of Ulysses or reason. For it is a much more difficult thing to subdue satisfactorily the stubbornly barricaded soul with temperance and virtue, or to drive out corruption, than it was to conquer Troy. They conceive that the same city endured siege for ten years, yet Penelope was not able to be overcome in twenty. Therefore, the ancients in many writings praise her as a singular model to be imitated.[30]

In likening her to Penelope, Spenser is showing us that Britomart has finally matured in her love for Artegall, possessing now in actuality those qualities of constancy, trust, and understanding which Merlin had foretold were potentially hers. Britomart's metamorphosis is all the more

---

[30] *Mythologiae* (1637), p. 552.

remarkable when it is recalled that it was she who could wait only three months for Artegall's return before becoming jealous and falling into despair.

The scene also serves to validate Artegall's new character; for just as Penelope's veil has fallen by right upon Britomart so has the wisdom commonly attributed to Ulysses come to Artegall. This too is consistent at every point with Spenser's theme, since the poem has already demonstrated that Artegall gained wisdom through humility.[31] While keeping the parallel characters, Spenser has neatly reversed the action, making Britomart (Penelope) the heroic suitor and Artegall (Ulysses) the successful defender of his honor from the false wooers. Artegall has successfully resisted the temptations of Radigund and Clarin, as Ulysses once resisted the charms of Circe and the enervating strains of Calypso.

> How many paines susteyned Ulisses, in that longe wandering? when both to women he did service (yf Circe, and Calipso are to bee named women) and to al men in al his talke he woulde be faire spoken: and also at home dyd beare the spight of the slaves, and nieces, that he might once attaine to the thing, which he desired.[32]

If the fastidious reader should raise his eyebrows at Spenser's "innovation" of implicitly relating the wise Ulysses to Hercules, he should remember the praise of Cato in Seneca's *De constantia sapientis.*

> As touching Cato, I besought thee not to trouble thy selfe about him, for I told thee that a wise man could neyther be injured by words or deedes: but that the

---

[31] See my discussion of *humilitas est sapientia* in Chapter II, pp. 133-140.

[32] Cicero, *De officiis*, Grimald trans. (1568), pp. 49-50.

immortal Gods had given us in Cato a more living example of a wise man, than either *Ulysses* or *Hercules* in former ages. For these have our Stoicks pronounced to be wise men, invincible in labours, contemners of pleasure, and conquerours in all Countries.[33]

Seneca writes as if the comparison were common knowledge, and Maximus of Tyre, the Neoplatonic philosopher, has no difficulty in regarding Ulysses, Hercules, and Socrates in common.[34] With the symbolic metamorphoses of Britomart into the faithful wife and Artegall into the wise husband, Spenser completes the first phase of Merlin's prophecy, which was reinforced by the vision in the Church of Isis.

Because in these two cantos Britomart is Spenser's chief concern, he is soon to put her new-found resolve to the test. After Artegall is sufficiently recovered from the debilitating effects of his long imprisonment and poor diet, he resumes his quest to free Irena and establish peace.

> Full sad and sorrowful was *Britomart*
> For his departure, her new cause of griefe;
> Yet wisely moderated her owne smart,
> Seeing his honor, which she tendred chiefe,
> Consisted much in that adventures priefe.
> The care whereof, and hope of his successe
> Gave unto her great comfort and reliefe,
> That womanish complaints she did represse,
> And tempred for the time her present heavinesse.
>
> (V.vii.44)

Britomart now has all the attributes of a perfect wife. To

---

[33] *The Workes of . . . Seneca,* trans. Thomas Lodge (1620), p. 661 [1.2].

[34] *Sermones e Graeca in Latinam versi Cosmo Paccio interprete* (Basel, 1519), p. 92 [xxii].

all intents and purposes, her long journey in *The Faerie Queene* is over. It has been a weary way, with many turnings; but it has led from darkness into the light, from love in nature to love in grace. For she now knows that "love does alwayes bring forth bounteous deedes,/ And in each gentle hart desire of honour breeds" (III.i.49.8-9).[35]

[35] Britomart's journey in *The Faerie Queene* is the maturing of a lovesick young girl, a progress from unqualified desire, through simple love, culminating in mature love. For the Renaissance, I suspect, Britomart's real achievement is her perfection in virtuous love. Spenser's treatment of the development of Britomart's character in her love for Artegall reflects the common concern of the Renaissance *trattati d'amore* about the relationships and differences of desire and love. In addition, Britomart's progress here seems quite consistent with the modifications and reconciliations which these treatises effected between the two, particularly as revealed in the most popular of these dialogues, the *Dialoghi d'amore* of Leone Ebreo [Judah Abrabanel] written in 1501 and published in 1535. The topic of the first dialogue between Love and Wisdom is desire and love (*Philosophy of Love*, trans. F. Friedeberg-Seeley and Jean H. Barnes [London, 1937], pp. 3-66). For similar treatments of desire and love in the Renaissance see Pietro Bembo's *Gli Asolani*, trans. Rudolph B. Gottfried (Bloomington, 1954); Mario Equicola's *Libro di natura d'amore* (Venice, 1554); Francesco Cattani's *I tre libri d'amore* (Venice, 1561); Flaminio Nobili's *Tratto dell'amore humano* (Lucca, 1567; republished Rome, 1895); Guido Casoni's *Della magia d'amore*; Tommaso Buoni's *Problemes of Beautie and All Humane Affections*, trans. S. L. Gent. (London, 1606).

CHAPTER IV

Justice and Peace

W HATEVER character defects Artegall had when he began his quest to free Irena have been largely purged away by his self-imposed intellectual humiliation during his imprisonment. Upon his release by Britomart, he can now truly begin his mission. But even before he leaves, he must prove his newly acquired resolve by overcoming a most difficult test, a proposal to linger longer with his beloved.

> Yet could it not sterne *Artegall* retaine,
> Nor hold from suite his avowed quest,
> Which he had undertane to *Gloriane*;
> But left his love, albe her strong request,
> Faire *Britomart* in languor and unrest,
> And rode him selfe upon his first intent:
> Ne day nor night did ever idly rest;
> Ne wight but only *Talus* with him went,
> The true guide of his way and vertuous government.
>
> (V.viii.3)

Artegall's determined behavior symbolizes his emancipation from the false attractions of woman's beauty. While it is true that Britomart's victory frees him from physical bondage to Radigund, her efforts should be read as an external manifestation of his own escape from moral error. His willingness to resume his search, despite the "strong request" (later withdrawn) of Britomart, signifies this newly achieved maturity. Although Artegall is now better qualified to undertake his quest than the Salvage Knight, who fought for beauty at Satyrane's tournament, or the Solomon-Hercules, who released Sanglier with only a single strand of restraint, or the Hercules, who cannot brook the insults of Hippolyte and was "wrapt in the fetters of a golden tresse," he is never to be free of the obstacles to justice that they represent. After many false starts, Artegall is just beginning his true quest for justice. In the following cantos, Spenser has presented his hero with situations deliberately analogous to those that revealed his past failings but which now demonstrate his commitment and capabilities. These new labors Artegall shares with Arthur, the knight of magnificence, who is the cohesive element binding together all the adventures in *The Faerie Queene* since his appearances are related to the primary virtue of each book. This chapter will consider the function of Arthur in *The Faerie Queene*, especially as it is adapted to the narrative demands of Book Five. By resisting all the temptations to which he initially succumbed, Artegall can accomplish the purpose of his quest: the establishment of peace by freeing Irena from Grantorto. At the moment of his greatest success, he meets his greatest challenge and proves conclusively that he has established his own interior peace.

i

After Artegall leaves Britomart, he does not have to go far before he is forcefully reminded of the decadence of the land through which he is traveling, and he is called once again to quell injustice. This time the quest is the customary stock-in-trade of *The Faerie Queene* and all romances before and after—the damsel in distress. In the distance Artegall sees a terrified woman on a speeding horse chased by two knights, who are pursued in turn by a single knight. When the lone knight forces one of the others to give up the chase and engage in battle, Artegall himself attacks the remaining knight "to save her from her feare" and soon overthrows the recreant. Meanwhile the lone knight has disposed of the other tormentor and turns to who he thinks is the remaining enemy.

In stead of whom finding there ready prest
Sir *Artegall*, without discretion
He at him ran, with ready speare in rest:

Who seeing him come still so fiercely on,
Against him made againe. So both anon
Together met, and strongly either strooke
And broke their speares; yet neither has forgon
His horses backe, yet to and fro long shooke,
And tottred like two towres, which through a tempest
    quooke.

                        (V.viii.9)

Evenly matched, the two knights are about to continue the
battle with their swords when the damsel, seeing that the
cause of their conflict is mistaken identity, calls upon them
to stay their hands by telling them she is the "wrong'd"
maiden they have already released from her pursuers.

Whom when they heard so say, they lookt about,
To weete if it were true, as she had told;
Where when they saw their foes dead out of doubt
Eftsoones they gan their wrothfull hands to hold,
And Ventailes reare, each other to behold,
Tho when as *Artegall* did *Arthure* vew,
So faire a creature, and so wondrous bold,
He much admired both his head and hew,
And touched with intire affection, nigh him drew.

                        (V.viii.12)

Artegall asks forgiveness for raising his spear and sword
against the Briton Prince, and vows to perform whatever
penance the other requires. Similarly, Arthur sees that he
himself was equally mistaken; and since "neither is en-
damadg'd much thereby," he suggests amends may be
simply made.

So can they both them selves full eath perswade
To faire accordaunce, and both faults to shade,
Either embracing other lovingly,

And swearing faith to either on his blade,
Never thenceforth to nourish enmity.
But either others cause to maintaine mutually.
(V.viii.14.4-9)

Having reached full accord with the Briton Prince, Artegall asks details concerning the late adventure with the two outlaw knights.

Built upon two of the most rickety clichés in romance, this elaborate scene which brings Artegall and Arthur together seems to serve no purpose, since Spenser simply could have arranged for them to meet each other along the way. The meager amount of scholarly comment upon this encounter is confined to technical matters which seem to imply that it is unimportant. Osgood has seen in the description of the combatants reeling and tottering from the impact of the first onslaught (9.9) another indication that "Spenser had an eye for towers and masonry, especially when they were 'ruinous and old.' "[1] Upton started a controversy about an even more recondite point when he questioned the source of Spenser's knowledge for having Artegall and Arthur swear fealty to each other on their swords (V.viii.14.7).[2] Yet for all its neglect, this episode is most important; it shows the new development of Artegall's character and illustrates the function of Arthur in *The Faerie Queene*.

If we temporarily defer consideration of the attendant circumstances which precipitated the initial conflict between these two noble knights (the fleeing maiden, mistaken identity) and direct our attention to the imagery of the battle and its immediate aftermath, we will uncover an elaborate poetic design which embodies its own meaning. When Artegall and the unknown knight first charge with their spears, neither is able to force the other to leave his horse.

---

[1] *Variorum, Book Five*, 224.
[2] For an outline of this controversy see *Variorum, Book Five*, 225.

Instead, both break their spears; both waver; and both totter "like two towres, which through a tempest quooke" (V.viii.9.9). Spenser has carefully developed the idea that both knights are equal in skill and strength. After heeding the maiden's entreaties to cease from further battle, Artegall sees Arthur to be "so faire a creature" and asks forgiveness for his mistake, vowing to make whatever amends are required. When Arthur does likewise, the coincidence of their courteous behavior proves the equality of their chivalry. To confirm their likeness to one another, Spenser describes their "faire accordaunce," "Either embracing other lovingly, / And swearing faith to either on his blade"; then he implicates each in the other's work, as both promise "either others cause to maintaine mutually" (V.viii.14.9).

To follow his poetic logic to its proper and consistent end, it appears unmistakable that Spenser has directed his energies toward depicting an Artegall who is equal to the Briton Prince in strength, courtesy, and purpose. This vividly completes the metamorphosis of Artegall's character. Arthur, the magnificent knight, possesses all the virtues plus wisdom. Artegall, the patron of justice, also represents all the virtues, since justice was commonly understood to subsume them all,[3] and as we have already seen, he has gained wisdom through humility. In a way this confrontation is inevitable since Artegall's whole journey has been a process of gradually fulfilling the potential of his name. In Book Two, Guyon has, significantly enough, pointed out for us that at Gloriana's court Arthur would be esteemed *as much as* Artegall and Sophy, that is, justice and wisdom.

> Said *Guyon*, Noble Lord, what meed so great,
> Or grace of earthly Prince so soveraine,

---

[3] See Aristotle, *Nichomachean Ethics*, v.i.15-20; and Cicero, *De officiis*, iii.vi.28: [justitia] "haec enim una virtus omnium est domina et regina virtutum."

But by your wondrous worth and warlike feat
Ye well may hope, and easely attaine?
But were your will, her sold to entertaine,
And numbred be mongst knights of *Maydenhed*,
Great guerdon, well I wote, should you remaine,
And in her favour high be reckoned,
As *Artegall*, and *Sophy* now beene honored.

(II.ix.6)

At this place in the narrative in Book Five, Artegall has become exactly what his name signifies—*Art-egal*, Arthur's peer.

The events prior to the mistaken, but highly revealing, encounter between the two noble knights are symbolic of Arthur's province in *The Faerie Queene*. When Artegall sees the distressed maiden pursued by two paynim knights, he is presented with an example of injustice which a single knight, however strong, would have difficulty in rectifying before harm is done to the innocent. It could very possibly happen that while Artegall is engaging the one, the other could carry out Adicia's orders, of which we later learn, and the damsel would be "dishonoured and shent" (V.viii. 23.4). Arthur, however, appears at this time to obviate any such possibility. Hence, even before Artegall and Arthur formally swear "either others cause to maintaine mutually," they have already demonstrated their similarity of purpose in equally serving the cause of justice—by destroying the recreant knights, by rescuing the distraught damsel.

Arthur's appearance here is typical of his other appearances in *The Faerie Queene*: he either makes it possible for the particular knight of each book to complete his task or he specifically shares in his work. In Book One, when Arthur defeats Orgolio and descends into his dungeon to release the imprisoned Red Cross, he is the necessary physical agent leading to Red Cross's spiritual regeneration. After convalescing in the House of Holiness, Red Cross, now St. George, defeats the Dragon. The pattern in Book Two is similar, but with a slight variation. After rescuing Guyon from Pyrochles and Cymochles, Arthur goes with him to the Castle of Alma and defends her from the forces of Maleger, while Guyon, the naturally temperate man, overthrows the Bower of Bliss and captures Acrasia. The problems in Books Three and Four are of a different nature; but here, too, Arthur helps to relieve some of the burden from the titular character, Britomart, since he sets out with Guyon to save Florimell from the Foster, "breathing out beastly lust." Later in Book Three Britomart rescues Amoret from the lustful Busyrane. Book Four has Arthur succoring the terrified Amoret, unintentionally abandoned by Britomart, and then freeing Britomart herself from crippling discord, an act which enables her to continue her search for her lover (IV.ix.31-37). Book Six seems to present special problems, but Arthur's role is clearly defined in relation to its hero, Calidore, the exemplar of courtesy. Inasmuch as a requisite for a society in which courtesy is to flourish is the approval of its inhabitants, Arthur ensures this approval by defeating Disdain and Scorn (VI.viii.4-30). Only then can Calidore bind the Blatant Beast, Slander. In every Book of *The Faerie Queene* Arthur's assistance contributes measurably in differing fashion to the successful completion of each knight's quest. By enacting the primary virtue of each Book, Arthur not only sets the symbolic pattern for the particular hero to follow but also makes it physically possible for the hero to carry out his mission.[4]

---

[4] This is reinforced by the narrative sequence of each book and is most rigidly defined in those books treating the quests of the Knights of Maidenhead. In each case, Arthur performs his task before the titular hero is able to complete his mission. Arthur defeats Orgolio and Duessa's Beast (i.vii.3-24) before Red Cross meets the Dragon (i.xi.8-55); he slays Maleger (ii.xi.42-46) before Guyon binds Acrasia (ii.xii.47-83); he discomfits Scorn and Disdain (vi.viii.4-30) before Calidore binds the Blatant Beast (vi.xii.26-38).

In Book Five, however, Arthur's particular role is somewhat muted. This does not mean it is less important than in the previous books, but here Arthur has met his match in strength, courtesy, and purpose. Earlier, Arthur was clearly superior to the other Knights of Maidenhead; now he shares his glory with Artegall, his namesake. Since the episode of the two paynim knights and the mistaken encounter metaphorically and actually confirm their equality, Artegall and Arthur, strictly speaking, now undertake a dual journey in the poem. If we consider the structure of the ensuing narrative, we will discover how carefully Spenser has worked to establish thematic and actual parallels between these two knights. Together, Artegall and Arthur defeat the Soldan and Adicia, thwart Malengin, and hear the trial of Duessa at Mercilla's Palace. A situation similar to the one that first brought them together then arises which separates them: at the conclusion of Duessa's trial, word is brought to Mercilla of another worthy woman in distress, the lady Belgae. Since Artegall cannot rescue Irena (the object of his long search) and Belgae without risking the possibility that one would succumb while the other was being saved, Arthur volunteers to champion the cause of Lady Belgae. Even when Artegall and Arthur part, they follow parallel courses to achieve the end of justice—peace. The one reestablishes Irena; the other creates peace for Belgae (V.xi.18.7).

ii

Existing within this larger framework of the quest for peace is a smaller, more tightly ordered cosmos in which the drama of the former is mirrored in the latter. It is a sort of poem within a poem. Beginning with the rescue of the fleeing maiden and ending with Mercilla's judgment of Duessa, it presents once again the obstacles to justice (but in reduced scale) and is the most patently allegorical part of the entire book. The context of this world is established by Samient, the rescued damsel, when she relates the circumstances of her late predicament and tells of her services to a maiden queen, Mercilla. Although she is highly respected and honored, Mercilla unfortunately has enemies who envy her happy and prosperous reign, chief among whom is a proud, ungodly tyrant, who seeks by force or bribery to overthrow her. He is provoked day and night into such flagrant acts by his wife, Adicia, a self-professed "mortall foe/ To Justice" (V.viii.20).

> Which my liege Lady seeing, thought it best,
> With that his wife in friendly wise to deale,
> For stint of strife, and stablishment of rest
> Both to her selfe, and to her common weale,
> And all forepast displeasures to repeale.
> So me in message unto her she sent,
> To treat with her by way of enterdeale,
> Of finall peace and faire attonement,
> Which might concluded be by mutual consent.
>
> (V.viii.21)

It should be noted here that Mercilla is most conciliatory and through her emissary Samient is bending every effort to achieve "finall peace." Adicia, "disdayning all accord," violates the diplomatic code, reviles Samient, and casts her out. Her subsequent charge to the two false knights to dishonor Samient is thwarted only by the timely appearances of Artegall and Arthur.

Given such a report of tyranny and injustice, of which the Samient episode is symptomatic, Artegall and Arthur willingly undertake to defend Mercilla's kingdom. They devise a stratagem which will enable them to proceed simultaneously against both defenders, a plan in which Artegall agrees to disguise himself in the armor of one of the fallen paynim knights and to use Samient as a decoy to gain entrance to Adicia's Castle. Once Artegall is in the castle, Arthur is to appear demanding Samient's release in order to provoke the tyrant, Soldan, into battle. When the first part of the plan is successful, Arthur issues his challenge.

> Wherewith the Souldan all with furie fraught,
> Swearing and banning most blasphemously,
> Commaunded straight his armour to be brought,
> And mounting straight upon a charret hye,
> With yron wheeles and hookes arm'd dreadfully,
> And drawne of cruell steedes, which he had fed
> With flesh of men, whom through fell tyranny
> He slaughtered had, and ere they were halfe ded,
> Their bodies to his beasts for provender did spred.
>
> (V.viii.28)

This stanza shows the true extent of Soldan's depravity. Fury and blasphemy are not unexpected reactions from one so named, since the name Soldan (Souldan, Sultan) marks him as an unbeliever. Nor should we be surprised when Soldan, despising common chivalry, takes unfair advantage in battle by fighting from a chariot. The most revealing details of the battle preparations, however, are the tyrant's man-eating steeds, which provide an explicit link with the underlying structure of Book Five, put the ensuing battle in proper perspective, and unmistakably identify the tyrant's character.

These unnatural beasts are of the same breed as the Horses of Diomedes and recall the labors of Hercules, for which Spenser provides his own annotation.

Like to the *Thracian* Tyrant, who they say
Unto his horses gave his guests for meat,
Till he himselfe was made their greedie pray,
And torne in peeces by *Alcides* great.
So thought the Souldan in his follies threat,
Either the Prince in peeces to have torne

With his sharpe wheeles, in his first rages heat,
Or under his fierce horses feet have borne
And trampled downe in dust his thoughts disdained scorne.

(V.viii.31)

Mentioned by Ovid,[5] the defeat of Diomedes by Hercules
is related at length by Apollodorus[6] and Diodorus Siculus.[7]
Basically, this labor is an example of retributive justice,
with the proud tyrant being subjected to his own punish-
ments. Mignault reads Hercules' victory as a triumph over
barbarity.[8] To Bersuire it meant victory over the tyrants
of the world.[9] Arthur's assuming the role of Hercules in
combating the Soldan/Diomedes is another indication of
his compatibility with Artegall.[10]

Since Soldan is mounted high on his hooked chariot, he
enjoys an early advantage over Arthur, who has great
difficulty approaching him. After a long period of travers-
ing to and fro, in a vain effort to get close enough to use
his spear, dodging both the hooked chariot and the steel
shafts of the tyrant, Arthur uncovers his magic shield, the
shield which blinded Duessa's seven-headed beast. It has

[5] *Metamorphoses*, ix. 183-184.

[6] *The Library*, II.v.8.

[7] *Library of History*, IV.xv.3-4.

[8] Alciati, *Emblemata* (1614), p. 496: "Nono, Diomedem Regem
Thraciae crudelissimum, qui sanguine et carnibus humanis equos
alere consueverat, perdomuit, et eius exemplo ipsum suis equis dedit
pablum, quod significat, Herculem eloquentiae et sapientiae viribus
barbariem et ferocitatem ab omnibus, quas incoluerit, regionibus sub-
mouisse."

[9] *Metamorphosis Ovidiana* (Paris, 1509), folio lxix. Bersuire
expands upon this idea and reads Diomedes as the devil and Hercules
as Christ (folio lxx).

[10] Arthur as a type of Hercules is a recurring motif in *The Faerie
Queene*. When he strangled Maleger before the House of Alma, he
reenacted Hercules' battle with Antaeus (II.xi.42-46). Later in
Book Five, he defeats Geryoneo, as Hercules once defeated his father
Geryon.

a similar effect upon Soldan's horses, and they take the bits in their teeth and flee headlong over the countryside.

> As when the firie-mouthed steeds, which drew
> The Sunnes bright wayne to *Phaetons* decay,
> Soone as they did the monstrous Scorpion vew,
> With ugly craples crawling in their way,
> The dreadfull sight did them so sore affray,
> That their well knowen courses they forwent,
> And leading th'ever burning lampe astray,
> This lower world nigh all to ashes brent,
> And left their scorched path yet in the firmament.
>
> Such was the furie of these head-strong steeds,
> Soon as the infants sunlike shield they saw,
> That all obedience both to words and deeds
> They quite forgot, and scorned all former law;
> Through woods, and rocks, and mountaines they did draw
> The yron charet, and the wheeles did teare,
> And tost the Paynim, without feare or awe;
> From side to side they tost him here and there,
> Crying to them in vaine, that nould his crying heare.
>
> (V.viii.40-41)

The analogy with the fall of Phaethon is appropriate since the Soldan has also unlawfully presumed authority. With the chariot completely out of control, Soldan is thrown out, falls upon its cruel hooks, and is torn to pieces—killed like Diomedes by his own horses.

Becoming enraged when she sees Arthur's victory and thinking to avenge her husband's death, Adicia rushes furiously at Samient with knife in hand, wrongly thinking her a prisoner.

> But *Artegall* being thereof aware,
> Did stay her cruel hand, ere her raught,
> And as she did her selfe to strike prepare,
> Out of her fist the wicked weapon caught:

With that like one enfelon'd or distraught,
She forth did rome, whether her rage her bore,
With frantic passion, and with furie fraught;
And breaking forth out at a posterne dore,
Unto the wyld wood ranne, her dolours to deplore.

(V.viii.48)

Having frustrated Adicia's wrathful intent, Artegall takes arms against her hundred retainers and chases them about until he has overcome them all (V.viii.50). After their defeat, Artegall opens the gates of Adicia's Castle for Arthur's triumphant entrance.

The overthrow of Soldan and the discomfiting of Adicia are by nature two separate but equal enterprises. By implicating both knights in each action, Spenser's epigraph to Canto VIII does not differentiate between them.

> *Prince Arthur and Sir Artegall,*
> *Free Samient from feare:*
> *They slay the Soudan, drive his wife*
> *Adicia to despaire.*

The husband and wife team of Soldan and Adicia is similar to the father and daughter team of Pollente and Munera. In the latter, the father uses force to extort money from the weak and passes it on to his daughter, who in turn uses it to subvert justice and increase the strength of her father. Soldan and Adicia employ similar methods to harass Mercilla, using force or bribery as the occasion warrants (V.viii.18). The marriage of convenience between Adicia and Soldan, quite obviously, reveals similarities of temperament, as both are proud and irascible, despiteful and malicious.[11] A difference in manner of execution, however,

---

[11] Even a cursory reading of Canto VIII reveals such characterizations of Soldan and Adicia. Spenser's relentless repetition of such phrases as *proud dame, proud Souldan, fell despite, deadly hate, disdaining all accord, with furie fraught, in despight, flaming with revenge,* and *furious despight,* leaves little doubt as to his intentions.

exists between husband and wife. It is Adicia, as her name implies, who "counsels" her husband to perform the acts of injustice so dear to her heart (V.viii.20). He is in effect her physical manifestation and carries out her policies; or to put it in other terms, Adicia is theory and Soldan is practice. When Arthur fights Soldan and when Artegall scotches Adicia, they are opposing the same foe, the barbarian Soldan and the "mad bytch" Adicia differing only in sex and method of operation. The degree of success Arthur and Artegall enjoy against their respective foes is exactly proportionate to the obstacle to justice each presents. Opposed by Arthur, the barbarous tyrant falls prey to his own barbarity. Thwarted of her felonious desires by Artegall, Adicia rushes madly into the "salvage woods" where she dwells among wild beasts, her fit companions. Although from this denouement, it appears at first sight that Arthur has had the greater success, in essence, however, each has achieved what it was possible for him to achieve. An individual tyrant may be completely crushed; but in the world of *The Faerie Queene* the principle of injustice (ἀδικία) will never be completely absent, no matter how far it is exiled from the company of men.[12]

Adicia and Soldan are the embodiment of malice and despite. To anticipate my argument for a moment: there are three things which the giant Awe keeps out of Mercilla's Palace, two of which are *Malice* and *Despite* (v.ix.22.7). The other is *Guyle*, whom Artegall and Arthur will shortly meet in the person of Malengin (v.ix.arg.).

[12] At the beginning of Canto IX, Spenser draws the proper distinction between the two exploits, giving 14 lines to Artegall and Adicia, 4 lines to Arthur and Soldan.

> What Tygre, or what other salvage wight
> Is so exceeding furious and fell,
> As wrong, when it hath arm'd itself with might?
> Not fit mongst men, that doe with reason mell,
> But mongst wyld beastes and salvage woods to dwell;
> Where still the stronger doth the weake devoure,
> And they that most in boldnesse doe excell,

iii

After the utter defeat of Soldan and the banishment of Adicia, Samient persuades the two noble knights to pay a visit to her queen, Mercilla, who lives nearby. On the way to her castle, Samient tells them the countryside round-about is robbed by a "wicked villaine" called Malengin, who is so crafty, "so light of hand," and "So smooth of tongue" that he can "deceive one looking in his face." Malengin's base of operations is an inaccessible cave to which he takes his booty and to which he runs when threatened by the law.

> Through these his slights he many doth confound,
> And eke the rocke, in which he wonts to dwell,
> Is wondrous strong, and hewen farre under ground
> A dreadfull depth, how deepe no man can tell;
> But some doe say it goeth downe to hell.
> And all within, it full of wyndings is,
> And hidden wayes, that scarse an hound by smell
> Can follow out those false footsteps of his,
> Ne none can back returne, that once are gone amis.
>
> (V.ix.6)

> Are dreadded most, and feared for their powre:
> Fit for *Adicia*, there to build her wicked bowre.
>
> There let her wonne farre from resort of men,
> Where righteous *Artegall* her late exyled;
> There let her ever keepe her damned den,
> Where none may be with her lewd parts defyled,
> Nor none but beasts may be of her despoyled:
> And turn we to the noble Prince, where late
> We did him leave, after that he had foyled
> The cruel Souldan, and with dreadfull fate
> Had utterly subverted his unrighteous state.
>
> (V.ix.1-2)

Of course, Adicia, in her many forms, will turn up again in Faery Land, an inevitable concomitant of the fallen world. The most cruel forms of injustice attack Artegall when he has completed his quest—*Envie, Detraction*, and the *Blatant Beast* (v.xii.28-43).

Malengin truly is a diabolical character and certainly deserves the epithet *Guyle* given to him in the epigraph to Canto IX. From the standpoint of theme and narrative structure the last four lines of this stanza are most important. Without them Malengin is just an exceedingly clever thief and flimflam artist who happens to live in a cave. As the learned John Upton remarked over two hundred years ago, these lines are reminiscent of Ovid:[13] "Proque domo longis spelunca recessibus ingens/ Abdita, vix ipsis invenienda feris" (*Fasti* I. 555-556; Heinsius text). Compare a related description in Vergil: "Hic spelunca fuit uasto submota recessu,/ Semihominis Caci: Facies quam dira tegebat,/ Solis inaccessam radiis" (*Aen.* VIII. 193-195).[14] The Ovidian description of a vast cavern with long recesses so well hidden that wild beasts could scarcely find it and the Vergilian cave receding to unplumbed depths, inaccessible to the rays of the sun, blend happily in Spenser's imagination to frame a symbol exactly appropriate to his theme. Spenser's "imitation" exploits the resonating qualities of the mythological image and gives it point. Both the Ovidian and Vergilian passages married in Spenser's stanza describe the residence of Cacus, the clever robber who once stole two (some commentators say more) prize heifers from Hercules.[15] It is to a similar place that Artegall and Arthur are going.

Of all the exploits of Hercules none is more indicative of his ingenuity than his encounter with Cacus.[16] A repre-

[13] *Spenser's Faerie Queene*, II (London, 1758), 626.

[14] I use Meyen's text (Venice, 1576), p. 729.

[15] The Cacus-Hercules confrontation attracted poets and historiographers alike. Besides those already mentioned, see Propertius, IV.ix; Juvenal, *Sat.* v.125; Martial, v.lxv.5-6; Livy, I.vii.4-7; Solinus, I.7.

[16] I exempt, with qualifications, Hercules' journey to the Garden of the Hesperides to obtain the golden apples. The apples, say the commentators, were indicative of those virtues abounding in wise and learned men. The apples are, after all, philosophical fruit. The dif-

sentative account may be found in Dionysius of Halicarnassus.

Hercules, being commanded by Eurystheus, among other labours, to drive Geryon's cattle from Erytheis to Argos, performed the task, and having passed through many parts of Italy on his way home, came also to the neighborhood of Pallantium in the country of the Aborigines; and there . . . he let them graze, and being overcome with weariness, lay down and gave himself to sleep. Thereupon a robber of that region, named Cacus, chanced to come upon the cattle . . . and longed to possess them. But seeing Hercules lying there asleep, he imagined he could not drive them all away without being discovered. . . . So he secreted a few of them in the cave, hard by in which he lived, dragging each of them thither by the tail backwards. This might have destroyed all evidence of this theft, as the direction in which the oxen had gone would be at variance with their tracks. . . . And while Hercules was puzzled to know how he should act in the matter, he hit upon the expedient of driving the rest of the cattle to the cave. And thus when those inside heard the lowing . . . they bellowed to them in turn and thus their lowing betrayed the theft. Cacus, therefore, when his thievery was thus brought to light, put himself upon his defense. . . . But Hercules killed him by smiting him with his club, and when he saw the place was well adapted to the harbouring of evildoers, he demolished the cave, burying it under its ruins.[17]

The detail about the theft of the heifers that first caught the eyes of the commentators on Vergil, Ovid, and Pro-

ference between the gathering of the apples and the killing of Cacus is the difference between wisdom and cleverness.

[17] *Roman Antiquities*, I.xxxix.

pertius and held their attention longest was the adroit manner in which Cacus planned to deceive Hercules. Everyone knew Cacus was a thief—that is in every text. But the manner in which the cattle were stolen indicated to the glossators that here indeed was an extraordinarily subtle thief, a master of fraud.[18] Bersuire, of course, saw here the work of that archdeceiver, Satan.[19] Germain Vaillant de Guélis, who had Ronsard's help in compiling his edition of Vergil, remarks simply that Cacus is deceit and his winding cave is a symbol of irremediable error.[20]

Spenser's characterization of Malengin and his account of his behavior are deliberately reminiscent of Cacus. In terms of the structure of Book Five this is not unexpected and it fits nicely into the theme of justice because Artegall succumbed earlier to guile when he agreed to battle Radigund on her own terms.[21] Here he faces the most highly refined practitioner of the devilish art, Malengin himself. Where Hercules previously succeeded singly, can two now fail?

Upon reaching Malengin's cave, Artegall and Arthur decide upon a ruse to draw the villain up out of its impenetrable depths. Samient, as before, is to be the decoy and is to stand near the cave and attract Malengin's attention by "Wayling, and raysing pittiful uprore,/ As if she did some great calamitie deplore" (V.ix.8.8-9). Drawn by the cries which attract him from his lair, Malengin appears

---

[18] I pass over in silence those few literal commentators who question the veracity of the story, either doubting whether a strong adult could drag a full grown heifer backwards the necessary distance to the cave or doubting whether an animal so treated would remain quiet and not awaken the sleeping Hercules.

[19] *Metamorphosis Ovidiana*, folio lxx. verso.

[20] *Aen.* viii.185ff. (*Opera* [Antwerp, 1575], p. 408). See also Paul Marsi's edn. of Ovid's *Fasti* (Venice, 1502), folio xxii; and Volscus' commentaries in Propertius' *Elegiae* (Venice, 1488), sig. K.iii.verso.

[21] "*Artegall fights with Radigund/ And is subdued by guile*" (v.-v.arg.).

in hideous aspect: almost the *semihominis Caci facies* of Vergil's text (V.ix.10). The necessary equipment of his trade is suggestive of his diabolical character.

> And in his hand an huge long staffe he held,
> Whose top was arm'd with many an yron hooke,
> Fit to catch hold of all that he could weld,
> Or in the compasse of his clouches took;
> And ever round about he cast his looke.
> Als at his backe a great wyde net he bore,
> With which he seldome fished at the brooke,
> But usd to fish for fooles on the dry shore,
> Of which he in faire weather wont to take great store.
>
> (V.ix.11)

Unlike Jesus, who teaches Simon and Andrew to be fishers of men in order to save men's souls (Mark i.17-18), Malengin fishes for "fooles" in order to imprison them in his cave, which "some do say, it goeth downe to hell" (V.ix. 6.5). Malengin diverts Samient's attention "with guilefull words"[22] and amuses her with feats of "legierdemayne."

> To which whilest she lent her inventive mind,
> He suddenly his net upon her threw,
> That oversprad her like a puffe of wind;
> And snatching her soone up, ere well she knew,
> Ran with her fast away unto his mew,
> Crying for helpe aloud. But when as ny
> He came unto his cave, and there did vew
> The armed knights stopping his passage by,
> He threw his burden downe, and fast away did fly.
>
> (V.ix.14)

Guyle has been trapped by guile.

Theoretically without hope of escape since he cannot return, Malengin immediately drops his intended prey and

---

[22] This was a common interpretation of a pertinent line from Propertius: [Cacus] "per tria partitos qui dabat ora sonos" (IV.ix.10).

dashes madly away, "leaping from hill to hill,/ And daunceing on the craggy cliffes at will" (V.ix.15.4-5). There is no reason for either Artegall or Arthur to dispatch Malengin personally since they have already frustrated his devilish designs by cutting him off from his base of operations, that inaccessible labyrinth from which no visitor returns, a bewildering maze whose sinuous windings suggest the deviousness of its landlord—Guyle. Talus, who is "swift as a swallow," follows Malengin so closely he is forced to abandon the mountain tops and return to the plain. In a final effort to escape the implacable pursuit of Talus, Malengin uses his fiendish skills to change himself into other shapes.

> Into a Foxe himselfe he first did tourne;
> But he him hunted like a Foxe full fast:
> Then to a bush himselfe he did transforme,
> But he the bush did beat, till at last
> Into a bird it chaung'd, and from him past,
> Flying from tree to tree, from wand to wand:
> But he then stones at it so long did cast,
> That like a stone it fell upon the land,
> But then he tooke it up, and held fast in his hand.
>
> (V.ix.17)

Given to Artegall, Malengin changes himself into an "Hedgehogge," pricking his hand and forcing him to relax his grip. He resumes his natural shape and runs away again; but Talus soon brings him back.

> But when as he would to a snake againe
> Have turn'd himselfe, he with his yron flayle
> Gan drive at him, with so huge might and maine,
> That all his bones, as small as sandy grayle
> He broke, and did his bowels disentrayle;
> Crying in vaine for helpe, when helpe was past.[23]

---

[23] Compare Livy's description of Cacus' death: "ictus clava fidem pastorum nequicquam invocans, morte occubuit" (*Hist.* i.vii).

So did deceipt the selfe deceiver fayle,
There they him left a carrion outcast;
For beasts and foules to feed upon for their repast.

(V.ix.19)

Despite all his machinations, Malengin loses his life, crushed by a club, as Cacus also perished.[24]

The description of Malengin and his elaborate metamorphoses may well be reminiscent of the Irish rebels,[25] although the details which critics have used to support this identification could very well apply to any clever robber or cozener.[26] Whether or not Malengin represents the Desmond rebels is of secondary importance to the major theme of the poem. The most original of Malengin's fiendish devices, however, his "wyde net" and his cave that "none can backe returne, that once are gone amis," are the most revealing details of his character.[27] They are both necessary for his successful deceptions, in which the Samient episode

---

[24] With the exception of Vergil, who votes for strangulation, Ovid, Propertius, Livy, and Dionysius favor the club.

[25] Quoted in *Variorum, Book Five*, 233. See Padelford, *ibid.*, 279; Upton, *Spenser's Faerie Queene*, II, 635.

[26] Terms like *wylie wit, crafty, light of hand, smooth of tongue, hollow eyes, uncouth vestment,* and *subtle.* See the description of Maleger's men (II.ix.13).

[27] It has been noted that some of the Irish insurgents lived in caves. This is a fact which proves nothing, since caves are the favorite hiding places of all sorts of thieves in literature—witness Cacus or Ali Baba's friends. Or for that matter see *The Faerie Queene*: the *Brigants* who steal Pastorella live in caves (VI.xi.43.1); Maleger's men are cave dwellers (II.ix.13.3). But these caves are undifferentiated, unlike Malengin's, or Errour's den, or Mammon's, or Night's, or Merlin's, or Proteus', or Malbecco's, or Lust's, or Adonis'—all singularly described, and all in *The Faerie Queene*. One wonders, perhaps unjustly, why Spenser, after spending so much time in describing the character and habitat of Malengin, carefully omitted a confirming hint if he wanted to make a definite historical identification. After all, he does go so far as to name Belgae, when her identity could not have been mistaken if she were named Griselda.

is a case in point. Although Samient is a trusted and qualified emissary of Mercilla and is her dedicated servant who
knows all about Malengin's devilish tricks, his depreda-
tions, and his labyrinthine home, she also succumbs to his
wiles and would have been added to the ranks of others
similarly deceived had not Artegall and Arthur arranged to
spoil his plans. Samient's capture, occasioned by impru-
dence, shows that even those thoughtfully forewarned may
become the prey of guile.[28] In *The Faerie Queene* Malengin is of the same family as Archimago and Dolon.[29] When
Malengin transforms himself into five different shapes,
proceeding from fox to serpent,[30] he fully reveals his
diabolical nature, so patently shadowed by his hellish cave
and net for fools.[31] As practiced by Malengin, guile subtly
undermines the foundations of society, disrupting justice
by diverting citizens from their proper tasks; but through
prudence, the prescribed antidote for guile, Artegall and
Arthur defeat Malengin.

iv

With Samient at their side extolling the virtues of her

[28] More precisely, a lack of prudence or practical foresight, since
she knows what to expect but does not prepare accordingly. The
distinction is made by Thomas Aquinas: "As stated above (ii.ii.Q.-
55.a.3-5) the vice directly opposed to prudence is cunning, to which
it belongs to discover ways of achieving a purpose, by guile in words,
and by fraud in deeds: and it stands in relation to prudence, as
guile and fraud to simplicity" (*Summa Theologica*, ii.ii.Q.111.a.
3-4).

[29] There is but a difference in degree between the δόλος who
seduces Britomart from the way and the Malengin [Dolus] who nets
Samient.

[30] This final mutation is not actually achieved, only attempted; for
when "as he would to a snake again/ Have turn'd himself," his
physical body is destroyed by Talus.

[31] In this context, we should recall that Milton's Satan also undergoes five metamorphoses, descending the Chain of Being from wolf
to serpent.

gracious queen, Artegall and Arthur continue on their way
to Mercilla's Palace, an impressive and stately structure
which well represents the virtues of its mistress. Its high
towers are dazzlingly bright.

And all their tops bright glistering with gold
That seemed to outshine the dimmed skye,
And with their brightnesse daz'd the straunge beholders
    eye.   (V.ix.21.7-9)

This external magnificence is equalled by the splendor of
the court itself, as Spenser makes Mercilla's throne of gold
"full bright sheene." The throne matches the cloth of state,

                bordred with bright sunny beams,
Glistring like gold, amongst the plights enrold,
And here and there shooting forth silver streames,
Mongst which crept litle Angels through the glittering
    gleames.   (V.ix.28.6-9)

Hamilton has shown us some of the important distinctions
Spenser makes in using light imagery, carefully marking
the true from the illusory. The light in Mercilla's Palace
is unequivocally true to its divine origins. Justice and mercy
are gifts of heaven; and Mercilla's Palace is the gentle bond
—reflecting in radiant glory the true source of peace. The
swearing of truth upon the Bible at any trial is formal confirmation of this relationship. Following Augustine, Thomas
Aquinas says the natural law was made known by an impression of divine light.

> The light of natural reason whereby we discern what
> is good and evil, which is the function of the natural
> law, is nothing else than an imprint on us of Divine
> Light. It is therefore evident that the natural law is
> nothing else than the rational creature's participation
> of the eternal law (*Summa Theologica*, I.ii.Q.9.a.2).

The image of light as justice also dominates the action

in Mercilla's Court and even manifests itself in the newly arrived justiciars. The throng of petitioners seeking justice through which Artegall and Arthur press cease clamoring and look at them, "all in armour bright as day,/ Straunge there to see, it did them much amaze,/ And with unwonted terror halfe affray" (V.ix.24.2-4).

Access to Mercilla's Court must be by ready and easy way. While her gates are never closed, they are guarded perpetually by the watchman, Awe.

> There they alighting, by that Damzel were
> Directed in, and shewed all the sight:
> Whose porch, that most magnificke did appeare,
> Stood open wyde to all men day and night;
> Yet warded well by one of mickle might,
> That sat thereby, with gyantlike resemblance,
> To keepe out guyle, and malice, and despight,
> That under shew oftimes of fayned semblance,
> Are wont in Princes courts to worke great
>   scathe and hindrance.
>
> His name was *Awe*; by whom they passing in
> Went up the hall, that was a large wyde roome,
> And full of people making troublous din,
> And wondrous noyse, as if that there were some,
> Which unto them was dealing righteous doome.
> By whom they passing, through the thickest preasse,
> The marshall of the hall to them did come;
> His name hight *Order*, who commaunding peace,
> Them guyded through the throng, that did their
>   clamors ceasse.   (V.ix.22-23)

It is revealing that the three *hindrances* to justice against which Awe guards Mercilla's porch—*guyle*, *malice*, and *despight*—are exactly the same three that Artegall and Arthur have just overcome. In defeating Soldan and Adicia, they turned back malice and despite, and the crushing of Malengin is self-evidently the crushing of guile. In the logic of the poem, Artegall and Arthur have earned their admission to Mercilla's Court, a world quite different from the World of Faery. It is a completely allegorical world, peopled with abstractions like Awe, Order, Zele, Reverence, Authority, Kingdomes Care, and Religion.

This new world is not the product of abrupt change but is the inevitable result of a process which began when Samient first rode across Artegall's field of vision pursued by two paynim knights. The bridge from Faery Land to Mercilla's Court is a brilliantly executed poetic transition. As Artegall and Arthur fight their way to her court, they gradually retreat from Faery Land proper, a retreat paralleled by similar changes in the kinds of adversaries they meet. From their first encounter with the "realistic" paynim knights, to their next with the symbiotic marriage of a tyrant and injustice, and finally with the personification of devilish guile in Malengin, Artegall and Arthur have been nudged closer and closer, both physically and metaphorically, to Mercilla's world of the concrete abstract—to a personified theory of justice.[32]

The giant Awe helps establish the tone of Mercilla's Palace, inspiring the reverential fear and respect so essential for the flourishing of justice. Calvin writes, "The first dutie of subjects toward their magistrates is, to thinke most honorably of their office, namely which they acknowledge to be a jurisdiction committed of God, and therefore to esteeme them and reverence them as the ministers and deputies of God."[33] Spenser thinks respect for authority is

[32] Mercilla's indifferent handling of justice serves as an object lesson for Artegall and Arthur, and Spenser's lavish description of her indicates her true place. Although she is seated on a throne, Spenser describes her and her court in celestial terms—cloth of gold, glittering gleames, angel-like (v.ix.28-29). As such she serves as a reincarnation of the late-departed Astraea.

[33] *Institutes* (London, 1592), p. 504 [iv.xx.22]; Thomas Aquinas is of similar mind (*Summa Theologica*, i.ii.Q.103).

so necessary for the execution of justice that he provides a moral example in the punishment of Malfont. Whether Malfont is Ulpian Fulwell or someone else from the squad of sour rhymers who heaped paper slanders upon fair Elizabeth is thankfully beyond investigation. Queen Elizabeth obviously had sensitive ears, and the successive statutes against libels and slanders enacted during her reign testify to their acuity. Spenser's contemporary readers probably had their favorite candidates for Malfont—but the more important issue in this episode is what he did rather than who he was. Malfont is disrespectful of Mercilla's godly office and his just punishment serves as a painful reminder of the giant Awe's swift retribution.

That order, peace, and justice are combined harmoniously is made exceptionally clear in the description of Mercilla on her throne. Her cloud-like cloth of state reminds us again that justice has its origin in heaven.

> All over her a cloth of state was spred,
> Not of rich tissew, nor of cloth of gold,
> Nor of ought else, that may be richest red,
> But like a cloud, as likest may be told,
> That her brode spreading wings did wyde unfold;
> Whose skirts were bordred with bright sunny beams,
> Glistring like gold, amongst the plights enrold,
> And here and there shooting forth silver streames,
> Mongst which crept litle Angels through the
>   glittering gleames.
>
> Seemed those litle Angels did uphold
> The cloth of state, and on their purpled wings
> Did beare the pendants, through their nimblesse bold:
> Besides a thousand more of such, as sings
> Hymnes to high God, and carols heavenly things,
> Encompassed the throne, on which she sate.
>   (V.ix.28-29.1-6)

Justice not only derives from heaven, but insofar as justice entails order it imitates the order that is in heaven, symbolized by the harmony of the spheres. In the Prologue to Book Five Spenser tells us that the celestial spheres fell out of harmony after man fell out of harmony with himself by sinning. The cloth of state suggests that when justice is dealt heavenly harmony is restored. Spenser was well aware that heavenly harmony is a natural symbol for the harmony that results from justice. The Oxford Aristotelian John Case, in his *Sphaera Civitatis* (1588), a Latin work based on the *Politics*, has as a frontispiece an astrological chart in which the heavenly spheres, each assigned a particular moral virtue, move around immovable justice (*justitia immobilis*) and the Astraea-like figure of Elizabeth presides over them all. The accompanying dedicatory poem addresses Elizabeth as the first mover, *tu mobile primum*.[34] In this scheme the magistrate is justice personified and the effect of her justice is harmony, a harmony Mercilla recreates both symbolically and actually.

Spenser's Mercilla is much more than a personification of justice. Around her throne sit allegorical figures, three of whom embody the ultimate perfections of justice.

> And round about, before her feet there sate
> A bevie of faire Virgins clad in white,
> That goodly seem'd t'adorne her royall state,
> All lovely daughters of high *Jove*, that hight
> *Litae*, by him begot in loves delight,
> Upon the righteous *Themis*: those they say
> Upon Joves Judgement seat wayt day and night,
> And when in wrath he threats the worlds decay,
> They doe his anger calme, and cruell vengeance stay.
>
> They also doe by his divine permission

[34] Fowler reproduces both the chart and poem in *Spenser and the Numbers of Time* and expands upon Frances Yates' discussion of Elizabeth as Astraea (pp. 196-200).

Upon the thrones of mortall Princes tend,
And often treat for pardon and remission
To suppliants, through frayltie which offend.
Those did upon *Mercillaes* throne attend:
Just *Dice*, wise *Eunomie*, myld *Eirene*,
And them amongst, her glorie to commend,
Sate goodly *Temperance* in garments clene,
And sacred *Reverence*, yborne of heavenly strene.

(V.ix.31-32)

Just as the dance of the Graces on Mount Acidale symbolically enacts the reciprocal pattern of virtuous love so
these three handmaidens of Mercilla prefigure the cooperative ends of justice. Each performs a different duty for
Mercilla and each fulfills the potential of her name—"just
judgment," "wise good law," and "mild peace." As we
have suggested, Artegall needs to establish justice internally before he performs adequately within the external
order of society—actions which ultimately lead to the harmonious order of peace. The three handmaids of Mercilla
form a hierarchy of justice, a hierarchy partially established
by Aristotle and completed by Renaissance Neoplatonic
jurists.

Sir Thomas Elyot keeps closely to the simple Aristotelian categories of justice in his *Governor*.

> Justice although it be but one entire virtue, yet is it
> described in two kinds or species. The one is named
> justice distributive, which is in distribution of honour,
> money, benefit, or other thing semblable; the other is
> called commutative or by exchange, and of Aristotle it
> is named in Greek *diorthotice*, which is in English cor
> rective. . . . Justice distributive hath regard to the per
> son; justice commutative hath no regard to the per
> son, but only considering the inequality whereby the
> one thing exceedeth the other, endeavoureth to bring
> them both to an equality. (III.i)

Commutative justice operates by arithmetical proportion,[35] and distributive justice by geometrical.[36] The former proper to the civil court is *just Dice*, the latter which distributes public goods, *wise Eunomie*. *Myld Eirene* flourished—in theory if not in practice—as the third part of justice in the Renaissance. Spenser makes peace the ultimate goal of justice in Book Five, and Renaissance political theorists never tired of making true justice, peace, the ultimate goal of government. In the last chapter of his *République*, Jean Bodin discusses peace and its implications, listing *eirene* appropriately enough with the other two allegorical daughters of Jove and Themis: "And it seemeth the antient Greekes in their fables, to have aptly shadowed forth unto us that which wee have spoken of these three kinds of Justice, giving unto *Themis* three daughters, *viz.* εὐνομία [*eunomia*], ἐπιείκεια [*epieikia*], εἰρήνη [*eirene*]; that is to say, Upright Law, Equitie, and Peace."[37] The three kinds of justice are not to Bodin any more than they are to Spenser equal aspects of the same virtue. They are on different levels, where the higher level encompasses the lower. *Eunomia, epieikia,* and *eirene,* Bodin explains, "are referred unto the three formes of Justice, Arithmeticall, Geometricall, and Harmonicall: howbeit that peace which shadoweth forth Harmonicall Justice, is the onely scope and summe of all the lawes and judgements as also of the true Royall government: so as is Harmonicall Justice the end both of Arithmeticall and Geometricall government also."[38] Bodin explains that just as the line contains the point and the surface contains the line, so geometrical justice contains arithmetical and harmonical justice contains geometrical.

[35] *Nichomachean Ethics*, v.iv. See also Aquinas, *Summa Theologica* II.ii.Q.61.aa.1-3.

[36] *Nichomachean Ethics*, v.iii. And Aquinas' *Commentary*, v.L.vi.

[37] *Six Bookes of a Commonweal* (1606), p. 792 [vi.vi].

[38] *Ibid.*

Since Mercilla is the embodiment of this harmonical justice, the two knights, conducted "by degree" to her throne, bow and give her their "myld obeysance." When she sees these two strange knights pay such homage to her, Mercilla, who had been dispensing justice "with indifferent grace" to all classes of society before their arrival, favors them by tempering her "Majestie and awe." Immediately pending is an important trial and the proceedings are temporarily stopped until Arthur and Artegall can be seated.

> But after all her princely entertayne,
> To th'hearing of that former cause in hand
> Her selfe eftsoones she gan convert againe;
> Which that those knights likewise mote understand,
> And witnesse forth aright in forrain land,
> Taking them up unto her stately throne,
> Where they mote heare the matter throughly scand
> On either part, she placed th'one on th'one,
> The other on the other side, and neare them none.
>   (V.ix.37)

It is quite clear that Artegall and Arthur are to be instructed in the niceties of the law, as Mercilla invites them to view the proceedings that they "mote understand,/ And witnesse forth aright in forrain land" (V.ix.37.4-5). The "forrain land" is the world of the reader and simultaneously Faery Land, from whence these knights have journeyed. Mercilla's "witnesse forth aright" indicates that she expects her guests to practice in their native land the principles of justice that they observe at her court. Once again, Spenser's grouping of the two knights at Mercilla's side confirms the complete equality of Artegall and Arthur (V.ix.37.8-9).[39]

Consonant with the change in allegorical technique, the trial itself is completely stylized. Yet for all its machinery,

---

[39] In this connection, it is significant that Spenser scrupulously avoids assigning to either knight the prestigious right side.

it strictly follows normal legal procedure: arraignment, presenting of charges, prosecution, and defense.[40] The defendant appearing at this bar of justice is a woman of "rare beautie." Although her vile and base condition has blotted her honor and defaced her titles of nobility, her "wretched semblant" has attracted the sympathies of the people (V.ix. 38). Against her, the prosecuting attorney, Zele, has carefully prepared his charge.

> First gan he tell, how this that seem'd so faire
> And royally arayd, *Duessa* hight
> That false *Duessa*, which had wrought great care,
> And mickle mischiefe unto many a knight,
> By her beguyled, and confounded quight:
> But not for those she now in question came,
> Though also those mote question'd be aright,
> But for vyld treasons, and outrageous shame,
> Which she against the dred *Mercilla* oft did frame.
>
> (V.ix.40)[41]

Rightly sensing that Duessa's defense will be based upon emotional appeals rather than upon facts, Zele refers to the distress brought to other knights beguiled by her appearance, while at the same time distinguishing this general analysis of her character from the specific charges against her—"treasons" against Mercilla. To prosecute his charge, he summons an impressive company of qualified witnesses: *Kingdomes Care, Authority, Law of Nations, Religion,* and lastly *Justice.*

[40] And, of course, verdict. Duessa's trial conforms in its essential pattern to that summarized by Thomas Smith, *De Republica Anglorum,* Book II.23.

[41] In a poetic aside (ix.41-42), Spenser reminds his readers about Duessa's past treacheries that were thwarted by "heavens grace" which guards just monarchs from treason. This anticipates the final disposition of her case.

The roles of the prosecutor Zele and the host of allegorical figures who speak out for the punishment or dismissal of Duessa are easily identifiable. What is important is how Mercilla makes her final judgment because it is here that Spenser shows us the place of mercy in the execution of justice. In the beginning of Canto X Spenser asks whether mercy is actually a part of justice (V.x.1) because he knows that strictly speaking it is not—it belongs to another cardinal virtue, temperance.[42] As a part of temperance, mercy is an aspect of the virtue by which the magistrate first establishes inner harmony before he can promote order in society. There are two kinds of mercy, however, which the moralists call clemency and meekness. Clemency moderates the external punishment while meekness only diminishes the passion of anger; this is the true meaning of Artegall's "humblesse meeke" in Isis Church.[43]

By observing Mercilla's behavior, we are now able to understand the full significance of Britomart's dream in Isis Church. As Britomart is happily doing sacrifice to Isis in her dream, a hideous tempest rises throughout the

---

[42] Aquinas, *Summa Theologica*, II.ii.Q.157.a.3; Cicero, *De Inventione* II.liv. Miss Tuve writes "Misericordia became not occasionally but commonly and properly one of the faces of justice" (*Allegorical Imagery* [Princeton, 1966], p. 67); that is precisely why Spenser asks the question. As he so often does at critical places in the text, Spenser provides his own poetic documentation to point the meaning. He has already shown the relationship of mercy to temperance by having "goodly *Temperance*" and "sacred *Reverence*" commend Mercilla's glory (V.ix.32.7-9). When at the beginning of Canto X he asks whether mercy is part of justice, Spenser is neither avoiding the question as Professor Nelson thinks (*Poetry of Spenser*, p. 267) nor is he setting "aside the abstraction of clerks" as Miss Williams writes (*Spenser's World of Glass*, p. 177). Rather, since he has already demonstrated the exact relationship of mercy to justice through temperance in Mercilla's just action, he now slyly apprises the reader of its true effect.

[43] Aquinas, *Summa Theologica*, II.ii.Q.67.a.4.

temple, fanning the embers of the altar into "outrageous flames" which threaten to consume everything.

> With that the Crocodile, which sleeping lay
> Under the Idols feete in feareless bowre,
> Seem'd to awake in horrible dismay,
> As being troubled with that stormy stowre;
> And gaping greedy wide, did streight devoure
> Both flames and tempest: with which growen great,
> And swolne with pride of his owne peerelesse powre,
> He gan to threaten her likewise to eat;
> But that the Goddesse with her rod him backe did beat.
>
> Tho turning all his pride to humblesse meeke,
> Him selfe before her feete he lowly threw,
> And gan for grace and love of her to seeke.
>
> (V.vii.15-16.1-3)

Miss Williams seems to think these lines show Artegall's character (the Crocodile) in a pejorative light—that he either fights or fawns, is all pride or "humblesse meeke." Such an interpretation is extremely misleading. In the episode in Isis Church, Spenser not only affirms the true love between Artegall and Britomart, he also presents the true relationship between justice and equity.

Despite her splendid palace and throngs of worshipful admirers, Mercilla naturally displays the salient traits of humility and meekness because any justiciar who has not wrapped the mantle of humility and meekness about himself and his office will be unable to dispense justice fairly. That a judge should not be proud but humble in the performance of his duties is rather obvious and should not require further comment. Usage, however, has eroded the original meaning of meekness from the true aspects of gentleness and mildness. But in the Renaissance, the philosophers, theologians, and poets—at least—knew Aristotle's observation that meekness was the antidote for anger, the mean mitigating its effect.[44] Moses, the first lawgiver, "was very meeke, above all the men which were upon the face of the earth" (Numbers xii.3). Henry Ainsworth reads this verse through Aristotelian eyes when he writes that meekness "is a virtue which keepeth a measure in anger, and avenging of ourselves when we are offended."[45] At the beginning of Book Five, Artegall is proud and wrathful and an unfit justiciar. In captivity, in Britomart's dream, and before Mercilla, Artegall is humble and meek. He learns, as does Arthur, the true exercise of mercy from its chief embodiment upon earth, Mercilla. Instructed by Astraea, taught by bitter experience, confirmed in love for Britomart, and illumined by Mercilla, Artegall becomes an exemplary justiciar. At the end of his quest, Artegall is milder than the "mildest man alive" (V.xii.42.3), the living, breathing law and true reflection of the divine.

The magistrate cannot always diminish punishment but must always suppress wrath, which is the moral meaning of the lion beneath Mercilla's throne. In this way mercy is reconciled with judicial severity. Such is the case with Mercilla's judgment of Duessa. The judge cannot pass judgment always in favor of the criminal because his first consideration must always be the common good (V.ix.44. 7-8).

Confronted with such strong witnesses giving evidence against her, Duessa defends herself with touching appeals —exactly as Zele had anticipated. Her parade of supporters include *Pittie, Regard of Womanhead, Daunger, Nobilitie of Birth*; and lastly "*Griefe* did pleade, and many teares forth powre" (V.ix.45.9).

> With the neare touch whereof in tender hart
> The Briton Prince was sore empassionate,

[44] *Nichomachean Ethics*, iv.v.

[45] *Annotations upon the Five Bookes of Moses* (London, 1639), p. 74.

And woxe inclined much unto her part,
Through the sad terror of so dreadfull fate,
And wretched ruine of so high estate.

$$(V.ix.45.1-5)$$

It is not the arguments of the different advocates that move Mercilla's decision, however much they move Arthur and Artegall. In the trial Spenser balances five reasons against Duessa and five in her favor (V.ix.43-45). *Pittie* pleads against *Kingdomes Care; Regard of Womanhead* against *Authority*. While Duessa's punishment is demanded by positive international law, the jurists' *jus gentium* ("law of *Nations*," V.ix.44.3), the demands of practical international politics urge her release: "And then came *Daunger* threatning hidden dread,/ And high alliance unto forren powre" (V.ix.45.5-6). Contrasting with the appeal of the common people against Duessa is the appeal to her noble birth. Lastly, *Griefe* pleads against *Justice*. Spenser tells us that only Arthur is moved by the arguments in her behalf since he does not see that the arguments in her defense are balanced by equal, if not stronger, arguments against her. Spenser does not intend us to assume, however, that just because Artegall makes the correct decision about Duessa he is any more perfect in justice than Arthur. On the contrary, we have the suggestion that just as Arthur one-sidedly inclines to the part of the would-be pardoners of Duessa, Artegall one-sidedly turns his heart away. When Spenser describes Artegall's position with the phrase, "zeale of Justice" (V.ix.49.5), he associates him with the prosecutor Zele, who is determined, as a prosecutor must be, to have Duessa punished no matter what the others say: "But *Artegall* with constant firme intent,/ for zeale of Justice was against her bent" (V.ix.49.4-5).

Unlike Arthur who is moved by emotional appeals, and unlike Artegall who has pre-determined Duessa's guilt, Mercilla condemns Duessa only after it is clear to her that

Duessa has condemned herself. Ate's appearance as a witness allows Duessa to incriminate herself.

> [Zele] brought forth that old hag of hellish hew,
> The cursed *Ate*, brought her face to face,
> Who privie was, and partie in the case:
> She, glad of spoyle and ruinous decay,
> Did her appeach, and to her more disgrace,
> The plot of all her practise did display,
> And all her traynes, and all her treasons forth did lay.
>
> (V.ix.47.3-9)

Ate, Spenser has told us, is the enemy of mercy and concord, "So much her malice did her might surpas" (IV.i. 30). As the enemy of mercy and concord, Ate rejects both justice and the goal of justice. Ate, the mother of discord, has power on earth because Duessa knowingly and wilfully raised her up from hell:

> Her false *Duessa* who full well did know,
> To be most fit to trouble noble knights,
> Which hunt for honor, raised from below,
> Out of the dwellings of the damned sprights,
> Where she in darkness wastes her cursed daies and nights.
>
> (IV.i.19.5-9)

In the Mercilla episode Ate shows the nature of Duessa's guilt, but her person as described by Spenser in Canto I of Book Four makes it equally clear that Duessa's actions in wilful confederacy with Ate have involved the destruction of justice and order. The catalogue of Duessa's other sins is only anticlimactic, for Duessa has already put herself outside the scope of mercy. Mercilla has no choice but to condemn Duessa. She cannot mitigate the punishment, which is to exercise that part of mercy called clemency. The greatest mercy she can show is through the virtue of meekness, or the suppression of wrath. That this is the meaning of Mercilla's judgment and the tears she sheds (V.ix.50.

6-9) is obvious from the beginning of Canto X when Arthur and Artegall praise her mercy.[46]

> Much more it praysed was of those two knights;
> The noble Prince, and righteous *Artegall*,
> When they had seene and heard her doome a rights
> Against *Duessa*, damned by them all;
> But by her tempred without griefe or gall,
> Till strong constraint did her thereto enforce.
> And yet even then ruing her wilfull fall,
> With more then needfull naturall remorse,
> And yeelding the last honour to her wretched corse.
>
> (V.x.4)

Having learned from Mercilla the true goal of justice, Arthur and Artegall are prepared to continue their quests.

v

Immediately after the just disposition of Duessa's case, Mercilla hears a petition of a different kind from two young men seeking aid for their widowed mother, Belgae, whose land has been invaded by a strong tyrant. Belgae was formerly a lady of great worth and wealth, blessed with the fruitful heritage of seventeen sons. The son of Geryon, whom Hercules overthrew, offered himself to her service after her husband's death. But as soon as Belgae commits her sovereign power to his hands, the tyrant, Geryoneo, sets up an image of his father as the new religion and gives her children one by one to a "dreadfull Monster to devoure" (V.x.13.7). Left without means, Belgae has no recourse but to ask Mercilla for help. Since Artegall already is burdened with the quest to free Irena and since

---

[46] Miss Tuve is correct when she writes encompassing mercy is beyond the scope of Mercilla—that, after all, is God's work. Yet it is a mistake to imply Mercilla's tears are useless. Her gentle weeping is a deliberate act ("let instead thereof to fall/ Few perling drops") and indicates she is not vengeful.

no other knight present at the court volunteers to bring relief to Belgae, Prince Arthur steps forward and requests Mercilla to "graunt him that adventure" (V.x.15.9), and she immediately assents. Early the next morning, Artegall and Arthur part, each to pursue his Herculean task—the establishment of peace. Their ways are now separate but parallel; their destinies different but related. The freeing of Belgae is but an aspect of the freeing of Irena.[47]

Leaving Mercilla's Court, Artegall "streight way went/ On his first quest, the which him forth did call" (V.xi.36.2-3). The emphatic language indicating the renewal of his quest deliberately recalls Britomart's conversion (V.vii. 24.6-9), and shows Artegall is indeed ready for the task ahead. His former winding way has become a straight course to Irena, leading from the shadows of indecision to the light of commitment. Before he comes to his destination, he meets Sir Sergis, a knight "well-shot in years" who formerly was Irena's champion, from whom Artegall naturally asks of Irena's present state.

> To whom he thus; She liveth sure and sound;
> For by that Tyrant is in wretched thraldome bound.
>
> For she presuming on th'appointed tyde,
> In which ye promist, as ye were a Knight,
> To meete her at the salvage Ilands syde,
> And then and there for triall of her right
> With her unrighteous enemy to fight,

---

[47] Arthur continues the Hercules pattern when he fights with Geryon's son. After defeating Geryoneo, the temporal force suppressing Belgae, Arthur undertakes to root out the blasphemous, sphinx-like monster which remains to corrupt the populace. As Hamilton has noticed, this furious battle is similar to Red Cross' battle with Errour, a similarity which is deliberate.

In political terms Arthur, having disposed of temporal and ecclesiastical power, now must expunge the heretical, soul-destroying errors persisting. Arthur's goals are similar to Artegall's since Belgae desires him to establish "my peace" (v.xi.18.7).

Did thither come, where she afrayd of nought,
By guilefull treason and by subtill slight
Surprized was, and to *Grantorto* brought,
Who her imprisond hath, and her life often sought.

And now he hath to her prefixt a day,
By which if that no champion doe appeare,
Which will her cause in battailous array
Against him justifie, and prove her cleare
Of all those crimes, that he against her doth reare,
She death shall by.

(V.xi.38-40.1-6)

As the shades of Artegall's former defections return to haunt him, he now realizes that his wayward behavior is largely the cause of Irena's present woe. His personal confession underscores his new maturity; and finding that he has but ten days to reach her shores, guarded night and day by Grantorto's men, he again pledges his life to her assistance (V.xi.43.1-4).

Pressing on, they soon see a rout of brutish people chasing a single knight to and fro, seeking to oppress him and bring him to bondage. Some of their number have imprisoned a lady who is crying out for help to the lone knight, who holds his own and even attacks their greater numbers. But the battle is wearisome and they are so many; and battering upon his shield, they force the knight to abandon it. Artegall and Talus ride to his rescue and soon disperse the rude band. Upon being questioned about his plight, the battered warrior, Burbon, tells of his love for the imprisoned lady, Flourdelis. Since Grantorto also has vied for her hand and has wooed her away with "golden giftes and many a guilefull word" (V.xi.50.4), she now rejects Burbon's suit; and Grantorto's men have thwarted his efforts to win her back.

When Artegall criticizes him for throwing away his shield, "the badge, that should his deedes display" (V.xi.

52.5), Burbon thinks he has an adequate explanation in necessity. Burbon was dubbed knight by Red Cross, who gave him the shield with "His deare Redeemers badge upon the bosse." For a long time Burbon fought many battles with it without suffering wounds or loss, even holding Grantorto himself at bay and often defeating him in the field (V.xi.53).

> But for that many did that shield envie,
> And cruell enemies increased more;
> To stint all strife and troublous enmitie,
> The bloudie scutchin being battred sore,
> I layd aside, and have of late forebore,
> Hoping thereby to have my love obtayned;
> Yet can I not my love have nathemore;
> For she by force is still from me detayned
> And with corruptfull brybes is to untruth mistrayned.
>
> (V.xi.54)

Artegall grants that Burbon's case is hard but tells him nothing should induce him to abandon his shield, his "honours stile"—not even the threat of death. Critics who have remarked upon this exchange note that it is highly ironic to hear Artegall lecture Burbon on the virtues of his shield since he himself was guilty earlier of a similar offense when he willingly surrendered his own badge of justice to Radigund. These critics are mistaken and have missed Spenser's point. There is no irony here, conscious or unconscious, for if there is any one Knight of Maidenhead in *The Faerie Queene* who has earned the right to instruct anyone about the meaning of his shield, it is Artegall. He has learned from most bitter and humiliating experience exactly what happens when a knight abandons his "honours stile."

Attempting to justify his wayward behavior to Artegall, Burbon pleads necessity and holds "That to temporize is not from truth to swerve" (V.xi.56.3). Although Burbon promises to take up his shield again when the time is convenient, Artegall tells him "truth is one in all" and *accidia* is the enemy of virtue. Artegall offers to help Burbon redeem his lady and then subdues all of Grantorto's captains while Talus puts to flight all the foot soldiers. Coming to Flourdelis, they see a fair woman in robes and costly jewels, whose raiment has been "fouly rent and shamefully defaced" by Grantorto's men.

> But *Burbon* streight dismounting from his steed,
> Unto her ran with greedie great desyre,
> And catching her fast by her ragged weed,
> Would have embraced her with hart entyre.
> But she backstarting with disdainfull yre,
> Bad him avaunt, ne would unto his lore
> Allured be, for prayer nor for hyre.
>
> (V.xi.61.1-7)

Artegall reminds her that such light regard for her troth and ready acceptance of the love and gifts of a stranger will compromise her honor. She is much abashed by his counsel but does not answer, and despite the fact that she had been unfaithful to him, Burbon takes her up on his steed and carries her away "nor well nor ill apayd" (V.xi. 64.9). Here Artegall encounters the last of the false lovers in Book Five: the squalid squire and his damsel; Sanglier and his gay lady; Braggadocchio and the snowy Florimell; Amidas and Philtera; Bellodant and Radigund; and finally, Burbon and Flourdelis.[48] Where before he did not recognize the difference between true and false love, he now fully understands the exact distinction.[49] The fidelity in love he demonstrated during his imprisonment, he now confirms: "Dearer is love than life, and fame than gold;/ But dearer then them both, your faith once plighted hold"

---

[48] He does not meet but only hears of Bellodant.

[49] We remember here that Artegall once fought at Satyrane's Tournament of Beauty.

(V.xi.63.8-9). At the opposite pole from Britomart and Artegall, Flourdelis and Burbon equally befit each other in an ultimate parody of love.

vi

When Artegall and his party reach the sea coast, they find a ship ready to sail; and in a day's journey they reach landfall, where they are met by a troop of Grantorto's men who forbid them to disembark. With Talus in the van dispersing all who dare to oppose him, Artegall and Sergis march toward the town. Hearing of their approach, Grantorto gathers all his forces and marches against them but is again repulsed with heavy losses by Talus. Artegall calls a truce and directs a herald to tell Grantorto he did not come for such slaughters "but for to trie the right/ Of fayre *Irenaes* cause with him in single fight" (V.xii.8.8-9). Grantorto agrees to dispute Irena's case the following day.

That night Sir *Artegall* did cause his tent
There to be pitched on the open plaine;
For he had given streight commaundement,
That none should dare him once to entertaine:
Which none durst breake, though many would right faine
For fayre *Irena*, whom they loved deare.
But yet old *Sergis* did so well him paine,
That from close friends, that dar'd not to appeare,
He all things did purvay, which for them needfull weare.
(V.xii.10)

Artegall's order for complete seclusion is yet another reminder by Spenser that this is the "new" Artegall, the knight of justice fully committed to the task at hand. His careful preparations here contrast to the casual manner in which he encamped after the first day's fighting with Radigund. Where previously he had his "pavilion to be richly pight/ Before the city gate" (V.iv.46.4-5), he now orders his tent "to be pitched on the open plaine." The night before the battle with Radigund, he entertained her emissary, Clarin, succumbed to "guyle" by agreeing to her terms, and gave her "gifts and things of deare delight" (V.iv.51.1-6). Now he forbids all visitors—friends and well-wishers; and Sir Sergis "all things did purvay, which for them needfull weare." The contrasts between past daring and present caution, companionship and isolation, excess and simplicity, could not convey a plainer meaning.

Since Irena herself has no knowledge of the coming of her champion, she awakens with a heavy heart the next morning, the day appointed for her death.

> Then up she rose, and on her selfe did dight
> Most squalid garments, fit for such a day,
> And with dull countenance, and with doleful spright,
> She forth was brought in sorrowfull dismay,
> For to receive the doome of her decay.
> But comming to the place, and finding there
> Sir *Artegall*, in battailous array
> Wayting his foe, it did her dead hart cheare,
> And new life to her lent, in midst of deadly feare.
>
> Like as a tender Rose in open plaine,
> That with untimely drought nigh withered was,
> And hung the head, soone as few drops of raine
> Thereon distill, and deaw her daintie face,
> Gins to looke up, and with fresh wonted grace
> Dispreds the glorie of her leaves gay;
> Such was *Irenas* countenance, such her case,
> When *Artegall* she saw in that array,
> There wayting for the Tyrant, till it was farre day.
>
> (V.xii.12-13)

These beautiful lines depicting Irena's sudden transformation anticipate Artegall's victory over Grantorto. In this regard, the terms which Spenser uses to describe her joyous blossoming forth are most important. Without the life-giving presence of redemptive justice, Irena is in a death-like lethargy of body, mind, and spirit, described in the text as *dull countenance, dead hart,* and *doleful spright.* New life "with fresh wonted grace" is lent her at the very sight of Artegall, her redeemer. When justice enters the field, peace revives.[50]

Grantorto, armed in iron plate and wearing a steel cap, finally comes in great presumption, "as if he feareless were."

> And in his hand an huge Polaxe did beare,
> Whose steale was yron studded, but not long,
> With which he wont to fight, to justifie his wrong.
>
> (V.xii.14.7-9)

Huge in stature and skilled in battle, Grantorto is depicted as being of indeterminate nature: "whether man or monster one could scarse discerne" (V.xii.15.9). In keeping with the theme of justice, Artegall's defense of Irena is announced as a trial by combat, with emphasis falling equally upon the aspects of *trial* and *combat.* Grantorto, whose name signifies both a legal and moral offense, has himself established the tenor of the encounter. For we have already learned from Sergis the legalistic framework within which Grantorto considers Irena's case.

> And now he hath to her prefixt a day,
> By which if that no champion doe appeare,
> Which will her cause in battailous array
> Against him justifie, and prove her cleare

---

[50] Artegall's rescue of Irena is similar to Hercules' rescue of Hesione. Renaissance commentators read Hercules' victory over the monster as Christ's deliverance of *Sancta Ecclesia* from the dragon (see T. A. d'Aubigné, *L'Hercule Chrestien* and Nicholas Reusner, *Emblemata* [Frankfort, 1581], p. 254, for examples of this reading). Spenser uses Christian imagery; but instead of specifying the church, he points to peace.

Of all those crimes, that he gainst her doth reare,
She death shall by.

(V.xi.40.1-6)

Grantorto couches his immoral threat to Irena in legal
terms, attempting to hide his unjust actions in the machinery of the law. That his accusations have no basis in
fact is indicative of the threat Grantorto holds for Irena
in particular and society in general. In this connection we
should remember that trial by combat was one of the three
types of trial legally sanctioned in sixteenth-century England.[51]

As we have learned to expect from Spenser's technique,
within this legal pattern the details of the battle proper
reveal the personalities of each combatant. At the trum-
pet's sound, the tyrant thunders his blows "with such force
and furie violent" that Artegall is painfully wounded.
When Artegall sees his style, he prudently avoids his
furious rushes and patiently waits for an opening. Seeing
the "cursed felon" raise his club to strike him mortally,
Artegall seizes the advantage and grievously wounds him.

Yet the huge stroke, which he before intended,
Kept on his course, as he did it direct,
And with such monstrous poise adowne descended,
That seemed nought could him from death protect:
But he it well did ward with wise respect,
And twixt him and the blow his shield did cast,
Which thereon seizing, tooke no great effect,
But byting deepe therein did sticke so fast,
That by no meanes it backe again he forth could wrest.

(V.xii.21)

[51] "By order and usage of Englande there [are] three ways and
manners, whereby absolute and definite judgement is given, by
parliament which is the highest and most absolute, by battle and
by the great assise" (Thomas Smith, *De Republica Anglorum* [Lon-
don, 1584], p. 48). See also Cowell's *Interpreter* (1637).

Artegall, who previously lectured Burbon on the virtues of his shield, uses his own to good advantage. The meeting of Grantorto's club with Artegall's shield is emblematic of their whole struggle. The tyrant uses his club "to justifie his wrong" (V.xii.14.9), while the shield of justice defends the right. Metaphorically and actually Grantorto has been confounded by the doctrine of true justice, because his "argument" is now powerless. Artegall realizes that further "dialectic debate," symbolized by tugging back and forth and his being drawn "all about," would be futile. Since the shield of justice has already done its work and has rendered injustice powerless, Artegall, personifying the justice the shield protects, can free it with impunity and exact sentence upon Grantorto: "He lightly reft his head, to ease him of his paine" (V.xii.23.9).

Immediately the populace rejoices in his success and offers worship not to Artegall, who is the means, but to the end for which he has been working—Irena, who is peace. They adore her with "due humbleness" and sound his "glorie" over all. To make sure his readers do not miss the complete significance of Artegall's quest, Spenser specifically indicates the result of his victory.

> Who streight her leading with meete majestie
> Unto the pallace, where their kings did rayne,
> Did her therein establish peaceablie,
> And to her kingdomes seat restore agayne;
> And all such persons, as did late maintayne
> That Tyrants part, with close or open ayde,
> He sorely punished with heavie payne;
> That in short space, whiles there with her he stayd,
> Not one was left, that durst her once have disobayd.
>
> (V.xii.25)

The work of justice is peace, and as far as any man can, Artegall has reestablished the kingdom of peace.

vii

Before Artegall is able to complete his task in reforming
Irena's realm, his course of justice is necessarily halted
when he is called back to Faery Court: "So having freed
Irena from distress,/ He tooke his leave of her, there left
in heavinesse" (V.xii.27.8-9). Artegall's sadness is symptomatic of all the quests in *The Faerie Queene*. For in Faery
Land, the model of the fallen world, no man ever completely succeeds. Although Spenser sometimes fondly remi-
nisces over the golden times of honor, chivalry, and love,
he never sentimentalizes the present condition of man.
After many attempts Red Cross Knight finally defeats the
dragon and frees Una's parents, yet later he is found before Malecasta's Castle still struggling against the lures of
the flesh. Guyon becomes perfected in temperance in order
to bind Acrasia, yet in the very next canto he succumbs to
wrath after his unhorsing by Britomart (III.i.9.1-4).
Britomart herself finally achieves maturity in love when
she realizes that "love does always bring forth bounteous
deedes/ And in each gentle hart desire of honour breedes";
yet when it comes time for Artegall to leave on his quest,
she tries her best to detain him. Calidore in fighting the
Blatant Beast is no exception to this pattern.

> Thus was this Monster by the maystring might
> Of doughty *Calidore*, supprest and tamed,
> That never more he mote endammadge wight
> With his vile tongue, which many had defamed,
> And many causelesse caused to be blamed:
> So did he eeke long after this remaine,
> Untill that, whether wicked fate so framed,
> Or fault of men, he broke his yron chaine,
> And got into the world at liberty againe.
>
> (VI.xii.38)

For Artegall, as for any other Christian, the struggle against temptation and human frailties can never end.

Although Spenser considers patterns of human conduct —ethical, moral, social, psychological, religious—he wisely declines to provide a simple formula for success because his poem has taught him the education of a truly virtuous gentleman is an impossible task. This is a humbling thought and it is no coincidence that each of the major exemplars of virtue in the poem humbly recognizes his infirmity—Red Cross in the House of Holiness; Guyon and Arthur to Alma; Artegall in captivity; and Britomart in Isis Church. Spenser's characters are not psychological types, each automatically assuming the vice he is fighting— psychological pawns in the novel of life. Nor are they archetypal projections of the subconscious, dancers swaying to the music of *anima mundi*. Nor are they allegorical examples, aged veterans of the *psychomachia*. Each of these methods of analyzing character creates its own variety of futile disputations. Spenser is a better teacher than Aquinas precisely because he is not a teacher in the strict sense of the term. His technique works not by precept nor by description but by example. Spenser's shrewd use of Calvin, Aquinas, the Bible and its commentators, and the emblem makers for his own purposes—not theirs—defines his aesthetic. Such practice denies the reduction of Spenser to a didactic and "philosophically serious" poet and reveals him as a poet who is serious in a highly subtle and sophisticated way.[52] His is a poetry of awareness, not resolution.

To emphasize for gentle readers his point that man's life is a continuing physical and spiritual battle even if individual victories may be won, Spenser fashions an unwholesome welcoming committee for Artegall upon his return. As soon as he sets foot upon the beach (V.xii.28),

[52] I am indebted here to Professor Allen's remarks on poets and philosophers (*Four Poets on Poetry* [Baltimore, 1959], pp. 8-14).

he encounters two ugly hags. The older of the two, whose hideous outer form vividly depicts her true inner nature, is gnawing upon a venomous snake.

> Her name was *Envie*, knowen well thereby;
> Whose nature is to grieve, and grudge at all,
> That ever she sees doen prays-worthily,
> Whose sight to her is greatest crosse, may fall,
> And vexeth so, that makes her eat her gall.
> For when she wanteth other thing to eat,
> She feedes on her owne maw unnaturall,
> And of her owne foule entrayles makes her meat;
> Meat fit for such a monsters monsterous dyeat.
>
> (V.xii.31)

Equally ill-favored and complementing her is the murderess of reputations, Detraction, who serves as the public manifestation of envy. To assist them in their hateful acts, they have the Blatant Beast, the power of slander. One by one, they rush at noble Artegall and attack him with their specialized weapons of vilification. Envie throws her half-dead snake at him which "Bit him behind, that long the marke was to be read" (V.xii.39.9); Detraction accuses him of prostituting the cause of justice, of oppressing innocent people, and of defeating Grantorto by treachery; the Blatant Beast deafens him with the roar of his hundred tongues.

That Artegall is beset by such hideous creatures should not lead us (as it has led other readers and critics) to believe Spenser is criticizing his present behavior or past actions and is compromising his achievement in any way. *Invidia* and her relatives are the unpleasant but unavoidable companions of anyone who has achieved prominence and success in public office. Although Pindar taught his readers man is only a dream of a shadow, he also never ceased cautioning his victors about *invidia*, the nightmare in palpable form which always accompanies praiseworthy endeavor.[53] In his *Delectable Demaundes* Alain Chartier shows that the one who desires to reign and govern must "learne above all things" to "Susteine Envie with great courage."[54] That Artegall returns home after the successful completion of his arduous quest only to meet with reproach, calumny, and backbiting envy, is one of the necessary ironies of life in Faery Land—and the world.

From the opening encounter with Sanglier, the descendant of the Eurymanthean Boar, to the freeing of Irena-Hesione, Artegall's quest is true to the Hercules pattern. It is consistent with Spenser's poetic design that Artegall's final labor in *The Faerie Queene* be the confrontation of *Invidia*, Hercules' last opponent. (See Plate III, following page 68.) The *locus classicus* for his ultimate struggle is Horace's *Epistola ad Augustum*:

> He that did crowse, and did culpon once
>   *Hydra* of hellish spyte,
> And monsters knowne with fatall toyle
>   to fetters frusshed quyte,
> Perceaved this by experience,
>   that monsters all do fall
> Through manliness: envie is tamed
>   at death, or not at all.[55]

All the commentators important for Renaissance readers reaffirm what is already plain in the Horatian text: the

---

[53] See Olympian II, VI; Pythian I, II, VII, XI; Nemean IV; and Isthmian II.

[54] Folio 62 verso.

[55] *Horace His Arte of Poetrie, pistles, and Satyrs Englished* . . . trans. Thomas Drant (London, 1567), sig. F.viii. Drant's is an inflated and expanded version of lines 10-12 of the Augustus:

> diram qui contudit hydram,
> notaque fatali portenta labore subegit,
> Comperit invidiam supremo fine domari.
>   (Heinsius' text)

struggle against envy is an unending battle which only death overcomes.[56] The unholy trinity attacking Artegall is Spenser's compliment to Horace which provides the final test for his hero's character and reveals him as the new Hercules, the worthiest of justiciars, and the true prince whose exploits admirably equip him to fulfill the providential plan.

Perfectly shaped by the integrity of Spenser's artistic vision, Book Five has come to its just close: it begins with Artegall's struggle with the intemperate boar Sanglier and ends with the assault by the Blatant Beast. Between these points, Artegall's character has undergone radical change. Once proud, wrathful, and concupiscent, he has learned the wisdom of humility. At the moment of his greatest triumph, the establishment of peace with the rescue of Irena, when he could rationally hope for praise and respect, Artegall withstands his greatest temptation, in which Envie, Detraction, and the Blatant Beast unleash the full fury of their rancor.

And still among most bitter wordes they spake,
Most shametull, most unrighteous, most untrew,
That they the mildest man alive would make
Forget his patience, and yeeld vengeaunce dew
To her, that so false sclaunders at him threw.
And more to make them pierce and wound more deepe,
She with the sting, which in her vile tongue grew,
Did sharpen them, and in fresh poyson steepe:
Yet he past on, and seem'd of them to take no keepe.

(V.xii.43)

Artegall's internal peace is now so firmly established it

[56] See Badius' edn. of *Sermones et epistolae* (Paris, 1503); the edn. with variorum notes of Acro, Porphyrion, Mancinellus, Badius, and Bonzo (Paris, 1519); Lambin's edn. (Venice, 1565); Cruquius' edn. (Antwerp, 1579); and *L'Opere D'Oratio*, commentary of Giovanni Fabrini (Venice, 1573), p. 330.

manifests itself in humility which bears, unmoved, taunts that would anger "the mildest man alive," a display of stoical resolve which marks him as similar to Plutarch's Hercules, who took less heed of grievous words and slanders than he did of flies.[57]

Concurrent with the maturing of his character, Artegall has also followed the progress of Hercules in the conquest of the West, the movement with which Book Five began.

Next Hercules his like ensample shewed,
Who all the West with equall conquest wonne,
And monstrous tyrants with his club subdewed;
The club of Justice dread, with kingly powre endewed.
(V.i.2.6-9)

While the Hercules pattern informs the thematic structure of Book Five, traditional interpretations provide the texture and significance which have fleshed out that pattern. Such an interpretation of Spenser's artistic plan is readily evident in the well-known Senecan plays[58] and was available for the common reader in Arthur Golding's translation of *De beneficiis*: "Hercules winning nothing too himself, traveled over the whole world, not conquering it, but setting it at libertie. For what could he win, that was an enemye too the evill, a defender of the good, and a pacifyer bothe of sea and Land?"[59] It is in this magnanimous sense of unselfish endeavor that the actions of Artegall must be understood. Spenser shows us that Artegall tri-

---

[57] *How one may take profits of his enmyes* (London, 1533), sig. B.ii.verso; see his *Moralia*, 90 D-E.

[58] *Hercules Furens* and *Hercules Oetaeus*; see especially the chorus in *Herc. Fur.* (882-894): *Pax est Herculea manu.* . . . In his study of the prevalence of the adaptation of some Herculean types to the demands of drama, Eugene M. Waith underscores the influence of the Senecan plays (*The Herculean Hero in Marlowe, Chapman, Shakespeare and Dryden* [London, 1962], passim).

[59] *The Work of that excellent Philosopher . . . Seneca concerning Benefyting*, trans. Golding (London, 1578), p. 9 verso [I.xiii].

umphs over injustice and overcomes the ultimate challenge of Envie and Sclaunder, who attempt to denigrate his efforts. Artegall's quest is the spiritual biography of the princely justiciar, that unique and perfect justiciar who is the embodiment of the ideal of justice left by his teacher, Astraea. Because the achievement of this ideal in Faery Land (the little world), is an heroic task, Spenser portrays Artegall as a type of Hercules. For Spenser's gentle readers who are to be instructed in virtue, Artegall's long journey in *The Faerie Queene*, from his shameless participation in the Tournament of Beauty to the restoration of Irena and the establishment of his own inner harmony, is an "ensample" of the education of a true exemplar of justice whose works are of great benefit to mankind and reflect an equanimity of soul.

Index